Book One of a Curiously True Trilogy

TRAPPED IN A FANTASY

A Strong Desire Meets a Stranger

A true story.

KARLEE CHRISTOPHER

Internationally Published Author

These are actual emails shared between two real people.
Proper names of individuals and of some places have been
changed for obvious reasons.

This book contains sexually explicit material.

For Jack…
You ignited my sexual soul.

Story Synopsis

When recently divorced Karlee Christopher, a successful Midwest business consultant, solicits for a casual encounter on the internet and travels across the country to meet her selected candidate, she apprehensively steps into a risky and potentially dangerous night that will forever alter her life.

A true story, *Trapped in a Fantasy* (A Trilogy) is part memoir, part sexually-charged emails shared between two people who meet as strangers on the internet. After their first night together, a sexual explosion for both of them, Karlee and Jack find themselves on personal expeditions, sharing intimate details of their lifelong suppressed sexual fantasies. Wrapped in an endearing friendship raw with yearning and desire, Karlee finds herself in love with her sexual soul mate, Jack, who often appears emotionally desolate and plagued with professional unrest, yet touches her sexuality to the depths of her core. Ill-equipped to offer her a desired conventional relationship, Karlee finds her heart in a 10½ year tug-of-war between the man who continues to ignite her sexually in every way and the abyss of her desire for requited love.

*T*his is how it all began . . .

Sunday, June 27, 2004 7:55 AM

Hot, Fun Woman Looking for New Experiences—45—w4m

I will be in Las Vegas July 6-10. I am looking to have fun with a young, well-built, clean, attractive male. We can meet for a drink, dinner, or a swim at my hotel pool (I'll be staying at one of the Strip properties) and see where it goes from there. Recently divorced and in need of some exciting sexual experiences! Not looking for anything outrageous; just good, hot sex. Must be willing to wear condoms (I will supply) for both oral and intercourse, provide photos, and have at least one telephone conversation with me before I head out. Non-smokers only. I am attractive, 5' 2", a size 8 with great breasts, blonde hair, and blue eyes, and fun, fun, fun . . .

----- Original Message -----
From: Jack
To: Karlee
Sent: Monday, June 28, 2004 1:25 PM
Subject: Fun in Vegas with a fun guy . . . in Vegas

Hi, anonymous craigslist personal ad poster!

I'm guessing that you've probably received hundreds or thousands of responses to your ad by now, but don't delete me yet! Give me the chance to arouse, titillate, annoy, or repulse you first! That's all I ask.

I was supposed to be working, but I'm taking a break. I was distracted and found myself perusing the ads. I have had an ongoing fantasy in my life to have an illicit sexual meeting. I don't know why, but the idea of meeting a stranger and having sex is tremendously exciting for me. You might wonder why, if that's the case, I don't just go off and hire a prostitute—well, I've never done that and it just isn't the same. There's something about a mutual attraction; a raw carnal desire that I'm drawn to.

Throughout my life I've only ever had sex with women that I've gotten to know over time. It's not that I'm shy; I love sex and I've been thinking about sex nearly non-stop since I was...born. Okay, maybe not exactly that long, but pretty close. In any event, other than thinking about it, I've never propositioned anyone for sex, as I always thought it wasn't respectful, or maybe I've had in the back of my head that it wouldn't be meaningful if there wasn't a deep connection to my partner.

So, obviously, I must be trying to change my way of thinking on that matter.

I loved reading your ad. Every six months or so, I'll browse the personals, but I never have written to anyone because I never see an ad that sounds like anything I'd be interested in...until today. I can't imagine a more perfect scenario. I know exactly where you're coming from and I think I would be the perfect choice for you to meet up with. A whole fantasy has popped into my mind from the moment I read your ad, and even while I type this, I'm very excited thinking about the possibility. I don't know what sort of physical specimen you're looking for, or what really "turns you on," but I'm sure that I could go a long way towards your need for some exciting sexual experiences. I'm not into anything "fancy" or "weird," just extremely passionate sex. I would, of course, wear condoms, and I am STD free, too.

I don't know if you've already made other plans. Even if you have, maybe you want to meet up with more than one man. I hope you'd like to know more about me. If so, please let me know. I live here and work here, and I could make time to be available to come to you. I'd be happy to describe some of my fantasies to you, send you a picture, and speak with you on the phone. I would be very happy to take this experience for what it is, and I'm extremely eager to learn more about you. You won't find a guy who's more passionate, and that goes a long way!

I'm 6' 1", 34 years old, and in pretty good shape. I work out regularly.

I hope to hear from you soon!

--Jack

----- Original Message -----
From: Karlee
To: Jack
Sent: Monday, June 28, 2004 2:48 PM
Subject: Re: Fun in Vegas with a fun guy . . . in Vegas

Hi Jack,

Wow—I don't even know where to begin. Your email definitely hit a chord in me.

Up until your email, I hadn't shared any of my story with the many men (not to mention women and couples—yikes!) who responded to my ad. Fact is, I've never done anything like this before and I keep wondering if I'm crazy for going down this road. I guess it's one of those internal dialogues—fighting between the "good girl" I've been all my life and the wild woman inside me that wants to come out and play! I, like you, have never allowed myself to have sex with someone I just met or was not involved with emotionally. At my core, I know that is what I still prefer. But I'm giving myself permission to explore what so much of the rest of the world seems to do!

Your timing was good. I have been getting close to deleting my ad, since I have doubted if I could really even go through with this. But earlier today I told myself to leave it at least until tonight, as I said to myself, "Maybe some really nice, normal guy will send a note." And there you were! Before we get into the fantasy (until you mentioned that, I hadn't really looked at this that way, and when I did, I found myself aroused at the idea!), I'd like to see a photo. It's not that I have some specific criteria; I just know that chemistry will be important to me.

Thanks for taking the time to write and I look forward to hearing back from you.

Karlee

----- Original Message -----
From: Jack
To: Karlee
Sent: Monday, June 28, 2004 3:49 PM
Subject: Re: Fun in Vegas with a fun guy . . . in Vegas

Hi Karlee,

Well, you asked for it, you got it. Or is it, "you've gotten it"? Either way, here it is...a photo of me. Now, keep in mind, I don't have a lot of photos of myself. This one will give you a general idea of what I look like, although I'm sure I must be much more attractive in real life. I decided it'd be a good thing to show you a truly horrendous photo, so that if and when you see the "real me," you'll be overcome by a wave of uncontrollable desire. Pretty clever, huh? I think I'm taller with bigger muscles than is evident in the photo.

>>*Wow—I don't even know where to begin. Your email definitely hit a chord in*

me.

I'm glad! I hope it was a C Major 7th chord...I always liked that chord.

>>*wondering if I'm crazy for going down this road. I guess it's one of those internal dialogues—fighting between the "good girl" I've been all my life and the wild woman inside me that wants to come out and play! I, like you,*

Exactly. You wrote exactly what I was thinking myself. (I mean, except for the "good girl" part—good boy would be more appropriate for me.) The desire has always been there, but I guess what has always stopped me from exploring it was that I imagined anyone who would do such a thing would be the kind of person I wouldn't want to do such a thing with. That's why I liked your ad and your email so much...you sound like you're on exactly the same page as me, and knowing that we've both never done anything like this before, but both want to, is—well—very exciting.

>>*involved with emotionally. At my core, I know that is what I still prefer. But I'm giving myself permission to explore what so much of the rest of the world seems to do!*

It's also what I prefer...and yes, I'm also giving myself permission to see what it's like. And knowing that you're not someone who ever does this, it would be perfect! Co-explorers, we are.

>>*Your timing was good. I have been getting close to deleting my ad, since I have doubted if I could really even go through with this. But earlier*

My timing isn't the ONLY THING that's good! See? I can be sexually suggestive, too.

>>*today I told myself to leave it at least until tonight, as I said to myself, "Maybe some really nice, normal guy will send a note." And there you were!*

Well, yes, I am nice and normal, though those are not big selling points when you're potentially about to meet someone for red hot passionate sex in a hotel room. I'm glad you think they're positives!

>>*Before we get into the fantasy, (until you mentioned that, I hadn't really looked at this that way, and when I did, I found myself aroused at the idea!)...I'd like to see a photo. It's not that I have some specific criteria; I just know that chemistry will be important to me.*

I've attached a photo (unless of course I forgot which is usually the case whenever I try to attach a file on an email). I hope there's some chemistry. If there isn't, I'll understand. I mean, if I were Brad Pitt, I probably wouldn't have grown up concerned with respect and emotion in regards to sex...I'd have been beating women off with a stick. I understand that everyone has their own personal tastes, so if I'm not your cup of tea, just let me know. Of course, you would be missing out on the best, hottest, steamiest, most fun sexual experience of your entire life. No pressure, though!

That's the other thing, of course...if you like my photo and you decide you want to proceed, I think it's really important that you realize that I'd have no expectations. What I mean is, if you got cold feet and didn't want to go through with it, I would be disappointed, but I wouldn't push, and if at any point you (or I) felt weird, I think we should both understand that we'd stop.

I like so much of what I've read from you, though, I hope that you like my picture. I hope I haven't broken any rules of the internet by sending you just a boring old picture of my head, rather than an extreme action close-up of my genitals. As I understand it, sending nude photos is almost mandatory—so please forgive me if I've done you wrong by not doing so. Let me know and I'll fix that situation in my all-nude self-photo studio.

I hope to hear back from you!

--Jack

----- Original Message -----
From: Karlee
To: Jack
Sent: Monday, June 28, 2004 6:55 PM
Subject: Re: Fun in Vegas with a fun guy . . . in Vegas

Hi Jack,

Thanks for the photo, and it was fine. Your sense of humor is great.

I laughed at the idea of a self-photo studio! Actually, many men felt it necessary to send photos of "the goods" and it pretty much freaked me out. Not because I am freaked out by male body parts; it just goes back to the whole, "I can't believe this is me involved in this!" Most photos were just normal, like the one you sent.

After more anxiety and deliberation, I've pretty much decided that I don't think I can really do this. I did delete the ad.

Perhaps we can keep in touch via email and see if it makes sense to talk on the phone before I head out.

Take care,
Karlee

----- Original Message -----
From: Jack
To: Karlee
Sent: Monday, June 28, 2004 10:17 PM
Subject: Re: Fun in Vegas with a fun guy . . . in Vegas

Hi Karlee,

I guess placing an ad that results in various male body parts being sent to you (aka "the goods") is an important part in having the complete internet experience. I've never been sent such photos, so I feel like I'm not a true internet guru.

So, you've pretty much decided that you can't do this. I can understand that. But, keep in mind, you were motivated enough to start the process, so there must be some part of you that wants to explore it. I think I went through exactly what you're going through, although for me, it was a question of whether I'd even look at ads (I tried internet dating several years ago, although it was for "traditional dating" and it seemed like it wasn't the way to go for

7

me). Once I decided that it was okay, that was my big hurdle. Actually following through with it, I don't think would have been a problem. It's just that—well—you're the only one, and you seem right on the same page! So, I'm not trying to talk you into anything. Actually, that's not true. OF COURSE I'm trying to talk you into something, but not something you don't want to do. And, I'm just presenting arguments. Why? Because if we are on the same page, then I have a good idea, I think, of why you might have decided it's a bad idea.

Do you feel a weird sense of nervous guilt? That's kind of what I'd go through. When I was looking through the ads, I felt like this was the sort of thing that I'd never do. What if someone found out? It would be embarrassing. And, I'm not the kind of person who'd do something like this. But, you know, I *am*...I know I want to; it's just that I want to do it in the right situation, with the right person... it's a hard mixture. I want to live out that fantasy, but I don't want to be thought of as the kind of person who does such things, even thought of that way by myself. I have those desires, but I don't want to suddenly find myself wearing cotton shirts unbuttoned to the navel with big gold chains and calling everyone "babe."

I guess part of the nervousness for me is that I'd want it to be between just you and me. I don't mean it'd be a secret, but the idea of this becoming a story that people tell at work seems kind of tawdry. I don't think it is tawdry; I think it's hot and exciting, but if people knew, they might judge me in one way or another. But you know...I'm pretty sure I'd like it. I'll go out on a limb and say that I'm pretty sure you might, too.

If it actually causes you anxiety, then you shouldn't worry about it. As I said, there's no pressure here. There's a willingness and a mutual curiosity, and I'd hate to think that I'd finally found someone who was exactly where I am and decided not to try it for the wrong reasons. But, you don't need any reason. All I'm saying is you wouldn't be the only one who is nervous about the idea. As soon as I sent you my picture, I started imagining what would happen if you were interested. Could I go through with this? I could. Does this make me a bad person? I don't think so. Should I forget about it? No. I've thought about it for a long time, and I think it would be a good thing to try.

I would definitely like to talk to you on the phone. I promise I won't keep pestering you if you're set against it. I'm just trying to make sure you don't miss out. (And by miss out, I mean on the best sex you've ever had in your entire life!) And, I don't want to miss out, either.

It'd be fun to talk about this, for me, whether we do it or not. And, all the sexy stuff aside, I think it'd be fun to chat with a kindred spirit. I don't know who else I'd be comfortable talking with about this. But, since it's already out there for us...

Anyway, do keep in touch. I'd like to hear what you're thinking.

--Jack

----- Original Message -----
From: Karlee
To: Jack
Sent: Tuesday, June 29, 2004 7:06 AM
Subject: Viva Las Vegas?

Hi Jack,

Good morning. So much swimming through this complex little head of mine!

My mom passed away three years ago and whenever someone like you comes into my life, I think it's her sending me an angel! (Of course I don't know if I want you to be angelic or devilish!) After reading your note this morning, I was thinking how some people might go through an entire lifetime and never share at the level of intimacy that we have shared in only two days! I find that fascinating. For a very long time now, I have wondered what it would be like to have a partner that would be excited about exploring our sexualities together.

Okay, so here's where I am today. (And I am a woman so this could change on a daily basis—you're seeing that already!) I say let's continue to move forward with no attachment to the outcome. What

I mean by that is...let's just keep corresponding and see where it goes. That takes the pressure off of me having to say "yes" or "no" right at this moment. Even if I said yes right now, you're not here and I'm not there so we couldn't act on it anyway. If we take one step at a time, we'll either end up together or we won't. Regardless, I believe we will both have been grateful for "finding" someone we feel comfortable sharing our thoughts with. Does that work for you?

And unless something really changes, at this point, I know I would be open to at least meeting you while I'm in Vegas and saying hello. I like the way you think and you have a great sense of humor and that is really appealing to me. I actually have a great sense of humor, also. It might be over-shadowed at the moment amidst the seriousness of me trying to decide what the heck I was doing placing a personals ad on craigslist!

If it doesn't get in the way of your fantasy of being with a "stranger," can I ask you some questions? I know if we get to know each other too well, we're no longer strangers and I don't know if that will ruin it for you! I'm just curious about some of the basics—how long you have lived in Las Vegas, your birthday, what kinds of things you enjoy doing when you're not involved in illicit sexual fantasies, what kind of work you do...that's probably enough. I don't want you to feel like you're being interrogated. I'm just a really curious person. And, of course I'm willing to share those same answers, if you have an interest.

I am definitely open to phone conversation. What is a good number to call? And best time of day?

Looking forward to speaking with you. And, hearing your voice!

Karlee

----- Original Message -----
From: Jack
To: Karlee
Sent: Tuesday, June 29, 2004 1:58 PM
Subject: Re: Viva Las Vegas?

Hi Karlee,

I'm very happy to have found a note from you in my inbox this morning!

I'm so sorry to hear about your mom; I can't even pretend to know your loss. But, if she's responsible for sending me to you, then I owe her my thanks! Boy, I wish I had the kind of mom who would help me find hot sex with a guy I hadn't yet met in Vegas.

I mean—find hot sex with a lady.

But my mom hasn't passed away, and I think it's highly unlikely she put you up to this. At least, I hope not. You know, now that I think about it, I'd rather my mom not have any involvement in helping me in that department in any way.

I've never understood people who aren't able to talk about sex. I mean, to some degree I guess I can. I've always felt like my thoughts about sex and sexuality weren't appropriate to discuss with people until "a certain point." When? How long do you have to know someone? I've seen people I knew who would be very open and up front about such things from the beginning, and it seemed right for them. Why is talking about such things bad? How will someone ever know what you want unless you can talk about it? And hey... sometimes both people want the same thing but they don't know it unless they can talk.

I had a relationship in the past with a woman who wouldn't talk about what she wanted. She felt guilty and uncomfortable and at a certain point I realized that we were two separate people rather than a couple. Intimacy is more than just sex; it's being able to talk and share and not be afraid of what someone else will think of you. I think everyone has thoughts and desires that they think might be "weird," and most of those are probably completely normal.

>>*Okay, so here's where I am today. (And I am a woman so this could change on a daily basis—you're*

I'm glad to hear that you are, in fact, a woman.

Your thinking about not having to commit to any action is, I think, exactly the right one. I never thought there was any obligation on either part. I mean, I live here. If you wanted me to fly out to Saskatchewan, I'd feel like you might be obliged to say hello, but that's it. How can you be obligated to someone for sex? As much as I like the concept ("I lost a bet, so I guess I *must* have sex with you now"), I'd never expect such a thing. Hope? Sure. But if both people don't feel good about it, why would either person want to move forward?

In other words, yes, I agree. Your thinking is perfect. There is no pressure, other than to remain open to possibilities. Even if you said "yes" right now, I think I'd feel exactly the way you feel; perhaps after we talk some more, I would be game to dive in head first, but... this is new to me, too! I have a feeling I might be ready to do a triple-gainer off the high board before you are (with a twist), but you'd have to want to (shall we say) get wet, too. You know—it's a diving analogy.

And as for finding someone we both feel comfortable sharing our thoughts with, I'm already grateful and enjoying this very much, whether or not it leads to pillow-clawing, wall-rattling, thigh-trembling, gasp-inducing sexy sex.

As for your sense of humor, I don't think it's been overshadowed at all—it shines through in every email. I think that, perhaps, we shouldn't allow ourselves to get overly serious about this situation. I think we both have some deep thoughts on the matter, but in the end, it shouldn't be stressful or a burden or rigid (in terms of planning, not...well...you know, sometimes rigid can be a good thing).

You can always ask me questions. I don't think answering any questions ruins the "stranger" fantasy. I think a lot of what intrigues me about this possible scenario is that we'd be able to be direct and say what we want. That's kind of a fundamental thing about it for me. I so much like the idea of being able to say anything, or suggest anything and maybe you'd say, "no, thanks," or you could say "that sounds great!"

There are a few things I've never felt comfortable discussing, and I'm

hoping it'd be okay to talk about them. I certainly know that
anything you would want to discuss, whether it's a fantasy or a
thought or anything else, I'd not shriek and run away in horror. The
worst I'd say is, "it's not my cup of tea."

I'll tell you a bit about my background before I answer your
questions. I did a lot of martial arts growing up, and through that I
became involved in helping with women's self-defense classes.
These classes were taught by women and were kind of a
combination of group therapy for abused women as well as a self-
defense class. At the end of each session, they'd bring me and other
guys in so they could practice their techniques against men. We're
theoretically bigger and stronger than women, but practicing
against men has a different psychological impact. I sometimes loath
to admitting it, but I am a nice guy. I am completely non-
threatening. I'd introduce myself and chat with these women before
getting into the first technique, which is escaping from being
grabbed by the wrist. I'd say what I was going to do beforehand;
they'd trained on this for weeks. I wouldn't grab; I'd just hold. And a
lot of these women would crumble. Some had been raped, some
had been physically abused, some were afraid of men for other
reasons. They'd fall to the ground and cry. It just destroyed me. It
happened to all of the guys who helped with this course. It was part
of their healing process, I was told.

I was in my early teens and it had a huge impact on my dating life. I
became so afraid of ever doing *anything* that might be unwanted
that I always erred on the side of "nice." I'd see kids in my high
school and college grabbing each other and wrestling while they
flirted. I never felt right touching a woman without permission. I'd
always ask before trying to kiss someone. And, I was a very slow
mover in initiating sexual stuff because I'd want to make sure
everything was okay.

And, that seems like it's a good way to go, until you realize that a lot
of women don't find it particularly spontaneous or exciting to be
asked before you kiss or touch them. If you ask, they have to say
"sure" which is awkward for them. Add to that the fact that there
are a lot of women who believe they should tell a man to stop when
they actually want him to keep going, and you get me, a guy who
would leap backwards whenever a woman said, "stop." A girlfriend

once told me that she had a fantasy of being taken against her will and I wasn't able to do it.

The result for me is that I always suppressed even talking about things, because I didn't want to make anyone uncomfortable. It wasn't about my own embarrassment.

So here I am, years later, and the thought of walking up to a woman that I'm attracted to and who I think is attracted to me and saying, "I'd really like to make love to you," is something I've never done, because I imagine that if I'm wrong, it would be awkward for her. I've never just leaned in for a first kiss when it felt right; I've always needed to know it was alright.

Now, once in a relationship, things have always been fine. At that point, I know it's okay, and I'm not inhibited. But even then, there are a few things I've never been comfortable suggesting. If they had come up on their own, great, but otherwise, not.

Sorry to ramble. I guess I wanted to give you the long boring story of why I'm so intrigued by our whole situation.

Anyway, to answer your questions, here goes. I've been in Vegas for about 6.5 years. I moved here from Chicago. I'm a Midwest kind of guy. I am a writer/editor for a textbook company. And surprise—I also work with computers! I bet you never would have guessed by looking at my photo. When I'm not involved in illicit sexual fantasies, I enjoy spending time with friends, going to movies, playing racquetball, and occasionally playing music. I also have fun with a number of other traditional activities, like walking in the mountains, cooking, and nude skydiving. Okay, maybe not nude. And, maybe not skydiving.

So, I'd like to know anything about yourself that you'd like to share. What brings you to Vegas? I'd also like to know...are you offended by "graphic speech?" If I said "cock," would you swoon or would you drool? In other words, do you prefer a fully erect penis or a rock hard cock? Imagine you had the choice. You're on "Let's Make A Deal." Monty is offering you a fully erect penis behind Door Number One, a rock hard cock behind Door Number Two, or you can take what's behind the curtain. Which will it be?

>>*I am definitely open to phone conversation. What is a good number to call? And best time of day?*

The best number is 702-###-####. That's my cell. As for best time...hmmm. What time zone are you in? I'm in PST, and the best time for me is usually after 9 PM (because it's free minutes and by then I usually have my phone plugged in). But, I often don't pick up numbers I don't recognize (I must have a number similar to a hotel's number, because I get A LOT of wrong numbers).

I can almost always make myself available if you give me a time.

See how accommodating I am?

--Jack

----- Original Message -----
From: Karlee
To: Jack
Sent: Tuesday, June 29, 2004 6:21 PM
Subject: Hi!

Hi Stranger, (just practicing my lines—or is that your line? ☺)

Are you by any chance a [cell phone company] customer for your cell phone? (I am, so we would then have free mobile-to-mobile minutes.) I'm on EST, and 9:00 PM your time is midnight here. If I'm going to be having sex next week, I need all the rest I can get and have to get to bed early! I'm just kidding; however, I would prefer to talk earlier than midnight. I have unlimited long distance on my house line. IF you are comfortable with giving me your home phone number, I could call you. If not, I'll just call you on your cell. Will you be home tonight?

I am really looking forward to speaking with you!

Karlee

----- Original Message -----
From: Jack
To: Karlee
Sent: Tuesday, June 29, 2004 7:17 PM
Subject: Re: Hi!

Howdy stranger!

I am, in fact, a [cell phone company] customer! Hooray! I don't think I have the unlimited mobile-to-mobile. I think I picked 1,000 minutes, but unless we're going to talk for 16 hours straight, we should be okay. I signed up for this service and then everyone I knew on [cell phone company] switched to another carrier. I only know one other [cell phone company] person. Can it be that we're the only three left?

So, you can try me on the cell but I'll probably be going out for a meeting in the next hour or so. If you call right now from your [cell phone company] phone, you can talk to me! Lucky you!

I agree with your thinking about resting up, just in case you do decide to have sex. See, you're a genius. I knew it. You should go to bed now, and wake up when your plane leaves for Vegas.

I'm eager to talk to you, too!

--Jack

----- Original Message -----
From: Karlee
To: Jack
Sent: Tuesday, June 29, 2004 10:32 PM
Subject: Re: Here I am!

(4 photos attached)

Hi Jack,

I hope the rest of your evening was great. I enjoyed talking with you.

I tried to send some photos, but kept getting a "Delivery Failure" notification. So if this has come through a million times, that's why!

Also, you may already have this on your cell phone since you have to unblock for the mobile-to-mobile minutes. My cell phone number is 440-###-####. Feel free to call anytime.

I told you a little bit about my move on the phone. Here's a bit more…I started my own consulting company in 1995. I wrote and published my first book in 1999. After that, I moved away from the consulting and into more of a success coach role. It was in January of 2001 that my mom was diagnosed with lung cancer. About four weeks after getting the news, my mother-in-law (at the time) had a stroke. She passed away the first week in March and my mom eight weeks later, almost to the day. The first few months were the hardest. Finally in July, I decided it was time to get back to the real world. Then September 11 [2001] came. Now, I'm certain the attacks didn't have the impact on me like they did for so many others; however, that day did affect me quite profoundly. Then it was in October that my husband of almost 17 years and I started the divorce process. I moved out of our home in June of 2002. I rented an apartment for the first year and last year bought a condo. When I moved out, I gave myself permission to take some time off to figure out my life! (I thought, how long could this take—one week, two weeks at the most, right?!!!) Over the course of time, hard as I tried, I just couldn't get excited about my business. Finally, I decided to call it "semi-retired" and let go. Soooo, I have no idea what kind of work I will do in Las Vegas. I am very interested in working in a casino. And I want to do something fun. Perhaps working at the front desk of a luxury casino/hotel, an event planner, a cocktail waitress, who knows. I have many skills and talents. It's just a matter of finding something fun that I will enjoy. That's my main focus. I am currently working on two more books; not extremely focused on them at the moment, although when I'm in the flow, I really enjoy writing.

Off to bed. I must get up early. Only six days left for panty shopping! ☺

Enjoy your day!

Karlee

----- Original Message -----
From: Jack
To: Karlee
Sent: Wednesday, June 30, 2004 3:57 AM
Subject: One more try . . .

Hi Karlee,

I just got home from my meeting, which turned into dinner (free dinner, even better!) and then a long hang-out session while I waited for my colleagues to go off to see a midnight showing of Spider-Man 2. Hmmm. Life in Vegas—the excitement never stops.

I did, in fact, get the photos. I got three emails from you: the first two each had a different photo; the third one had no attachment. For some reason, the body of the email was the same for all three messages, except for one of the last sentences of one of the last paragraphs, which was chopped short in the first two messages. I know that's not particularly interesting, but I didn't want you to think that all I thought about was sex.

Speaking of sex, NICE PHOTOS! I'm afraid I won't be able to be objective about us having sex now—you're sexy! As I'm sure you've been told many times. Now it's going to seem like a very long week until you arrive in town. Are you here yet? Why not?

In a word, HUBBA-HUBBA! Okay, so that's two words.

How are those essays coming?

As for work in Vegas, I don't know all the details about working in casinos, but don't they require some kind of state card or something? You might be able to start on that paperwork while you're here, in case it takes a while (I believe they do background checks, etc). I, myself, think being a dealer would be fun. But, you have to go to school and then it's a battle to get that first job. Still, it'd be interesting, I think.

Did I mention HUBBA-HUBBA?

Good night!
--Jack

----- Original Message -----
From: Karlee
To: Jack
Sent: Wednesday, June 30, 2004 1:33 PM
Subject: Re: Still here ...

Hi Jack,

I'm still here, but barely! I woke up this morning with a twitch in my right eye. Nervous, perhaps?! Then I had a long conversation with one of my best male friends. And of course the big brother role kicked in and he told me all the reasons this was wrong. I'm not ready to close the door yet. I just want to be upfront with you, as I believe that it's all part of this process.

It's back to that ongoing internal struggle between good and bad, right and wrong, safe and dangerous, panties vs. no-panties (for me, not you!)...does it ever stop!!!

Your email made me smile. Thanks—I needed that!

Hope you're having a great day and I look forward to hearing from you.

Karlee

----- Original Message -----
From: Jack
To: Karlee
Sent: Wednesday, June 30, 2004 3:07 PM
Subject: Re: Still here ...

>>*I'm still here, but barely! Woke up this morning with a twitch in my right*

eye. Nervous, perhaps?!

Either that or you're playing poker and bluffing.

>>*Then I had a long conversation with one of my best male friends. And of course the big brother role kicked in and he told me all the reasons this was wrong.*

That's good, I think. I mean, you want the people who watch out for you and care about you to think about all the potentially bad sides. That's their job. We should both want to make sure we're safe, first and foremost.

But, on the other side, not everyone is going to see the upsides, either. It could be good—it could be great—or even better! Is it really any different from saying you're going out to meet someone at a bar? Or meet someone through on-line dating? We've already determined we're going to see how it goes, so is it really any different from meeting a stranger for dinner? I guess the difference is that we both know we're having very sexual thoughts. Well, I suppose traditionally that's a secret and people have several meetings over days or weeks before they decide it's appropriate to move into a physical relationship. I think we're just disposing of some of the pretense.

If you told your man-friend that you were planning on meeting someone in a bar and might want to have sex, I'd imagine he'd give you the same warnings. The idea that you have less information about people on the internet seems odd to me; you've got more information on me than if we'd met at a party or on the subway (which would be difficult since there isn't a subway here). I think it's always good to be cautious and take precautions, but I really don't think this is nearly as scary as meeting someone in a bar or even a blind date.

>>*I'm not ready to close the door yet. I just want to be upfront with you, as I believe that it's all part of this process.*

I agree. What are his concerns? Maybe there are things I should be worried about, too.

>>*It's back to that ongoing internal struggle between good and bad, right and wrong, safe and dangerous, panties vs. no-panties (for me, not you!)...does it ever stop!!!*

If your friend is telling you why this is wrong, it's probably a case of him trying to impose his own sense of right/wrong on you. I think you know this within yourself. If you've been thinking about it for a long time and keep coming back to it, I think you owe it to yourself to explore it. If you shut yourself off, you'll certainly come back to it again. The question is: If you were to fully act out everything you fantasize about, do you think it would make you a bad person? You mentioned you'd had a couple of "one night stands." Are you somehow a lower person because of it?

By the way, my guess would be that the worst part about a one-night stand is that you probably don't know what you're getting into at the start. Unless the guy says, "I'd like to be with you for one night only," the assumption is probably that things are great and maybe this will lead somewhere. I'd think that expectation followed by— nothing—would be bad. What we're talking about, we both have a good idea of how things could work out. Maybe it's multiple nights, maybe it's one night, maybe it's zero nights. Who knows? Nothing's written in stone or entirely ruled out, but there aren't any hidden agendas.

>>*Your email made me smile. Thanks—I needed that!*

Good, I'm glad I'm good for something! I'll just add here that I'm much better in bed than I am at writing emails! Think how much more you'd be smiling!

>>*Hope you're having a great day and I look forward to hearing from you.*

I've got a teleconference call in a few minutes; once that's over, my day will be better. It'll be even better still if I hear more from you today!

--Jack

----- Original Message -----
From: Karlee
To: Jack
Sent: Wednesday, June 30, 2004 4:52 PM
Subject: Re: Still here...

Hi Jack,

What size condoms should I bring?

I'll write more later. Just thought I'd throw that out to keep the energy alive!

Karlee

----- Original Message -----
From: Jack
To: Karlee
Sent: Wednesday, June 30, 2004 5:05 PM
Subject: Re: Still here . . .

They come in sizes?! Who knew?

Personally, I usually go with a couple of Hefty bags and some bungee cords...

Okay, maybe not.

So, how DO they make crotchless panties, anyway? Do they take existing panties and cut the crotches out? What do they do with those crotches? It'd be a shame to waste that.

Any size you would like to bring will be fine. If they're too small, I'll squeeze in. If they're too big, I'll stuff some socks in there. Or...are you trying to subtly ask me a specific question? You know, if there's anything you want to ask, all you have to do is ask...

And anything that I actually know the answer to, I'll tell you.

How are your essays coming? What sorts of things have you

fantasized about? What sorts of things do you like the most? You know, sexually...

--Jack

----- Original Message -----
From: Karlee
To: Jack
Sent: Wednesday, June 30, 2004 5:43 PM
Subject: Essay #1

Hi Jack,

Okay, so I haven't spent a lot of time today as I'm concentrating more on getting rid of this upper respiratory thing. Can't get things down my throat if I'm coughing every five minutes!

Ya know, this may sound really boring, but there is one thing I always wanted to do and have yet to have the opportunity...play one of those erotic board games. Foreplay is really big for me because the prolonging is so totally good. ALMOST, and I said ALMOST to the point of begging to be taken!

Another scenario that I found myself thinking about was you coming to my room on behalf of the hotel. Your job is to make certain that as a guest, I am totally and completely satisfied. It might start with you standing close behind me as you point out the highlights on a city map, perhaps a massage to help heal that pulled muscle in my inner thigh, or undressing me for a relaxing bath...

That's not 1,500 words I know—but it's a start.

Your turn...

Karlee

----- Original Message -----

From: Jack
To: Karlee
Sent: Wednesday, June 30, 2004 6:08 PM
Subject: Re: Essay #1

>>*Okay, so I haven't spent a lot of time today as I'm concentrating more on getting rid of this upper respiratory thing. Can't get things down my throat if I'm coughing every five minutes!*

Well, you should take care of yourself. You want to be healed up before you get to Vegas, because the dry air probably won't help. And I...Hey! Wait a minute...when you say, "can't get things down my throat," are you being dirty? Or are you just talking about food? I can't tell! And I like it!

>> *Ya know, this may sound really boring, but there is one thing I always wanted to do and have yet to have the opportunity...play one of those erotic board games. Foreplay is really big for me as the prolonging is totally good. ALMOST, and I said ALMOST to the point of begging to be taken!*

I'd certainly be up for playing such a game...but, I'm already big on foreplay. That can be the best part (well, certainly in the top two)! And, if you felt the need to beg to being taken, I would certainly honor that request, because I am nothing if not polite.

>>*Another scenario that I found myself thinking about was you coming to my room on behalf of the hotel. Your job is to make certain that as a guest, I am totally and completely satisfied. It might start with you standing close behind me as you point out the highlights on a city map, perhaps a massage to help heal that pulled muscle in my inner thigh, or undressing me for a relaxing bath...*

Perfect. Wow. That's such a perfectly erotic fantasy. I like it A LOT. You wouldn't have to try very hard at all to get me into that scenario.

>>*Your turn...*

Well, let's see...I've got to run to the UPS store (I mean, in the next few minutes, not in my fantasy) but I'll try to give you one. There are many. As I've said, as I write to you and talk to you, various little scenarios like the one you described run through my head. So, for example, I've always had a bit of a voyeur fantasy. I'm hugely turned on by the thought of watching you undress. I am also wildly turned on by the thought of you wearing nothing but a towel (or lingerie, or any number of things). So, I like the idea of being in your hotel room while you excuse yourself for a minute, and then you go to another room (I guess my fantasy requires a suite or several rooms). I sort of lean around the corner, and see you undressing, maybe getting ready to take a shower, or maybe getting dressed after a bath, or changing clothes.

I guess I may as well just tell you the whole fantasy, since I agreed to not hold back...it's kind of embarrassing to put yourself out there...kind of worried you might read something and think, "Oh YIKES! That's freaky." But, you know, it's just thoughts. For me, part of getting into this with you is to allow myself to put myself out there a bit, but nonetheless, there's kind of a fear that you might see something as being too dirty. If so, let me know. It's just fantasy.

Anyway, as it plays out in my head, I lean around the corner and you're getting ready for a bath. You don't see me, but I'm so turned on that I unzip my pants quietly and begin to touch myself. You go into the bathroom and I follow, looking at you through the open door. You're so attractive (and soapy!) and I try not to touch myself as I watch you, but the way you move your hands over your body is so sensual. You get out of the tub, and start to dry yourself off, when you catch a glimpse of me in the mirror, my (I'm going to go with the term that seems appropriate here) hard cock in my hand. For a second, it's as if we're both caught in the headlights; we both freeze. I'm vulnerable and embarrassed, as are you, yet we're both intrigued and turned on by what's happening. Neither of us moves for a moment. I open the door all the way and walk towards you slowly. You step up to me so we're face to face. I'm breathing very heavy, unsure of what you want. You touch my chest with your fingers and slowly trace down to my leg, then even more slowly you move your hand up to my cock and caress it. I lean in for a kiss, our bodies push together. I lift you up onto the sink and kiss your breasts, massaging them with my hands as my tongue runs over your nipples. You throw your head back and...

Well, you know. You get the general idea.

That's the sort of stuff I think about. Hopefully describing it in detail doesn't put you off.

--Jack

----- Original Message -----
From: Karlee
To: Jack
Sent: Wednesday, June 30, 2004 6:12 PM
Subject: Re: Essay #1

I changed my flight. I'm on my way NOW!

----- Original Message -----
From: Jack
To: Karlee
Sent: Wednesday, June 30, 2004 7:09 PM
Subject: Re: Essay #1

No you're not!

Are you?

--Jack

----- Original Message -----
From: Karlee
To: Jack
Sent: Wednesday, June 30, 2004 8:42 PM
Subject: Question...

Hi Jack,

Of course I'm not on the plane, but I was just about ready! The whole bathroom thing really did it for me!

So here's a question. Earlier you wrote: I am also wildly turned on by the thought of you wearing nothing but a towel (or lingerie or any number of things). I know what a towel is and I know what lingerie is, but...tell me about the "or any number of things." I need to know if there are other "things" I should put on my shopping list!

I was totally comfortable with what you shared. None of it freaked me out and I didn't think it was "too dirty." And I was relieved that it was actually very erotic, which is more of what I'm looking for and comfortable with.

Looking forward to Essay #2. That will probably have to wait until tomorrow. I'm still recovering from (and enjoying in my head) the bathroom scene!

Karlee

----- Original Message -----
From: Jack
To: Karlee
Sent: Wednesday, June 30, 2004 10:18 PM
Subject: Re: Question...

Hi Karlee!

>>*Of course I'm not on the plane, but I was just about ready! The whole bathroom thing really did it for me!*

When you say that it did "it" for you, what exactly is "it"? Is "it" a good thing, I hope? How many times did "it" get done for you?

>> *So here's a question. Earlier you wrote: I am also wildly turned on by the thought of you wearing nothing but a towel (or lingerie or any number of things). I know what a towel is and I know what lingerie is, but...tell me about the "or any number of things." I need to know if there are other "things" I should put on my shopping list!*

Since you ask: I think the sexiest lingerie is satin "teddies" I think they're called. Kind of like a short slip, with spaghetti straps, coming down to the upper thigh. I guess they also make those types of things as dresses, too. I also find the ultra-short mini-boxers to be very sexy...kind of like cotton hot pants, I guess they're called. (See, this is hard when you don't know the terminology.)

I believe I told you on the phone that I've always had a weakness for skirts and dresses. A black miniskirt with pantyhose underneath (the kind that are individual leggings); also a full dress with buttons and "regular" pantyhose.

Then there's the look of wearing just an over-sized T-shirt or man's button-down shirt with nothing else. That's great, too.

In terms of bras, I like them all. I guess black might be my preference, although other colors are nice, too. Red, silver... whatever. I must have a thing for satin. Who knew? As for panties—I know the kind that I find the sexiest, but I don't know what they're called. Tap pants? Maybe not. They sort of look like shorts; usually lacey or frilly. But, you know, I like just about any kind of underwear. Let's not forget things like corsets, baby doll nighties, even traditional (satin) pajamas! And, while we're at it...the French Maid is always a good look.

Whew. It sure is hard...I mean...difficult...to think about this. I'm picturing you in all of these things and it's getting me all worked up. But that's a pretty good list of my top things.

How about you? What sort of clothing do you find to be the sexiest on a man? I ask a bit reluctantly because I would not put "style" in the column of my best attributes. I've never been much of a clothes horse, but hey...maybe you have a weakness for old sneakers!

>>*I was totally comfortable with what you shared. None of it freaked me out and I didn't think it was "too dirty." And I was relieved that it was actually very erotic, which is more of what I'm looking for and comfortable with.*

Well good! I'm very happy then!

>>*Looking forward to Essay #2. That will probably have to wait until tomorrow. I'm still recovering from (and enjoying in my head) the bathroom scene!*

While I hope that you fully recover from your respiratory ailment, I think it would be okay if you were still woozy from thoughts of the bathroom scene! That's the kind of thing you shouldn't rush to recover from!

--Jack

----- Original Message -----
From: Jack
To: Karlee
Sent: Wednesday, June 30, 2004 10:38 PM
Subject: Re: More questions ...

So...are there any other things you've thought of? Things you are or are not turned on by?

For example, I'll give you the information that I'm not turned on by EVERYTHING. Yes, it's true. I'm not particularly titillated by, for example, "water sports" (other than water polo, which fascinates me). I have no interest in pain (giving or receiving), animals (only as friends), and I'm not a great fan of anal activities.

That being said, there's not very much that I can say I'd be OPPOSED to. I find it thrilling to be able to do something that would give another person so much pleasure. If there were something you always wanted to try, I might be willing. I might not, but really there's nothing I can think of that you'd say, "I've always wanted to try this," that would leave me disgusted. I've tried several things that weren't things I'd ordinarily be interested in.

I guess I bring this up because that whole bathroom scene I described earlier is kind of an exhibitionist/voyeur fantasy. It isn't the same as having sex on a bus or looking into someone's window; it's play.

I guess that leads me into another fantasy I have...it's about the only thing I've ever been too embarrassed to talk about "in the moment," because I feel like it's too much like a porno film, and if someone were opposed by it, it seems like you just suggested something crazy.

Well, we're not holding back, so...okay, here goes...the thing I'm thinking of is this...after hours of hot, sweaty, ravenous intercourse, I find the idea of pulling out my (again, I think the appropriate term) cock and hovering over you, looking into your eyes, and stroking myself until I can't keep control any longer and I spurt hot cum all over your breasts—that idea appeals to me. There's something kind of primal about it. It's kind of exhibitionistic. I don't think it's degrading...for anyone, I think it would be degrading for me. But, I guess I've always thought that a woman might think it was degrading or disgusting.

You know, the more I write to you, the more I'm beginning to realize that I might be something of an exhibitionist/voyeur. Because I also find the idea of touching myself in front of you while you touch yourself to be extremely erotic. Maybe as part of foreplay...it seems so deeply personal and private. It's the kind of thing I typically would do by myself (not that I do that kind of thing, of course—that would be wrong!).

I dunno. Just more thoughts. Don't worry...this is about as "out there" as I get. I'm not into goats or auto-asphyxiation or being whipped with leather straps. I've not done any of those things.

But if you make a good case, I might be up for just about anything!

--Jack

----- Original Message -----
From: Karlee
To: Jack
Sent: Thursday, July 1, 2004 9:33 AM
Subject: Next week is getting closer . . .

[I don't know if you already got this message. I sent one this morning and got a message from the "Delivery" people saying a message didn't go through. So, I'm thinking maybe it was this one.]

Hi Jack,

Well, we're almost through this week and then next week...

I'll be writing more later, but since I have started to get used to having mail from you in the morning, I thought I would do the same for you.

I thought I'd start your day with a response to this...

You asked... *When you say that it did "it" for you, what exactly is "it"? Is "it" a good thing, I hope? How many times did "it" get done for you?*

I went to bed as usual last night and the more I thought about that bathroom scene, the more aroused I became. All I can say is, "Thank goodness for vibrators." I do, however, prefer the real thing!

I'll be back later to answer your questions, (which I'm very glad you asked) and maybe another essay!

Karlee

----- Original Message -----
From: Jack
To: Karlee
Sent: Thursday, July 1, 2004 9:33 AM
Subject: Re: Next week is getting closer . . .

Hi Karlee!

>>*Well, we're almost through this week and then next week...*

Thank goodness. This may be the longest weekend ever. Actually, I wind up doing more work on weekends than during the week, so maybe that'll help the time go by.

>>*I'll be writing more later, but since I have started to get used to having mail from you in the morning, I thought I would do the same for you.*

That's mighty nice of you.

>>*I thought I'd start your day with a response to this...*

What better way to start the day? It beats the heck out of Wheaties.

>>*I went to bed as usual last night and the more I thought about that bathroom scene, the more aroused I became. All I can say is, "Thank goodness for vibrators." I do, however, prefer the real thing!*

Hmmm...This is like a ping-pong game of arousal. You get aroused; I get aroused more...I like it! However, what do you mean, "all you can say"!? You can say more! You can say all you want! You can even say more than that! I don't mind details. There's a lot of good stuff in details.

>>*I'll be back later to answer your questions, (which I'm very glad you asked) and maybe another essay!*

I'll be here!

--Jack

----- Original Message -----
From: Jack
To: Karlee
Sent: Thursday, July 1, 2004 1:40 PM
Subject: Re: More questions . . .

>>*I don't know if you already got this message. I sent one this morning and got a message from the "Delivery" people saying a message didn't go through. So, I'm thinking maybe it was this one*

I did get this one, in fact, and just replied to it. If you sent anything else today, I didn't get it. There must have been a network problem.

But why are you reading this? Why aren't you answering my questions and writing essays? I hope you don't come to me the day it's due and ask for an extension! (I may have a special extension for you, though, if you know what I mean!)

(I mean my penis.)

--Jack

----- Original Message -----
From: Karlee
To: Jack
Sent: Thursday, July 1, 2004 7:04 PM
Subject: Essay #2 on the way . . .

Hi Jack,

I hope your day has been great. I just got back from the doctor and told her I was having hot sex next week and needed to feel better NOW! I did go to the doctor, but I didn't tell her all that! Just know I will be in tip-top shape by Tuesday!

Well, since neither of us is into giving or receiving pain, it doesn't make sense for me to be purposefully late with my essay just so that I can be disciplined! It's in the next email. No peeking ahead!

Here are responses to your earlier message...

>>So...are there any other things you've thought of? Things you are or are not turned on by?

I have to tell you that before "meeting" you, I really hadn't given a whole lot of thought to my own personal fantasies. Yes, I read erotic material and watch movies and some scenarios turn me on more than others. But I had never actually put ME into the scene. It was just a turn-on to read about other people doing it. Well, now that I can see it's much more fun to put ME into it, it changes the whole dimension. Most of the time, I just yearn for having good sex and a lot of it. One of the reasons the bathroom scene turns me on so much, I suppose, is that I would have to say that I am limited on variety. Most of my lovemaking has been rather traditional and pretty much missionary style or me on top. So many new things to explore.

>>For example, I'll give you the information that I'm not turned on by EVERYTHING. Yes, it's true. I'm not particularly titillated by, for example, "water sports" (other than water polo, which fascinates

me). I have no interest in pain (giving or receiving), animals (only as friends), and I'm not a great fan of anal activities.

We're on the same page there. Although I have been skinny dipping and enjoy that. As far as animals—NO / Anal—NO / Pain—NO and one more—NO friends, family, or co-workers! I'm not saying I would never go down those roads; I am just not interested in it for now. Plus I'd probably have to be realllllly drunk and I don't plan to be reallllly drunk when I'm with you.

Maybe there are a lot of things I've always wanted to do and just don't know it yet!

>>No, the thing I'm thinking of is this...after hours of hot, sweaty, ravenous intercourse, I find the idea of pulling out my (again, I think the appropriate term) cock and hovering over you, looking into your eyes, and stroking myself until I can't keep control any longer and I spurt hot cum all over your breasts—that idea appeals to me.

I am totally open to that. I don't find it disgusting at all. If you feel guilty about it, you can make it up by taking a nice, warm wash cloth and gently wiping off my body!

I know men are turned on by watching women touch themselves. I'm not sure about that one. That would definitely have to be a part of the bathtub/bathroom scene. Not sure about just lying on the bed next to each other and masturbating.

>>How about you? What sort of clothing do you find to be the sexiest on a man? I ask a bit reluctantly because I would not put "style" in the column of my best attributes. I've never been much of a clothes horse, but hey...maybe you have a weakness for old sneakers!

Probably for me, the most important thing about clothes is that they're clean and in nice condition. I'm kind of a clean freak—not obsessive, but personal hygiene and grooming are definitely a part of my "turned-on" / "turned-off" package. Since we're not holding back, I'm going to just put it out there. This is probably more uncomfortable for me than the fantasy part—primarily because I believe in letting people be who they are—except when they're in bed with me!!! Now some of these may sound so simple, and I think they are to most people. However, you'd be surprised how many men I met through the internet that didn't seem to have a clue! So here goes:

*Freshly showered / deodorant and I lovvvve cologne, but not too much
*Clean fresh breath—no garlic!
*A nicely shaven neck is a turn-on. I love kissing a man's neck, but not when there's hair on it
*I am into nice feet. Now I know not everyone has nice feet and that's okay. (If you have nice feet, and you're comfortable with it, I'll probably want to kiss them, so I'd prefer they are clean and that your toe nails are clipped.)
*Clean hands and finger nails
*And last on the Jay Leno list...trimmed (doesn't have to be shaved) pubic hair is always a plus for someone who loves oral sex.

Oh my god, I sound like a mother! (Well, except for the pubic hair—not from my mom anyway!) Oh well, I guess that's all a part of the package!

As far as underwear on men, silk boxers are probably my favorite. If you're a briefs guy, no need to make a special purchase, as underwear is probably pretty far down on my list of importance.

I'd better move along...I know you're eager to get to that next email!

Karlee

----- Original Message -----
From: Karlee
To: Jack
Sent: Thursday, July 1, 2004 7:08 PM
Subject: My homework assignment!

Essay #2
YOU: Doctor
ME: Patient

I'm a young female virgin coming in for her first gynecological exam. You're a kind, almost fatherly-like, middle aged doctor. You know I am very frightened about this exam, not knowing what it entails. You begin by having me lie down on the bed and slowly undressing me. You tell me that you're going to help me relax by stroking a feather (I'll get one) all over my body. Soft, gentle, tender caresses. My legs are closed tight because I am so afraid. After some time, you begin examining my breasts. Squeezing, circling, and gently pinching my nipples. You tell me everything looks good there, and that a part of the breast exam involves wearing nipple clamps while you do the rest of the exam. My legs are still closed tight. You tell me that the best way for you to proceed is to let you kiss me "down there" so that I can see that this exam won't hurt. Because you are so kind, I open my legs partly for you to come in with your tongue and mouth. (And if I don't explode by then—hey, when I'm aroused, it doesn't take much, so don't spend too long on any one part!) You tell me it's time to insert the tool for the exam and that I will need to spread my legs wide so that you can do the exam. At that point, you reach for my vibrator which is on the night stand in ice water, (YIKES, I can't believe this is me!), and start to probe.

Your turn...

----- Original Message -----
From: Jack
To: Karlee
Sent: Friday, July 2, 2004 5:08 AM
Subject: Re: Essay #2 on the way!

Hi Karlee,

>>*I hope your day has been great. I just got back from the doctor and told her I was having hot sex next week and needed to feel better NOW! I did go to the doctor, but I didn't tell her all that! Just know I will be in tip-top shape by Tuesday!*

I'm glad to hear you're on the mend. I'll remember to tell my doctor that I'm going away for hot sex the next time I'm feeling bad, and maybe I'll get a miracle cure, too.

>> *is I would have to say that I am limited on variety. Most of my lovemaking has been rather traditional and pretty much missionary style or me on top. So many new things to explore.*

I'd say there's nothing wrong with missionary style or you on top...but there are some positions that you've been missing out on! I personally think that a lot of the positions are more stunts or parlor tricks (Twister!) than actually pleasurable. But, you can let me know.

>>*NO friends, family, or co-workers! I'm not saying I would never go down those roads; I just am not interested in it for now. Plus I'd probably have to be reallllly drunk and I don't plan to be reallllly drunk when I'm with you.*

It seems like that's a good policy (friends, family, co-workers), but if you did go down that road, why would being drunk make it better? Seems like you'd want to go in perfectly sober so you'd know what was happening, rather than make a potentially friendship-ending, family-splitting, job-destroying mistake! But, I won't ask you to involve any of those people.

>>*I know men are turned on by watching women touch themselves. I'm not sure about that one. That would definitely have to be a part of the bathtub/bathroom scene. Not sure about just lying on the bed next to each other and masturbating!*

Well, you know...men ARE turned on by watching women touch themselves, so who can blame me? I am a man, after all.

>>*freshly showered / deodorant and I lovvvve cologne, but not too much, clean fresh breath—no garlic!, a nicely shaven neck is a turn-on / I love kissing necks, but not when there's hair on it, I am into nice feet. Now I know not everyone has nice feet and that's okay. (If you have nice feet, and you're comfortable with it, I'll probably want to kiss them so I'd prefer they are clean and that your toe nails are clipped!), clean hands and finger nails, and last on the Jay Leno list... trimmed (doesn't have to be shaved) pubic hair is always a plus for someone who loves oral sex.*

I shower regularly and use deodorant. I'm not much of a cologne guy, but maybe I can do something about that. Fresh breath isn't a problem unless I have just eaten pizza, so I'll make sure not to do that. Shaven neck...got it! I have feet...don't know if they're nice or not. I'm going to guess that they aren't...they're pretty flat. But I'll try to remember to clip my nails, too.

As for the pubic hair, I just trimmed it today!

>>*Oh my god, I sound like a mother! (Well, except for the pubic hair—not from my mom anyway!) Oh well, I guess that's all a part of the package!*

Ha ha! I'm glad your upbringing didn't include lectures on pubic hair trimming from your mom.

>>*I'd better move along...I know you're eager to get to that next email!*

You're right!

--Jack

----- Original Message -----
From: Jack
To: Karlee
Sent: Friday, July 2, 2004 5:09 AM
Subject: Re: Essay #2 on the way!

WOW!

Are you sure you've never done this before? That's a fantastic fantasy. Oh, my.

It's a very hot fantasy.

I'll have to give some thought to my next fantasy, but as it's 2 AM here and I've been working all day, I may have to wait a bit. Besides, I'm too busy thinking about yours. VERY GOOD.

You get an "A."

--Jack

----- Original Message -----
From: Karlee
To: Jack
Sent: Friday, July 2, 2004 10:42 AM
Subject: It's the end of the week...

Hi Jack,

Here we go...

>>I'd say there's nothing wrong with missionary style or you on
top...but there are some positions that you've been missing out on!

Can't wait to find out!

>>It seems like that's a good policy (friends, family, co-workers), but
if you did go down that road, why would being drunk make it
better? Seems like you'd want to go in perfectly sober so you'd
know what was happening, rather than make a potentially
friendship-ending, family-splitting, job-destroying mistake! But, I
won't ask you to involve any of those people.

You've got a good point. I guess because the whole thing is so
foreign to me, I always thought that being drunk would allow me to
loosen up enough to even begin the process. Have you ever gone
down that road?

>>Well, you know...men ARE turned on by watching women touch
themselves, so who can blame me? I am a man, after all.

(Oh dear god, I hope so!) Okay, maybe if you're a good boy, I'll let
you watch!

... and last on the Jay Leno list...actually, after I thought about it, I
think it's David Letterman that has the lists. I'm not much on TV.

>>I'm not much of a cologne guy, but maybe I can do something
about that.

If you're comfortable with this, how about I pick up a few samples of some cologne at the department store. As far as what I like, I don't have an exact one to tell you, anyway. Then you'll have a few to try. I don't need a lot and would also want you to be comfortable with how you smell, too!

Now about my fantasy...

>>*Are you sure you've never done this before? That's a fantastic fantasy. Oh, my.*

No, I've never done this before. I've just spent a lot of time walking around a store we have here with adult toys and lingerie wondering what it would be like to be with a man who is open to all these toys, gadgets, lotions and potions! I'm glad you liked it. Parts of it were a stretch for me. Glad to know it may have "stretched" you, too!

>>*I'll have to give some thought to my next fantasy, but as it's 2 AM here and I've been working all day...*

We're going to have to start getting you to bed early...I don't want you falling asleep on me during the exam!

>>*You get an "A."*

Okay, so I'm somewhat of an over-achiever. Is there something I could have added to make it an A+?

I'll be back soon.

Karlee

----- Original Message -----
From: Karlee
To: Jack
Sent: Friday, July 2, 2004 11:03 AM
Subject: Logistics time . . .

Me again!

Okay, so we're getting down to the nitty-gritty. I haven't jumped ship and you're still here! (Oh, yes, it still enters my mind from time to time!)

Assuming I'm feeling good enough, I might be away for part of the weekend. So I thought today might be a good day to start some dialogue about what next week might look like. I understand nothing is carved in stone and all is subject to change. But since there are (or were originally!) other parts to this trip for me, I'd like to start to get a better idea of what it might look like.

Do you know your schedule? I'll be in Tuesday afternoon. Should we plan to have our "initial screening" :-) on Tuesday evening? Since I know myself well enough to know I'll be worked up about this (some of that good, some nervous), it might be good for me to just find what happens out right away instead of allowing myself to be pre-occupied more than I need to be.

How familiar are you with the Strip? There's an area that has outdoor seating that is between Harrah's and I think Imperial Palace. One thing I know for sure... it's near Ghirardelli's Chocolate! Or we could pick a more visible landmark and walk to that area if you are not familiar with it.

What are your thoughts?

And how's your Essay #2 coming along? (Wink, wink!)

Karlee

----- Original Message -----
From: Jack
To: Karlee
Sent: Friday, July 2, 2004 1:39 PM
Subject: Re: Logistics time . . .

Hi Karlee!

>>*You've got a good point. I guess because the whole thing is so foreign to me, I*

always thought that being drunk would allow me to loosen up enough to even begin the process. Have you ever gone down that road?

Do you mean gone down the road of having something to drink to loosen up? I'm not much of a drinker myself, and I certainly don't think being drunk helps any situation. I knew some people in my younger days that would get drunk and use that as an excuse for their behavior. It sort of became a "secret identity," except instead of a cape and mask, it involved staggering and vomit. See? This is why I think drunk isn't the way to go. It may involve vomit and it's hard to be erotic and sexy when you're talking about vomit.

>>and last on the Jay Leno list....actually, after I thought about it, I think it's David Letterman that has the lists. I'm not much on TV.

I used to watch a lot of TV, but these days I don't watch much either. I think you're right, though, Letterman has the top ten lists.

>>If you're comfortable with this, how about I pick up a few samples of some cologne at the department store. As far as what I like, I don't have an exact one to tell you, anyway. Then you'll have a few to try. I don't need a lot and would also want you to be comfortable with how you smell, too!

I'm open to that. Although, I wouldn't say that I'm UNcomfortable with how I smell right now!

>> No, I've never done this before. I've just spent a lot of time walking around a store we have here that sells adult toys and lingerie wondering what it would be like to be with a man who is open to all these toys, gadgets, lotions and potions! I'm glad you liked it. Parts of it were a stretch for me. Glad to know it may have "stretched" you, too!

It was very, very, really, very good.

>>We're going to have to start getting you to bed early... I don't want you falling asleep on me during the exam!

I have problems sleeping and a wacky work schedule, but I don't think it's possible that I'd fall asleep during the exam!

>>*Okay, so I'm somewhat of an over-achiever. Is there something I could have added to make it an A+?*

I was going to give you an A+, but I wanted to leave room just in case a future essay was even better!

--Jack

----- Original Message -----
From: Jack
To: Karlee
Sent: Friday, July 2, 2004 1:58 PM
Subject: Re: Logistics time . . .

Oh, good; I always like the nitty-gritty.

I hope you feel well enough for a trip this weekend...don't let yourself relapse, though! I left Vegas for a few days to a more humid climate and when I came back, I felt very dry (especially my throat). Remember to drink LOTS of water. More than you think you possibly can. That'll help.

Other than that, my schedule is fairly wacky. Typically the worst days for me are Fridays, Saturdays, Sundays, and...Tuesdays. But! This Tuesday might be good. The trouble is, I might not know until Tuesday. Right now, it looks like I'll be free. I'm sure you'll want some time to unpack/settle-in, but earlier will be better than later, I think.

I'm familiar with the Strip. I believe I know the area you're talking about (it's more-or-less directly behind Harrah's, right?) Perhaps a different location might be better...it will be 105 outside, and if you like someone who is clean and refreshed, perhaps an indoor cafe/restaurant would be a good idea. The trouble is, I very rarely go to the Strip and have a hard time thinking of a place where we could meet. I guess inside the Ghirardelli's Chocolate might be one option.

The question is how we can contact each other. Is the number you gave me a cell phone? We could figure it out that way. I know that the amount of time it takes me to get to that part of the Strip is entirely random, so it would be good if I could give you updates.

>>*And how's your Essay #2 coming along? (Wink, wink!)*

I'm still thinking about it...it's in progress!

--Jack

----- Original Message -----
From: Jack
To: Karlee
Sent: Friday, July 2, 2004 2:54 PM
Subject: Essay

For the purposes of this fantasy, each of us are married or with someone, we've never met, and we're all vacationing in Vegas.

You've had a long, relaxing day on your vacation. Your partner went off and did his own thing, playing cards, then said he'd be going out late to check out the night life (probably the strip clubs). You spent the day at the pool, enjoying the solitude. Later on, you went to the spa in the hotel and had a massage, followed by a nice meal, and you decide to go to bed. You change into your comfy satin nightdress and get into bed.

I've had a long day, running around the Strip, attending some convention. I wanted to be having fun, but it's been work. All day, I've been exposed to scantily-clad models and half-naked women trying to sell their products. I've been thinking about sex all day, and I know my partner has been out doing her own thing all day, too. I think she won't be back at the hotel before me; she mentioned going to see a show, and I think that I may use the time alone to pleasure myself because I'm so worked up.

I get back to my massive hotel and look at my card key. I wonder why they don't put the numbers on the keys, and struggle to remember what part of the hotel my room is in. I'm pretty sure it's 872. If you'd been standing there, you could've told me that 872 is YOUR room. But, you were already in bed at that time, and we'd never met.

I find 872 and it looks like the right room from the hallway (they ALL look the same) so I dip my card in. It doesn't open. I try again. Nothing. A housekeeper is rolling her cart past me at that moment and I explain that my card doesn't work, and that I don't want to go all the way down to the front desk, and she very kindly opens the door for me.

I step into the room. It's dark; the curtains are drawn. From the light in the hall, I can see that someone's in the bed, so I know it must be my partner. She must've decided to go to bed earlier than I thought. I close the door and take off my shoes and socks, and very quietly undo my belt so I don't disturb her. You rustle slightly, so tired and relaxed, and fall deeper into your sleep.

I remove my pants and put them on the chair. I'm breathing in short excited breaths. I'm so hard. It's strange; perhaps something about the city has made my libido go through the roof. I step out of my boxers and toss them on the chair, and climb into bed next to you.

You're lying on the right side of the bed, facing away from me. I catch a whiff of your perfume—my partner's perfume. I lay on my back, my cock acting as a tent pole with the sheets. I know I can't sleep like this. I figure you've had a hard day and I don't want to disturb you, so I being to stroke myself slowly. I let out a little sigh, and in your sleep you hear it and also make a little noise. I stop. I whisper, "Are you awake?" as softly as I can. You think you're dreaming; you don't recognize the voice...it's that sleepy, floating sensation. You curl your body a bit more and your rear end rubs against my leg.

I trace my fingers along your back, very lightly. I run my hands up and down, caressing your bottom, brushing up against your inner thighs and the back of your knees. I kiss the back of your neck; you feel my hot breath as it gives you goose bumps. My fingers go down between your legs, ever so gently, touching your pussy. I stroke you softly for several moments as you sleep, until I feel you begin to get wetter and wetter.

You are having an amazing dream...it's not about a person; just about the sensations your body is enjoying. You begin to moan quietly.

As my other hand continues to rub your back and legs, I think how soft your skin is. Maybe you're using a new moisturizer? And you seem to be in better shape. How did I not notice this? Maybe I've been working too hard and neglecting my partner, or maybe I'm just finding myself more drawn to her because I'm feeling the charge of Vegas.

I roll onto my side and my cock brushes up against the outside of your pussy. I can feel your moisture. Still, you're asleep, and I don't want to wake you. I wrap my arm around your waist and hold you, but your pelvis has started to rock back and forth, pushing against me.

You push back and my cock slides slowly inside you. Deeper, deeper, it penetrates you until you feel your whole body is filled up. It's so slow, and wet, and I moan in pleasure. You also moan. I move my arms up and caress your breasts as I begin to thrust in and out of you, slowly and firmly. I notice your breasts seem so much fuller and that makes my cock even harder.

You can't sleep any longer and you have a strange sense of disorientation. You were dreaming, feeling enormous pleasure, and now you realize you're being taken from behind. Your partner came home early, you assume, but this isn't anything like making love to him. It's so...wonderful. You think that maybe Vegas had an impact on him, too.

As we both move together, the pace increases. You grab my hand as I cup your breasts. You become aware that things are different. Those hands are stronger, yet gentler. And something is definitely different about the hard flesh that's inside you. It's different in a good way.

I hear you moan and I wonder why your voice doesn't sound the same. Perhaps the dry air has changed the tone of your voice. That seems unlikely. I reach up and stroke your hair. It's totally different. Maybe you spent the day at the hair stylist?

As we both get closer and closer to orgasm, we call out our partners' names. At that moment, we both realize...what do we do? I freeze, my cock still inside you. My hands still hold your breasts. We're still intertwined, spooning together. Neither of us moves. What do I do? What will you do? I can hear my own heart thumping in my chest. You feel it too, along with your own heart.

We stay completely motionless for what seems like hours. Do we both know that we're in the wrong room? It feels so much better than either of us have ever experienced. We try to convince ourselves that maybe we are in the right place, after all...even though we know it isn't true.

I adjust my hips, ever so slightly and excruciatingly slowly. I want to know what will happen. I don't know what will happen, but I have to find out. You stroke my hand lightly, and then squeeze the muscles inside your pussy, grabbing onto my cock. I again start rotating my hips, thrusting in and out of you, gaining speed, going deeper and deeper. Suddenly, I roll you onto your back and push your legs apart as I climb on top of you. The room is dark, but we can see each other for the first time now...again, we pause...but not for long. I lean in to kiss you as I begin to make love to you more and more passionately. Our hands intertwine, and we look into each others' eyes. We're both screaming now, and I feel your body begin to shake and watch your back arch as you get close to cumming...this sends me over the top, I can no longer control myself, and together we reach the heights of ecstasy. The muscles in our bodies constrict, we throw our heads back, and we pull each other closer together. You feel my cock spasm inside you as my warm cum fills you. We collapse together, breathing hard and caressing each other.

So, there you go. That's a real stranger fantasy...it'll never happen, but the idea appeals to me. I can imagine it pretty vividly.

--Jack

----- Original Message -----
From: Karlee
To: Jack

Sent: Friday, July 2, 2004 3:43PM
Subject: Re: Essay

OH MY GOSH, JACK... My arms are like Jell-O. I can barely type on the keyboard.

This is amazing. I almost had an orgasm just reading it.

I'll be back to answer the other emails later. I need to go and recover!

----- Original Message -----
From: Karlee
To: Jack
Sent: Friday, July 2, 2004 5:13 PM
Subject: I'm speechless...

Hi Jack,

I don't know how you are even able to be at work. I don't know if this is turning you on as much as it is me. I'm just about going nuts over here. I was just in the bathroom and had a whole fantasy about you being here and us being in my Jacuzzi tub... You sitting on the edge, enjoying, as I am sucking your "fully erect penis"—OK—cock, while I'm having an opportunity to let one of the water jets bring me pleasure.

In a previous email, I asked you the question, "Have you ever gone down that road?" Your response was, "Do you mean gone down the road of having something to drink to loosen up?" No, I meant the road regarding my comment about no friends, neighbors, co-workers. Ménage-Trios? / Orgies?

>>Although, I wouldn't say that I'm UNcomfortable with how I smell right now!

I'm sure you do smell fine. And after Essay #2, you could be crawling out of a swamp and I'd be ready to throw you down on your back and mount your rock, hard cock. Okay, that was a stretch for me. Using the words with a stranger, I mean. Meaning it—no, that part was EASY!

>>I was going to give you an A+, but I wanted to leave room just in case a future essay was even better!

I'm not sure I can do another one. I'm barely able to function already.

Karlee

----- Original Message -----
From: Karlee
To: Jack
Sent: Friday, July 2, 2004 5:27 PM
Subject: Next week . . .

Hi Jack,

You wrote...

>>I hope you feel well enough for a trip this weekend...don't let yourself relapse, though! Remember to drink LOTS of water.

You really are a nice guy, aren't you? I am feeling better. The Rx must be working. Of course now I seem to have this problem with a constant throbbing between my legs and excessive secretions. I already know where I need to go to take care of that! WEST!

>>I'm sure you'll want some time to unpack/settle-in.

Yes, please give me at least 5 minutes! :-)

>>...it will be 105 outside,

Yes, and right now my body heat is at about 505, that's 610 and much too hot to be outside!

>>Perhaps an indoor cafe/restaurant would be a good idea.

What a great idea that is! Let me think of an option or two. I like the idea of a cafe/restaurant better than Ghirardelli's Chocolate. That place just seems too wholesome after what we've been up to! Hey, it's a family place!

>>*The question is how we can contact each other.*

Yes, my cell phone number is 440-###-####. We can communicate that way.

Karlee

----- Original Message -----
From: Jack
To: Karlee
Sent: Friday, July 2, 2004 5:31 PM
Subject: Re: I'm speechless . . .

Hi Karlee,

Wow, I'm glad you liked what I wrote!

>>*I don't know how you are even able to be at work. I don't know if this is turning you on as much as it is me. I'm just about going nuts over here.*

It's hard (so to speak) to be working. I think you would have been able to tell that I'm turned on!

>>*just in the bathroom and had a whole fantasy about you being here and us being in my Jacuzzi tub... You sitting on the edge, enjoying, as I am sucking your "fully erect penis"—OK—cock, while I'm having an opportunity to let one of the water jets bring me pleasure.*

That sounds... excellent. Sign me up!

>>*No, I meant the road regarding my comment about no friends, neighbors, co-workers. Ménage-Trios? / Orgies?*

I've gone down some roads...I mean, friends, definitely. I think friends are a great choice, unless they get weird, but if they're already your friends, you know whether they'll get weird or not. Co-workers, too. Co-workers is odd because it's seen as "inappropriate" and sometimes it's explicitly against policy...but, the reality is a lot of people get together at work because they spend so much time together. I've never gotten together with neighbors...maybe I don't leave my house enough. As for orgies... I suppose it depends how you define an orgy, but probably not by any definition I can think of. (Is two couples independently engaging in sexual activities in the same room an orgy?)

>>*I'm sure you do smell fine. And after Essay #2, you could be crawling out of a swamp and I'd be ready to throw you down on your back and mount your rock, hard cock. Okay, that was a stretch for me. Using the words with a stranger, I mean. Meaning it—no, that part was EASY!*

If it's all the same to you, I'll still plan on showering. No swamps in Vegas, anyway.

>>*I'm not sure I can do another one. I'm barely able to function already.*

I'm glad you'll have something to think about on your trip this weekend!

I'd like to know a bit about how you think we should proceed if we both decide we want to try to move forward. Like...what might we want to do? You know, you only get that first time once! It'd be nice if we could tell whether we were both ready to "take things further" without having to talk about it explicitly...at least, it would be nice from my point of view. I don't know; what are your thoughts? I'd like to try to make any of those fantasies happen to some extent, again only if we're both willing.

Tell me what would make you the happiest. No obligation, of course, and we'll make sure to find a way that's perfectly safe. I don't know, for example if you really wanted to sort of live out the essay I sent today, we could talk and meet for a while, and my signal to you that I'm interested might be that I say I have to get up and go to the bathroom. When I was away, if you thought you were also interested, maybe you could sneak a key to your room under my napkin, and when I got back, you could say, "Nice to see you," and head up to your room. If there was no key, I'd know you weren't interested. If I didn't go to the bathroom, you'd know I wasn't interested.

Of course, what if I REALLY had to go the bathroom? And what if you had to go the bathroom? I guess this isn't perfectly thought out, but I think you get the general idea of what I'm thinking. Right? We could work out the details (like, how I'd know which hotel and which room the key was for, so I didn't actually live out that fantasy for real!)

What do you think?

--Jack

----- Original Message -----
From: Jack
To: Karlee
Sent: Friday, July 2, 2004 5:48 PM
Subject: Re: Next week...

Okay, so just in case we were thinking everything was going too perfectly...

It turns out I do have a few commitments that will be tough (or impossible) to break. I have something at 7:30 that will last until at least 9:30 or 10:00, I'm guessing, but maybe I could get out at 9. That's on Tuesday. That leaves us a few options: beforehand (but I'd have to rush out, which is no good unless you get in very early in the afternoon) or after my commitment (which would be fine with me, but you'd be up late, late, late). We could wait until Wednesday (I've got something I'm supposed to do between 7–9ish but I think I'll skip it) but then we'd have to wait...and....well that's no good.

Thursday night I have another commitment, again 7–9ish. Friday afternoon I hope to be free, but Friday and Saturday will probably be bad for me.

All of those events are at the Palms, which isn't far away from where we're talking about meeting.

I think you'd have a tough time staying up until 10:00pm (1am your time) but who knows? What do you think? I might be out a bit earlier, but not much.

--Jack

---- Original Message -----
From: Karlee
To: Jack
Sent: Friday, July 2, 2004 8:00 PM
Subject: Re: Next week...

Hi Jack,

Sad news about your schedule! Is it subject to change again? If so, perhaps we should just wait a bit (a day or two) and see if the options are still the same. My preference would be to not get too worked up about any one scenario and then find out it won't work!

>>It'd be nice if we could tell whether we were both ready to "take things further" without having to talk about it explicitly.

I agree it would be nice and certainly adds to the excitement of it all. However, I'm not sure that will be an option on the first night. Although I love the idea of the room key fantasy, I know myself well enough to know that I would not give my room key to anyone I just met an hour ago. I know that was a part of your whole fantasy (sex with a stranger). I totally understand if you want to save all this for someone who is not so cautious! We agreed that there were no obligations. If it's meant to be, we'll figure out a way that works for both of us.

Considering how your week looks, although it may take away from some of the "excitement," maybe we should meet Tuesday after your meeting. If we're comfortable, we can move into Wednesday evening for a next step. As far as 10:00 being 1:00 my time, that's not a problem for two reasons. 1. I can take a nap when I get in! 2. When coming from the east coast, I always do my best to stay up as late as possible to help with the adjustment to a different time zone. So, Tuesday after your meeting might work.

Sounds like Thursday is out. I leave Saturday morning. That would possibly give us Friday afternoon if we want more!

Your thoughts?

Karlee

----- Original Message -----
From: Jack
To: Karlee
Sent: Friday, July 2, 2004 8:29 PM
Subject: Re: Next week ...

My schedule isn't likely to change (in fact, it didn't change; I just didn't realize that I had these events next week.)

I can certainly do late Tuesday. I can give you a call when I'm leaving the Palms (a little before 10pm) and we can meet up at a place of your choosing.

That schedule won't change, unless I wind up finishing slightly earlier.

As for the room key idea, I understand...no problem. I will plan to head home after our meeting and hope that you are up for a re-meeting on Wednesday (and/or Thursday or Friday). Thursday is a bit of a question mark for me, other than a couple of hours in the early evening. I might have the day free until 7pm, or not. Don't know that yet.

See, this part isn't nearly as fun as the essays...but at least it means we're getting closer to meeting, possibly!

--Jack

----- Original Message -----
From: Karlee
To: Jack
Sent: Friday, July 2, 2004 9:25 PM
Re: Next week . . .

Hi Jack,

I love that this whole experience has given me an opportunity to learn so much more about myself. I love personal growth and development work and this is some work!

Since a part of this is us being able to share what's on our mind with no attachment, please excuse my "rambling" for a few moments...

After I sent that last email, I ran (well drove, didn't run) up to the mall. While I was there, I started to question why I was so quick to "kick out" the room key idea. I know part of it is because I tell myself I am a smart woman. But what came up for me is that this is part of the reason I haven't had much sex! I have too many rules! And yes, rules are good and they serve us in many situations, even ones such as this. BUT, too many rules is exactly why I posted the personals ad in the first place. I'm tired of boxing myself in, or should I say out, of experiences because of my own fear. Even telling you that brings up fear, because I know they teach in self-defense classes to not appear afraid! I mean it goes back to what we talked about earlier in the week. This is not much different than if I was lying by the pool at my hotel, met some guy, felt a sexually charged connection and off we go. Now that's not my norm, and yet doing that would not be the worst thing in the world, right, and the risk would potentially be the same. I would know him no more than I know you. Maybe even less. By next week, I will probably know you better than the first guy I invited to my place and had sex with last year. I guess it's probably too much hype on "Internet Connections Gone Bad." Too much emphasis on people being able to be someone different than who they really are. But I am being who I am, so why would I think you're not really who you are? And would my mom really send me someone who would harm me?! I think not! So when the whole room key thing came up, I allowed my imagination to get out of hand. I'm not saying I have totally changed

55

my mind about it. I just wanted to see if I could get in touch with why that created me to start to put up a wall to this whole thing. I guess it was the whole idea of you being alone with my key and not knowing if you blah, blah...

Actually, I have been skydiving (not in the nude), and how much scarier can this be than jumping out of a plane?!?

What concerns do you still have with this? It sounded like there might be some based on your "If I don't go to the bathroom, it means I'm not interested in moving forward" comment.

Karlee

----- Original Message -----
From: Karlee
To: Jack
Sent: Friday, July 2, 2004 9:31 PM
Subject: Re: Room Number

>>I wonder why they don't put the numbers on the keys, and struggle to remember what part of the hotel my room is in. I'm pretty sure it's 872. If you'd been standing there, you could've told me that 872 is YOUR room. But, you were already in bed at that time, and we'd never met.

On a lighter note...if I check in on Tuesday and find I'm in Room 872, I'll know that's a sign to GO!!!!! Heck, I'll rush down to the Palms to look for you!

And yes, I was reading it again! Mmmmmmmm—Mmmmmmmmmm!

C'mon 872.

----- Original Message -----
From: Karlee
To: Jack
Sent: Friday, July 2, 2004 9:35 PM

Subject: Re: Scents

I'm still reading. ☺

>>*I catch a whiff of your perfume – my partner's perfume.*

Do you have scents that you are particularly fond of?

Back to the essay...

----- Original Message -----
From: Jack
To: Karlee
Sent: Friday, July 2, 2004 9:56 PM
Subject: Re: Next week...

Hi Karlee!

>>*I love that this whole experience has given me an opportunity to learn so much more about myself. I love personal growth and development work and this is some work!*

Me, too, although I guess I don't think of this as "work." Work doesn't typically leave me this aroused.

Regarding the room key idea, I understand your fear in that. I guess I didn't think about how it could be scary. In my mind, at that point, we will have decided to either move forward or not, and we could have a conversation ("So...what do you think?" "I think we should move forward!" "I agree wholeheartedly!" "Very well, then let us proceed to the elevator...") although I don't think the conversation would be that easy. My thinking was, at that point, you'd go up to the room, and I'd follow you a few minutes later.

From a safety standpoint, I guess I didn't see that as any riskier than going up with you. If you were worried that I could hand the key off to someone that could rob your room, I could understand. I guess I don't understand how at the point when I'd be coming up to your room would be any riskier than handing me the key, but that doesn't matter...if you are frightened by the idea, we certainly won't do it...not a problem at all.

>>*connection and off we go. Now that's not my norm, and yet doing that would not be the worst thing in the world, right, and the risk would potentially be the same. I would know him no more than I know you. Maybe even less.*

I think it's safe to say it would be considerably less. But your point about the hype of internet scare stories is a good one. I've heard many, although to tell the truth...and I've never really thought about this before...I don't think I HAVE heard many. I think maybe once or twice I've seen stories in the news about a teenage girl going off to meet a guy she thinks is 15 and who turns out to be 45, but I think the "everyone on the internet is dangerous" mentality is kind of like "never eat Halloween candy because it's filled with razor-blades." I had this idea that there was some kind of a trend of sick people putting razor blades in candy, but in reality, I don't know of a single case.

In any event, people do undoubtedly misrepresent themselves on-line. But, you can judge for yourself whether I am what I say I am. I'll be making the same assessment about you...that's why we'll meet.

All other things being equal, I really can't imagine a place that could be safer than a casino on the Strip. There are people around everywhere, security cameras on every floor and entrance.

I certainly don't mind talking to you and telling you if I find you very attractive and feel comfortable with you and want to go up to your room and make love to you. Having to do that wouldn't ruin it for me...I just like thinking about the exciting possibilities only if they're mutually non-threatening.

>>*Actually, I have been skydiving (not in the nude), and how much scarier can this be than jumping out of a plane!?*

I would think considerably less scary. But, I know more about me than you do, so there you go.

>>*What concerns do you still have with this? It sounded like there might be*

some based on your "If I don't go to the bathroom, it means I'm not interested in moving forward" comment.

Well, I'm in somewhat of the same boat as you. I want to meet you and see how that goes. Maybe you'd make me uncomfortable...it seems unlikely, but it's possible. Maybe I'd feel like you really didn't want to do this...who knows? I mean, if you suddenly decided you really wanted to live out that whole "wrong room" fantasy, and left a key in my name for your room at the desk and wanted that to be our first meeting...that would certainly be tempting, but I'd have my own hesitations. Keep in mind, almost everything that you think of in your "worst case scenario" could also affect me. I realize there are some risks, but I think they're minimal. Still...it's good to know what you're getting into. I mean, when I was a child, I was TERRIFIED to go to New York City. I'd see the news and it was murder, kill, robbery, rape, murder, murder, museum opening, mugging, murder. In my mind, I'd be instantly killed if I went there. But, you know...it's fine. I still vote for "play it by ear." We'll be in touch. Figure out what you're comfortable with; don't feel like you have to do ANYTHING that makes you nervous, because you don't. On the other hand, don't get too fearful...this is a high-anxiety situation, but it should be in a good way.

That's my two cents. Let's see how it goes.

--Jack

----- Original Message -----
From: Jack
To: Karlee
Sent: Friday, July 2, 2004 9:56 PM
Subject: Re: Room number . . . .

>>C'mon 872!

I'm glad you liked it!

--Jack

----- Original Message -----
From: Jack
To: Karlee
Sent: Friday, July 2, 2004 9:58 PM
Subject: Re: scents . . .

>>*Do you have scents that you are particularly fond of?*

You know, I'm sure I do...but I couldn't tell you what they are. There are a couple that I notice...I recognize, whenever I smell them, I spin around to see who smells so good, but I don't know what they are. Now I wish I did.

--Jack

----- Original Message -----
From: Karlee
To: Jack
Sent: Saturday, July 3, 2004 12:51 PM
Subject: Time to vote?

Hi Jack,

How are you today? At work?

I decided to stay home and get another good night's sleep in my own bed. I'm feeling better, but not yet 100%. My dad has a boat on Lake Erie and I was going to spend the day with him. I might go tomorrow just for the day.

I pulled out my suitcase this morning to start packing. Quite an interesting thought process than any other trip I've taken!

What I've been thinking as far as Tuesday...how about we meet as planned after your meeting. We'll chat for awhile and see where it goes. Assuming we are both interested in moving forward...we'll go to my room. Will you have been working all day plus into the evening at that point? I mean, I know when sex is involved a man can stay up late. But how many "hours" do you think you'd really have left? I was thinking we could either start with that board game or perhaps create another scenario that could lead to the bathroom scene. This is far from outrageous, but I think it would still be fun. Something like: I'm a horny, single woman on vacation. (Hey, how creative is that!) We meet, talk for awhile, and I invite you to my room. (If we go this route, we can come up with how we want that to unfold, i.e., I put my hand under the table and reach for your crotch and ask you if you would be kind enough to come to my room and help me with the city map, or I take my foot and rub it up your leg toward your crotch or something like that.) We go. We are getting acquainted. I walk over to the table and ask you to show me the highlights of the city on a map. I'm standing at the table. (I'm sure there will be some kind of Las Vegas guidebook in the room.) You start out next to me, but then for a better view of the book, you move close behind me so that you can look over my shoulder and point to the highlights. You start to tease me by nuzzling my neck and gently moving your pelvis to my back end. I can feel you are getting aroused and I am, too. I finally admit that I am ready to succumb to my temptation, but that I would really like to take a bath since I've been traveling all day. I excuse myself to the bathroom...and Take 2—The Bathroom Scene!

Now, another consideration...coming from, "What if this is just one encounter?" (It sounds like we are both open to more than one, yet we know it's too soon to tell for sure.) So, IF we only had one, which fantasy would you vote for? I really hope we can get to the Wrong Room fantasy. I'm just not comfortable starting with that one. But I have to know some things ahead of time so I know how to dress and what to have "prepared" for the room! So if we look at three—if you could choose only one—which would you choose? We've got 1. Bathroom Scene 2. You doctor/Me patient 3. Me: Hotel guest/You: Guest Services! I think my first choice would be the above scenario, either with the guide book or the board game. AND, we're in this together, so I want to hear what your preference is, too. And perhaps we'll take parts of all of them. I don't know—it's like trying to eat for a whole week in one day!

Another preparation question: Assuming we end up in my room, is there anything you would like me to have there for you? Something to drink? Pop, beer, wine? Water? Anything else that would make it a better experience for you?

Also, I'm not promising I will deliver on this one, but I am curious...how do you prefer your women? Shaved? Not? Something in between?

Looking forward to hearing from you!

Karlee

Hi Karlee!

I'm good today. I'm doing a little bit of work, but not much. I was going to play racquetball last night and the court was full, so my friend and I went to eat instead. So much for exercising and being healthy.

I'm sorry you're missing a trip to the lake. But, you know, you are about to go on vacation and you don't want to have a relapse and be sick in Vegas. That'd be less than perfect.

>>*What I've been thinking as far as Tuesday...how about we meet as planned after your meeting. We'll chat for awhile and see where it goes. Assuming we are both interested in moving forward...we'll go to my room. Will you have been working all day plus into the evening at that point?*

I will have been working, but I'll make a point of shifting my schedule a bit to start later. I'm never in bed before 1 or 2am and often awake and alert until 4 or 5am. I may even try to take a nap! And keep in mind..."work" isn't breaking rocks with a sledgehammer. I'll be wide awake.

>>*would still be fun. Something like: I'm a horny, single woman on vacation.*

(Hey, how creative is that!) We meet, talk for awhile, and I invite you to my room. (if we go this route, we can come up with how we want that to unfold, i.e., I put my hand under the table and reach for your crotch and ask you if you would be kind enough to come to my room and help me with the city map, or I

I think this idea is perfect. That seems very sexy and I think it leads perfectly into the bathroom scene, and it follows your "full service" fantasy, too! As an indication of just exactly how exciting I find it, I can barely type! Hmmm.

I think I have a change to that bathroom scene, though. Maybe you should take a shower rather than a bath. You know, it takes so long for the tub to fill up and all that...see, I'm always thinking!

>>aroused and I am too. I finally admit that I am ready to succumb to my temptation, but that I would really like to take a bath since I've been traveling all day. I excuse myself to the bathroom... and Take 2—The Bathroom Scene!

I don't want to be suggesting too much...because this is equally my fantasies and your fantasies, but from my point of view, there's no need for you to admit anything. I kind of like the idea of going up to your room with all of the flirting being somewhat restrained. Maybe my touches are accidental. You might just excuse yourself to take a shower after your travels, so that when I "sneak in" to watch, it's kind of more of a "surprise." I guess this is kind of silly, since we're talking about what could happen anyway, but I like the idea of that unspoken sexual tension. Is that appealing to you, or would you like things to be more...spoken?

>>Now, another consideration...coming from, "What if this is just one encounter?" (It sounds like we are both open to more than one, yet we know it's too soon to tell for sure.) So, IF we only had one, which fantasy would you vote for? I really hope we can get to the Wrong Room fantasy. I'm just not comfortable starting with that one. But I have to know some things ahead of time so I

If this is just one encounter, I think...it would be very hard to choose! I think the Wrong Room idea would be tough as a first encounter, too. Although, if I were to come back another night, that might be VERY exciting. I really like your doctor's appointment idea...too bad I don't have a doctor's coat and stethoscope.

If I had to choose, I think your idea above is the best of all worlds! For example...maybe instead of Guest Services, I'm just the extremely friendly Vegas host (which, in fact, I am!) We meet and talk, if you're interested in moving forward you ask if I could give you some tips about visiting Vegas. I could brush up against you, press my hips into you while standing behind you, and maybe give you a little light (clothed) massage...you wonder whether I'm interested in you or just a "nice guy." After a while you go for your shower, and then...well...my interest becomes very apparent!

I'm certainly open to the board game and other ideas, but I think we've come up with something MUCH better than the game. We're good at this.

>>*hear what your preference is, too. And perhaps we'll take parts of all of them. I don't know—it's like trying to eat for a whole week in one day!*

Exactly! We may have to meet more than once. I'm definitely interested in exploring the other ones, too.

>>*Another preparation question: Assuming we end up in my room, is there anything you would like me to have there for you? Something to drink? Pop, beer, wine? Water? Anything else that would make it a better experience for you?*

Maybe a can of soda...I have a feeling my mouth will be dry with nervousness! But, I'm sure we can find anything we need. How about you? Anything I should bring? Will you have a Vegas tourist map?

>>*Also, I'm not promising I will deliver on this one, but I am curious...how do you prefer your women? Shaved? Not? Something in between?*

That's a good question. I'm not sure what my preference is. I have very limited experience with shaved women, but I find it very appealing for oral sex. VERY appealing. Okay, I think the answer is shaved, because now the idea is turning me on...but any way you like is fine with me!

>>*We still have to figure out where to meet! I suppose that could be done on the day of...*

I'm REALLY looking forward to meeting you! This has been one of the most sexually charged weeks I can remember!

--Jack

----- Original Message -----
From: Karlee
To: Jack
Sent: Saturday, July 3, 2004 12:51 PM
Subject: Really close now

Hi Jack,

I hope you had (are still having) a good day. I'm back with some thoughts about your thoughts!

>>*I'm never in bed before 1 or 2am and often awake and alert until 4 or 5am.*

What kind of vitamins do you take?!!! You don't have to answer that. Just a rhetorical question!

>>*I think I have a change to that bathroom scene, though. Maybe you should take a shower rather than a bath.*

I actually was thinking the same thing. Wasn't sure if a shower would be as erotic as a bath, though. I guess that's my job, huh? I'll start practicing with my next shower!

>>*but from my point of view, there's no need for you to admit anything*

Actually, we're on the same page here. I was only having that dialogue in my head and didn't see myself actually "telling" you! Guess I was just thinking out loud!

>>like the idea of that unspoken sexual tension. Is that appealing to you, or would you like things to be more...spoken?

Unspoken is good for me. I've yet to be with a partner that encouraged a lot of dialogue, so that's kind of foreign to me anyway.

>>Exactly! We may have to meet more than once. I'm definitely interested in exploring the other ones, too.

And I'm sure we could come up with more if we needed to!

>>Maybe a can of soda...

What kind...Pepsi, Coke? Just let me know. I'm a big bottled water drinker, so I'm sure I'll be going to a store for that.

>>Will you have a Vegas tourist map?

I'll bring something that can act as a map, or possibly an actual map.

>>We still have to figure out where to meet!

I've got a few ideas in my head. I'll share those tomorrow or Monday. If at all possible, I'd like to have as much of this in place before I get on the plane. It will help with my anxiety and add to the excitement!

>>I'm REALLY looking forward to meeting you! This has been one of the most sexually charged weeks I can remember!

Same here. If I had a nickel for every thought I've had and the thoughts were burning calories, I'd be a size 2 millionaire!

By the way, I don't think I'll be bringing any cologne. I stopped at a couple of men's fragrance counters and evidently samples are not a big commodity. The one counter had a couple to give, and they just about gagged me. I think I'll take the chance that I will love your natural body scent!

Karlee

----- Original Message -----
From: Karlee
To: Jack
Sent: Saturday, July 3, 2004 9:13 PM
Subject: Another question

Hi again,

Do you have an image already in your head of what this stranger you fantasize about having sex with would be wearing? I won't be going shopping before I leave, but I can see if I have something in line with what might be pleasing to you. Maybe it will match what I already have in mind! Stockings are pretty much out of the question. It would be unusual for a woman to be wearing them in Las Vegas during the month of July, unless perhaps she's a professional, a dancer, etc. Most likely not a tourist!

Karlee

----- Original Message -----
From: Karlee
To: Jack
Sent: Saturday, July 3, 2004 9:53 PM
Subject: How does this sound?

Hi Jack,

Since you mentioned massage...

I just came across a brochure from the Canyon Ranch Spa at the Venetian that I picked up when I was in Vegas last year. Rather than helping me with sightseeing, do you like the idea of helping me to pick out a spa package?

Karlee

----- Original Message -----
From: Jack

To: Karlee
Sent: Sunday, July 4, 2004 12:41 AM
Subject: Re: Another question . . .

>>*Do you have an image already in your head of what this stranger you fantasize about having sex with would be wearing? I won't be going shopping before I leave, but I can see if I have something in line with what might be pleasing to you. Maybe it will match what I already have in mind!*

I have a feeling whatever you have will be great. I think my earlier email covered all the sorts of things I really like (although I may not have described them all adequately).

>>*Stockings are pretty much out of the question. It would be unusual for a woman to be wearing them in Las Vegas during the month of July, unless perhaps she's a professional, a dancer, etc. Most likely not a tourist!*

Hmmm...I never thought about that. I guess you're right. See, that's how little I know about fashion. But, it doesn't prohibit a dress or a skirt, right? MMmm...

--Jack

----- Original Message -----
From: Jack
To: Karlee
Sent: Sunday, July 4, 2004 12:51 PM
Subject: Re: How does this sound?

>>*I just came across a brochure from the Canyon Ranch Spa at the Venetian that I picked up when I was in Vegas last year. Rather than helping me with sightseeing, do you like the idea of helping me to pick out a spa package?*

Sure! I like that idea.

Is it Tuesday yet? Why not?!

--Jack

----- Original Message -----
From: Karlee
To: Jack
Sent: Sunday, July 4, 2004 9:42 AM
Subject: Two days

Hi Jack,

Today is Sunday (hey, Happy 4th of July!) and it was one week ago at about this same time that I posted my ad on craigslist. Looking back, I'm not really 100% certain what I was thinking the outcome would really be. But I can tell you that what we have created this week never entered my mind.

Anyway, back to the shower scene...(sorry that I keep making you have to think about me being all naked and wet in that shower; I know it must be very hard for you to do.) For the purpose of your excitement and how this scene is to progress...will it make any difference to you whether or not I get my hair (I'm talking about on my head) wet? That may seem like a silly thing to ask, but hey, I'm trying to cover all the bases. I know some men are turned on by being able to run their fingers through hair which is a different sensation with wet hair vs. dry.

I have finally come up with what I believe will work best for me and our initial meeting. Where, what, etc. It's pretty much the same as we last talked about it. I just filled in some details. I'll be back later tonight to share what I'm thinking and hopefully it will be comfortable for you as well. In the meantime, I'm going to head up to my dad's boat for the day.

Do you use text messaging on your cell phone? I know sometimes in the casinos it's hard to hear ringing, etc., so I thought that might be a back-up way for us to communicate on Tuesday.

Enjoy your day!

Karlee

----- Original Message -----
From: Jack
To: Karlee
Sent: Sunday, July 4, 2004 7:33 PM
Subject: Re: Two days . . .

Hi Karlee!

Happy 4th of July to you, too...

Wow, it's only been a week since you posted the ad? It seems like longer...I guess when you spend so many hours getting worked up and aroused, time goes slower. Nicer, but slower.

As for the shower question...hair wet or dry isn't a factor for me. Whatever you prefer is 100% fine with me. I'm Mr. Flexible.

I look forward to hearing your other details later tonight.

As for text messaging, I don't have it on my phone. I used to, but I was getting nothing but wrong messages and ads so I had it turned off. My phone has a vibrate mode, though, so I'll know if you're trying to reach me.

Enjoy the lake!

--Jack

----- Original Message -----
From: Karlee
To: Jack
Sent: Sunday, July 4, 2004 11:45 PM
Subject: Minor delay

Hi Jack,

I hope you had a great day. I enjoyed my time at the lake, although it was a quiet day. It ended up being just me, my dad, and my sister. Considering I was in almost all week getting well, it felt good to be out and about.

It's almost 11:45 PM and I need to head to bed. I want to be certain my head is clear when I write since we only have one more day to get the plans set for Tuesday. Look for an email from me tomorrow for sure!

I have to say that I have relaxed quite a bit about this whole thing and I am really looking forward to meeting you—regardless of what takes place or not. I'm saying the "regardless of..." for you, not for me, as I'm fairly certain that unless a huge red flag comes up when we actually meet—I'm good to go!

Just as a side note... I will not be meeting any of the other men who wrote to me. My intention from the start was never more than one in the first place, since I wasn't even sure I could do that. I'm telling you that not because you care or even would have given it any thought. It is probably more about me convincing myself that this isn't so bad since it's only one!

Enjoy your evening. I will write more in the morning AND see you in a couple of days!

Karlee

----- Original Message -----
From: Karlee
To: Jack
Sent: Monday, July 5, 2004 1:14 PM
Subject: Cold feet

Hi Jack,

When I wrote last night that I was "good to go," I really felt I was.

Then this morning I woke with a feeling of dread! I realized this was coming from the fact that the direction I had gone with you was not really what I had been intending to create when I placed the ad on craigslist. When I placed the ad, I knew I would only be able to move forward if I had the opportunity to spend a fair amount of time with this person before being alone with him. I allowed myself to get caught up in your fantasy about a "stranger." What isn't working for me is the fact that I know so little about you. Of course I know some things from our emails this week. But when I placed the ad, I was thinking that meeting someone for dinner or drinks or by the pool would give me an opportunity to get to know them on more of a personal level. I'm not sure why this is important to me. I just know it is and I have to honor myself and not give up what I need to make something like this work for me. I am eager yes; desperate, no.

The way I saw this playing in my head when I posted the ad was something like this: I would receive emails, sort through, etc., etc. Before I left, I would have had probably more than one conversation on the phone, although I know my ad said just one. Perhaps we (me and "this man") would have made arrangements to meet for a drink Tuesday evening. If there was a mutual interest, my expectation would have been for us to proceed through the week; perhaps dinner, playing slots in a casino, a walk down the Strip, time by the pool—almost like a "pretend boyfriend." Then, assuming the energy is there, this would have led to the sex.

It was never my intention to just meet someone and proceed to my room.

I was thinking a day or two ago how even more wildly excited I would be if I actually already knew you and we were already past the "uncertainty" phase. Like meeting a lover for a wildly outrageous rendezvous. I know; some of that fits. The reality is that you are not my lover. I don't even know your last name or where you work, or if you're in a relationship. You could be married and have a family. Heck, I don't know. All I know is having that kind of knowledge adds a comfort level for me.

I don't feel good about the fact that I allowed this to go as long as I did, knowing that I really doubted whether or not I could go through with it. I believe we agreed last week when I got cold feet about day two or three, that it would be okay at any time for either of us to change our mind. Your writing hit a cord with me and I guess I got drawn in and enjoyed it. But the truth is, I'm so worked up over this that it's starting to take away from me thinking that I'll even be able to enjoy my trip.

And since I want to trust that you are the nice guy you initially introduced yourself as, I know you would never want a woman to be doing this in fear.

That's where I am today.

Your thoughts?... Okay, so I haven't totally closed the door!

Karlee

----- Original Message -----
From: Jack
To: Karlee
Sent: Monday, July 5, 2004 3:08 PM
Subject: Re: Cold feet

Hi Karlee,

Well, I'm not exactly sure what to say in response to your last email. I'll start by saying that when you said you were "good to go," I thought that was nice, but it didn't change anything from my point of view. When you said you had cold feet the first time, it also didn't change anything from my point of view. When you have cold feet this time, same story.

All this talk about how things could play out is, and always has been (for me) talk about things I'd find to be exciting. I got the impression that you felt that way, too. But, all along, my expectation has never changed from meeting and seeing if we want to proceed. I don't see any of our conversations as a "blank check"; if we met and didn't feel comfortable enough with each other, maybe we'd just have a nice chat and I'd be on my way. If we liked each other and you felt that everything was good and you invited me up to your room, and suddenly you became uncomfortable, I'd leave. If we were half-way through one of the scenes we talked about and you suddenly decided it wasn't right, I'd go.

I'm not trying to coerce you to do anything you don't want to do. In fact, if I have cold feet about anything, it would be that I can't tell if you really do or really don't want to do this. My guess is that you do, but you've got a lot of issues you're trying to overcome before you'll truly believe this is something that, not only would be okay to do, but that you'd really like to do. Probably guilt? Maybe fear? I'm not sure. But if those things keep coming up, I worry a bit—if you did decide to move forward after meeting, but had the attitude of gritting your teeth and forcing yourself to do it in the spirit of self-empowerment...that's a scenario I wouldn't be interested in. I think of skydiving (which I haven't done) but imagine a lot of people hang in the doorway, trying to force themselves to jump out of the plane the first time. It's scary. Maybe at that point, they don't want to go. They close their eyes and psyche themselves up. Go. Do it. Jump! C'mon! You have to! Everyone expects you to! They do that for several minutes, and then force themselves to go. If that's what you're feeling, I guess I could understand that, but I wouldn't want to be that "first jump" (so to speak). I could see someone deciding to do this as an intellectual exercise or having it be all about personal growth. If it is, that's all great. But if that's ALL it is, well...it would defeat one of the major purposes, which is to have a fun, sexy, memorable, enjoyable time.

I mean, maybe none of that is happening. Maybe you're just going back and forth and I can understand that. I'm excited about possibly meeting you, and I absolutely imagine all kinds of great things that could happen, but I still don't have (and never have had) any expectations. Maybe your "cold feet" and "good to go" emails are just to keep me up to date about how you're feeling, and I do appreciate the information. I guess, though, that I don't worry as much...I plan to see how things go and trust myself to let me know if things feel right or not. Thinking about it and analyzing all the possibilities is a good idea...so you're smarter than me.

As for some of the other points in your email...you wrote about realizing that the direction we'd gone was not what you had been intending to create with your ad. Is that bad? Do you regret that direction? You mentioned that you know so little about me...I'm an open book, you know. I'd be happy to tell you all about my life...the things you mention are all things I imagine would have been talked about in person. They're all small talk, I think...are they crucial details? I suppose they are. I just don't think of them as being nearly as interesting or personal about any of the things we've talked about. I could certainly understand you wanting to know my last name, or where I work, or whether I am or ever have been married, what my favorite kind of food is, where I grew up, what my hobbies are...all of that paints a picture of who I am. I'll answer all of those. The only reason I haven't is that it seems so much less intimate than ANYTHING we've talked about. It's bar talk. I wouldn't feel like I was more comfortable with you if I knew your favorite color rather than if I knew you had these feelings or concerns, or if I knew that you're a fan of Madonna rather than knowing your doctor fantasy.

But if it makes you feel more at ease, I'm not hiding anything. You just haven't asked before. My last name is Smith. I grew up in Chicago. I have an undergrad degree in Education and an MBA. I've lived in Maryland, South Carolina, New York City, Frankfurt (studied abroad), and Las Vegas. I'm not married and have never been married. I'm allergic to cats, but more of a dog person anyway. I watch a lot of movies, and I don't read nearly as much as I used to. If I'm leaving anything out, it's not intentional; you can ask me whatever you'd like to know.

>>*interest, my expectation would have been for us to proceed through the week; perhaps dinner, playing slots in a casino, a walk down the Strip, time by the pool - almost like a "pretend boyfriend." Then, assuming the energy is there, this would have led to the sex.*

Ah, okay...that plan was never described to me. Is that the source of your concern? Do you think I've had (for lack of a better word) an agenda that I'm trying to get you to conform to? I don't. I'll say it again...if you want to meet and chat and then call it a night, that's fine. I have no expectations.

You know, I REALLY don't want you to do something that you'll regret. If you left Vegas and then felt bad about yourself...well, I want no part in that. Granted, all of that is within you. But I don't want to feel like I've pressured you in any way. So, I guess I'm getting some cold feet now, too.

>>*It was never my intention to just meet someone and proceed to my room.*

I didn't get the impression it was. As I remember it, we clicked over the idea that we could have someone we'd each be able to talk with about things we've always thought about and were excited by, and maybe that open communication could (not would, but could) lead to something we'd both be very excited by. Is that bad? I don't think so. I don't get the impression that you're really okay with your desires. That doesn't make you a bad person, and I would be delighted to help you through any obstacles on a quest for something you want. But if you don't really want it, I would absolutely not want to be the guy who pushed you out of the airplane on your first skydive.

And, if it had been your intention to meet someone and proceed to your room, I wouldn't have thought any differently about you.

>>*I don't feel good about the fact that I allowed this to go as long as I did, knowing that I really doubted whether or not I could go through with it. I believe we agreed last week when I got cold feet about day two or three, that it would be okay at any time for either of us to change our mind. Your writing hit a cord with me and I guess I got drawn in and enjoyed it. But the truth is, I'm so worked up over this that it's starting to take away from me thinking that I'll even be able to enjoy my trip.*

It makes me sad to read this...and if that's true, then maybe we should just forget it. Clearly, you've got REALLY cold feet. I mean, you've swung pretty wildly about this and while my point of view has never changed (I'm no more or less good to go than I was from day one), I don't know how I can tell if you'd really be okay. On the other hand, I can't make that decision for you, you have to. But, hmmm...

>>*And since I want to trust that you are the nice guy you initially introduced yourself as, I know you would never want a woman to be doing this in fear.*

True. I can't tell from email whether you really want to or really don't want to live out some of these fantasies. My guess is, from all of our conversations, that you do, but you're trying to overcome the thoughts that are stopping you. But those thoughts seem to run deep. It's possible, though, that maybe you'd like to be the kind of person who could live out those fantasies, but you're trying to convince yourself that you could do them and really you never could. I don't know...maybe you don't know. Who knows? I tend to think that when people think and dream about those things and suppress them, it's never a good thing...that's what they want, and that should be explored. Maybe this isn't the best comparison, but I had a friend who was very smart and was the son of two attorneys. He was going to be an attorney. They never pressured him, but that's what he knew and they supported and encouraged him. But, he was really into music. That was what he wanted for a career. He always thought about it and talked about it and when his friends would encourage him to give it a try or get more involved in music, he'd dismiss it because he felt that was a stupid kid's dream. He got through most of law school and then decided he couldn't force himself to follow that path anymore and he started doing music; he's much, much happier now.

So, I'm not sure where we are. As I've always said, no expectations. If you want to meet we can see how it goes, but after reading this email, I'm concerned that you may not really want to do any of this, and I don't want to feel like you're forcing yourself. Even if my pushing you out of an airplane would lead to your personal growth...I'm not willing to push you. I'll go with you, (and this is only an analogy—I'm not going skydiving!!) but you've got to make those decisions on your own.

What do you think?

--Jack

----- Original Message -----
From: Jack
To: Karlee
Sent: Monday, July 5, 2004 6:29 PM
Subject: Cold feet

So here's a silly question... Is today a holiday? I've been working for hours and can't get anyone on the phone. I thought Friday was the day people took off for the 4th weekend.

I bet you'll have a nice, empty flight on Tuesday. With any luck, you'll get a good movie, too.

--Jack

----- Original Message -----
From: Karlee
To: Jack
Sent: Monday, July 5, 2004 6:56 PM
Subject: Re: Cold feet

Hi Jack,

I'm at my computer working on my response to your email.
And yes, today is a holiday! Because the 4th was Sunday, the legal
holiday (banks, post office, etc.) was today. I know I'm not your
boss, but if I was, I'd say, "You've worked hard enough today. It's a
holiday. Go rest up. And, you've got a hot chick coming in from the
east coast to see you and you're going to need all the energy you
have."

Guess that gives you some indication what my reply will be! It will be
on its way shortly!

Karlee

----- Original Message -----
From: Karlee
To: Jack
Sent: Monday, July 5, 2004 7:59 PM
Subject: Finally, The Meeting Place!

Hi Jack,

I didn't respond right away. I wanted to make sure I wasn't going to
change my mind—again!

Here goes…

*>>But if those things keep coming up, I worry a bit—if you did
decide to move forward after meeting, but had the attitude of
gritting your teeth and forcing yourself to do it in the spirit of self-
empowerment...that's a scenario I wouldn't be interested in.*

Although I did say that I love personal growth and development, rest assured, my intent with this was never about self-empowerment. I'll stick to skydiving for that!

>>*In fact, if I have cold feet about anything it would be that I can't tell if you really do or really don't want to do this*

I really do. Perhaps at some point we'll have a conversation about what was going on for me; maybe not. Either way, for now, I'd rather concentrate on moving forward vs. talking about all the stuff that was holding me back.

>>*you wrote about realizing that the direction we'd gone was not what you had been intending to create with your ad. Is that bad? Do you regret that direction?*

I hope it's not bad, and no, I don't regret it. It was just recognition that I was facing aspects of this "meeting" and having to make decisions that I might not have had to if it had unfolded differently.

>>*I'd be happy to tell you all about my life...the things you mention are all things I imagine would have been talked about in person,*

What a relief that was. I can see now how part of my anxiety could have been alleviated if I would have asked more about that initial meeting. More about how long you thought it might be...A half an hour? An hour? It doesn't really matter at this point. BUT, what I know is that in my head I was envisioning you moving this along quickly and me having to know in ten minutes or having to make a decision before I was ready. That was all my own stuff. I know you have made it very clear about both of us needing to be comfortable, and I appreciate that.

>>*it seems so much less intimate than ANYTHING we've talked about.*

I agree. I was coming more from a safety standpoint. I guess I was thinking that this would be better if I could actually legitimize you! I'm okay with this now.

>>*Ah, okay...that plan was never described to me. Is that the source of your concern? Do you think I've had (for lack of a better word) an agenda that I'm trying to get you to conform to?*

No, I never felt that. And you're right. I never did describe that plan. I was just recognizing that this unfolded differently than I had originally pictured in my head. Again, neither good nor bad at this point. And, I'm an optimist! Maybe it will be better than anything I could have ever imagined anyway! After all, I can play the slots and hang out by the pool by myself. What we've talked about is best done with two people. That I do know!

>>*I can't tell from email whether you really want to or really don't want to live out some of these fantasies. My guess is, from all of our conversations, that you do, but you're trying to overcome the thoughts that are stopping you.*

I guess two points come up for me here. One, my main concern was originally a safety issue; and next, remember that my original intent with the ad was to find an exciting sexual encounter. (And I think I did!) But, it never initially had to do with "fantasies" per say. I really am okay with the fantasies. As long as I feel good chemistry with you (or like you, am attracted to, or however you want to word it), and I feel safe with you, I really will be good to go! Now I can't guarantee that will unfold on night one. But if we make it to my room, it will only be because I am ready and want to.

Okay, I guess I had three points. The third being is that I now realize that I was putting way too much pressure on myself about being able to do this the "right way." Since I've never been involved with anything quite like this, I think I started to wonder things like, "what if I don't do "it" the way he wants or the way he was hoping it would be or blah, blah, blah…hey, I'm a fantasy virgin! I was getting too caught up in all the role-playing and how it would all look and it added so much pressure to the whole first meeting. Now, I have in my head that this will unfold naturally and that's okay.

>>*So, I'm not sure where we are.*

We're close, very close! Close enough for me to say…

Let's meet at the Mirage. Do you know where the White Tiger Habitat is? (NOT to be confused with the Siegfried and Roy Secret Garden and Dolphin Habitat.) It's right at the end of that moving walkway that comes off the Strip. That area is not that big, so it should be relatively easy for you to spot me. (I'll be wearing a short black skirt and I believe a coral colored top.) From there, we can walk to one of the lounges or restaurants and have something to drink. I don't know if we need to talk about what you will say to me when you approach. I think it would work better for me if we start just as if we were meeting someone we hadn't ever met before. If we move forward, and the way I understand it, is that would unfold during our conversation, right? How about we say that the "Karlee is ready to move forward" cue is if I start to shift the dialogue to you being that friendly Las Vegas Host? Will that work? What else do we need to consider? Do we need to know what your "cue" will be? Also, please keep in mind that if I don't initiate a move forward tomorrow, it doesn't mean it won't happen. I'm open to the possibility that I might be so excited about the whole thing and decide I want to wait until Wednesday and move right into the Wrong Room scenario!

I will plan to be ready by around 9:30. I know you said you have a commitment until 10:00, but that you might be able to get out earlier. You'll be calling me when you are leaving, right? I'll need to know what time to be at the tiger display.

I look forward to hearing your reply! I'm off to finish my packing. Do you think 17 condoms will be enough... for the first night?

Hey, I'm lightening up!

Karlee

----- Original Message -----
From: Jack
To: Karlee
Sent: Monday, July 5, 2004 10:47 PM
Subject: Re: Finally: The Meeting Place!

>>*I didn't respond right away. I wanted to make sure I wasn't going to change my mind—again!*

You might change your mind again...who knows? I'd kind of be surprised if you didn't get nervous before meeting, to tell you the truth...that's the time I anticipate being the most anxious.

>>*What a relief that was. I can see now how part of my anxiety could have been alleviated if I would have asked more about that initial meeting. More about how long you thought it might be…A half an hour? An hour? It doesn't really matter at this point. BUT, what I know is that in my head I was envisioning you moving this along quickly and me having to know in ten minutes or having to make a decision before I was ready. That was all my own stuff. I know you have made it very clear about both of us needing to be comfortable, and I appreciate that.*

I don't have a timetable. I would guess that we'll enjoy each others' company (I hope) and I won't be watching the clock.

>>*I agree. I was coming more from a safety standpoint. I guess I was thinking that this would be better if I could actually legitimize you! I'm okay with this now.*

I'm glad I've reached a certain level of legitimacy! I'll show you my ID too, if you want.

>>*I guess two points come up for me here. One, my main concern was originally a safety issue; and next, remember that my original intent with the ad was to find an exciting sexual encounter. (And I think I did!) But, it never initially had to do with "fantasies" per say. I really am okay with the fantasies. As long as I feel good chemistry with you (or like you, am attracted to, or however you want to word it, and I feel safe with you, I really will be good to go! Now I can't guarantee that will unfold on night one. But if we make it to my room, it will only be because I am ready and want to.*

I hope you haven't misunderstood me here...I think it'd be great if you wanted to do any of those fantasies that we've talked about. If that somehow makes you more uncomfortable, we don't have to do it. There is a certain amount of "scripting" to what we talked about, but we don't have to do any of it. If you decide you want to go back to your room and "play it by ear," I'm agreeable to that, too!

>>*much pressure to the whole first meeting. Now, I have in my head that this will unfold naturally and that's okay.*

That's the right way of thinking about it, I think.

>>*Let's meet at the Mirage. Do you know where the White Tiger Habitat is? (NOT to be confused with the Siegfried and Roy Secret Garden and Dolphin Habitat) It's right at the end of that moving walkway that comes off the Strip. That area is not that big, so it should be relatively easy for you to spot me. (I'll be wearing a short black skirt and I believe a coral colored top.) From there, we*

I can certainly go there, though I don't know that I've ever driven to the Mirage, so I can't give you an accurate guess about how long it'll take me to get there (park, find the White Tiger Habitat). I wonder, though...do they have a Starbucks or some small cafe place? I just think it'd be so much more stressful to find someone in a big open area like that. If you're picking that because it's public and safe, I understand that, but I mean like a place with chairs inside the casino. I don't know. I'll bring your cell phone number and we'll try to find a way to find each other. I guess my hesitation is that I'm not sure I've ever been to the White Tiger Habitat. Unless it's that big aquarium (kind of white rocks and waterfalls) in a long hallway opposite a gift shop, I think. I believe I kind of know where that is.

I'll try to spot you... short black skirt (!) and a coral top. All I need now is to know what coral is. Is that blue-green? It seems that every color name I don't know ends up being blue-green or occasionally green-blue.

>>*me if we start just as if we were meeting someone we hadn't ever met before. If we move forward, and the way I understand it, is that would unfold during our conversation, right? How about we say that the "Karlee is ready to move forward" cue is if I start to shift the dialogue to you being that friendly Las Vegas Host? Will that work? What else do we need to consider?*

Is it easier if we just talk about what we're thinking? Does that remove some anxiety? I could say, "So, how do you feel? What do you think?" We could then decide what, if anything, we want to do.

I absolutely don't want you to think at any point that talking ruins the "illusion" of the fantasy...maybe you'll think of something you'd find appealing! Maybe you'll decide you really want to have me do or try something we didn't talk about. That's great! From my point of view, the fantasy is a playful thing, not a script we have to memorize. So, don't be shy to improv!

>>need to know what your "cue" will be? Also, please keep in mind that if I don't initiate a move forward tomorrow, it doesn't mean it won't happen. I'm open to the possibility that I might be so excited about the whole thing and decide I want to wait until Wednesday and move right into the Wrong Room scenario!

If you want to have a cue, I will take any reason you have for me to join you back at your room as a cue that you're feeling comfortable. How's that?   And if for some reason you want me to come back to your room and don't want me to do anything except go back to your room (maybe you need luggage moved) you can say 'come back to my room for nothing other than moving luggage.'

>>I will plan to be ready by around 9:30. I know you said you have a commitment until 10:00, but that you might be able to get out earlier. You'll be calling me when you are leaving, right? I'll need to know what time to be at the tiger display.

I'll call you when I'm done at the Palms, which is probably somewhere between ten and thirty minutes away from the Mirage, depending on how lost I get. How's that? And you have my number, I believe, but just in case, it's 702-###-####. My phone will be off until I'm done, but it'll get messages.

>>I look forward to hearing your reply! I'm off to finish my packing. Do you think 17 condoms will be enough for the first night? Hey, I'm lightening up!

Good! It's good to see! And no, it won't be enough!

(I guess I never told you about my balloon animal fantasy.)

 --Jack

----- Original Message -----

From: Karlee
To: Jack
Sent: Monday, July 5, 2004 11:30 PM
Subject: This should do it . . .

Hi Jack,

It's been almost three hours and I haven't once changed my mind nor had doubts! Progress!

>>I'd kind of be surprised if you didn't get nervous before meeting, to tell you the truth...that's the time I anticipate being the most anxious.

Actually, at the moment, I'm finally more excited than nervous! You're right though, I'm sure butterflies will kick in sometime tomorrow!

>>I don't have a timetable. I would guess that we'll enjoy each others' company (I hope) and I won't be watching the clock.

I like that!

>>I'm glad I've reached a certain level of legitimacy! I'll show you my ID too, if you want.

That's good to know. Feel free to ask to see mine! Although it would be great if we felt a comfort level that was beyond that. But the offer is good. Thank you.

>>There is a certain amount of "scripting" to what we talked about, but we don't have to do any of it. If you decide you want to go back to your room and "play it by ear," I'm agreeable to that too!

I like that, too!

>>Unless it's that big aquarium (kind of white rocks and waterfalls) in a long hallway opposite a gift shop, I think. I believe I kind of know where that is.

Yes, it is across from a gift shop. Believe it or not, for once(!), this choice wasn't because of the public and safety factor. I thought it would be easy, but if you self-park, it is kind of a hike. If you're open to valet parking, the registration desk is right in the front door. We could meet there. If you go to the website, there's a menu on the left. Click on Property Map and you can enlarge it and see the layout. Is that helpful? I want to make this easy for you, too. And…not have it take you an extra hour to find me! Are there other places or casinos that you are really familiar with as far as finding them and parking, etc.? The Mirage was just one idea. And if we move forward, it's fairly convenient to my hotel/room. Of course, I am open to meeting you someplace you are familiar with as well. I'm actually quite familiar and comfortable with most of the Strip. Speaking of finding me… coral is in the orange/red family. Some might call it a deep peach. I was going to tell you that originally. I thought I'd just wait to see if you asked!

>>*Is it easier if we just talk about what we're thinking? Does that remove some anxiety? I could say "So, how do you feel? What do you think?"*

That could be good. Let's just be ourselves and let it unfold naturally. I think that is the least anxiety-creating scenario!

>>*If you want to have a cue, I will take any reason you have for me to join you back at your room as a cue that you're feeling comfortable. How's that?*

Sounds good.

>>*I'll call you when I'm done at the Palms, which is probably somewhere between ten and thirty minutes away from the Mirage, depending on how lost I get. How's that? And you have my number, I believe, but just in case, it's 702-###-####. My phone will be off until I'm done, but it'll get messages.*

Okay. I'll stay put until I hear from you. 440-###-####.

>> *(I guess I never told you about my balloon animal fantasy)*

I'll bring the whole case! And...I think it would be great if this leads to hearing others that I haven't yet heard as well!

I think that about covers everything! Whew—what a week! Also, just an FYI. I'll be leaving for the airport around 11:00 AM (EST). I will probably shut my computer down around 10:30 AM or so. If you need to communicate with me after that, it's best to call my cell phone. I don't plan on taking my laptop with me and I doubt that I'll check email when I arrive.

See you soon! Less than 24 hours at this point!!!!! Not that I'm counting!

Karlee

----- Original Message -----
From: Jack
To: Karlee
Sent: Tuesday, July 6, 2004 12:11 AM
Subject: This should do it . . .

>>*Yes, it is across from a gift shop. Believe it or not, for once(!), this choice wasn't because of the public and safety factor. I thought it would be easy, but if you self-park, it is kind of a hike. If you're open to valet parking, the registration desk is right in the front door. We could meet there. If you go to the website, there's a menu on the left. Click on Property Map and you can enlarge and see the layout. Is that helpful? I want to make this easy for you, too. And not have it take you an extra hour to find me!*

The map helps and that seems like a fine place. So many tiger gardens in this town, it's hard to keep them all straight!

>>*Speaking of finding me, coral is in the orange/red family. Some might call it a deep peach. I was going to tell you that originally. I thought I'd just wait to see if you asked!*

See, I'm glad I asked! Of course, I've got your picture and you've got mine, so it won't be a total surprise. I'm guessing that I'll be wearing light colored cargo shorts, sneakers, and probably a polo shirt. Maybe a button-up denim shirt. Not sure yet.

The only place that would be more convenient for me might be the Palms, since I'll be there, but it's a pain to get to if you don't have a car, so the Tiger Habitat sounds good to me!

>>*I think that about covers everything! Whew—what a week! Also, just an FYI. I'll be leaving for the airport around 11:00 AM (EST). I will probably shut my computer down around 10:30 AM or so. If you need to communicate with me after that, it's best to call my cell phone. I don't plan on taking my laptop with me and I doubt that I'll check email when I arrive.*

Take a nap when you get in! You can try to call me anytime, too. It's less than 24 hours? Wow! I'll go cut my toenails, then.

Have a good flight! I'm looking forward to meeting you, however it plays out!

--Jack

----- Original Message -----
From: Karlee
To: Jack
Sent: Tuesday, July 6, 2004 10:27 AM
Subject: See you tonight!

Good Morning, Jack!

I'll be close to on my way by the time you read this...

>>*I'm guessing that I'll be wearing light colored cargo shorts, sneakers, and probably a polo shirt.*

Either way, I'll be looking for your shirt to be opened to the navel, with big gold chains and I know you'll be calling me "babe." ;-)

>>*Maybe a button-up denim*

I'd like to think of it as a button-DOWN! Mmmm!

>>*of course, I've got your picture and you've got mine, so it won't be*

a total surprise.

I'll make a mental note to tell you if I change my mind about my outfit. I chose it based on your fondness of skirts. If I was meeting you as say a "real first date," I would normally dress a bit more on the conservative side for a first meeting. Hey, maybe that's why I don't date much! Hmmm?

>>Take a nap when you get in!

That will be great if I can actually relax enough to fall asleep. I'm going to have to if I want to be up 'til the wee hours LV time! Hope you get to nap, too!

>>Wow! I'll go cut my toenails then.

You are funny! Can't wait to meet you!

Karlee

Part Two
Three Years Earlier

The Beginning of One Woman's Journey through
Death, Divorce, Dating, and Daring Adventure

June 3, 2001

Dear Mom,

It's been one month now since you died. I still feel a tremendous
loss—much harder than I ever imagined. I feel so empty and so
scared. You were such an important part of our family being whole
and now it's not. The disbelief of it all is raw. I still wait to find it
was all a mistake. But I know it wasn't. Why, why, why?

You looked so beautiful at the funeral. I've wanted to write to you
since it was first over as a way of capturing my thoughts. I feel a need
to recollect every detail. You died at about 3:15 PM on May 2. It was
a Wednesday. You were at home in the bed hospice had brought on
Monday. I was there. Rose, Dad, Mary and Aunt Rita. Your
breathing changed and boom—you were gone. I can't believe I was
at your side when you took your last breath. Very scary, yet almost
peaceful in a way. We were all yelling all these good-byes; it was like
trying to get a lifetime of messages to you in 30 seconds. Dad just
held your hand; his head down. Lou and Robert were out in the hall.
Chuck had just called to say he was on his way. I kept screaming,
"I'm going to miss you, Mom." And I do. Bye, Mom, Good-bye,
Mom.

We waited awhile before calling hospice. Then Debbie the nurse
came and she called the funeral home. She cleared out your medicine
and unhooked the IV. All while you were just lying there. Your
body. Your spirit—gone. You looked beautiful; so very peaceful.
You were at home for a few hours and then the funeral home came
and took you away. Mr. Lightner suggested we wait in the family
room. And we did. But we could hear the sounds. Leaving the
bedroom, down the hall, through the living room, onto the porch,
then the sidewalk, and into the hearse. And after they left, I walked
back into your room. Now just the bed was there. And no you.
There were others in the house, yet to me, it felt so empty. My heart
was aching, Mom. Aching an ache I hope I never have to feel again.

On Thursday, Dad and Mary and I went to the florist and ordered
flowers and to the church to pick out the songs. Then Mary and I
went to the mall to find a dress for you. We found two that we really

liked and brought them home. We picked the cream colored one and I was glad that we did. It was my favorite of the two. Very delicate and elegant. Then we had to take the dress and your shoes to the funeral home.

On Friday, I went to the mall to shop for me. Two sizes smaller, Mom! What a weight loss program. Not one I recommend. I bought you a Mother's Day ring. A gold band with M-O-M cut out and some small diamonds. It's with you now, Mom. I hope you like it. It was from just me.

Saturday was the first day of the viewing. Mom, you looked so beautiful. The dress was perfect. You were wearing your heart-shaped diamond necklace from Dad and we bought you some new earrings. Over 50 floral arrangements, Mom! You would have loved it. So many people said they have never seen anything like it. What we ordered from the florist was a spray of 100 yellow roses. On the bow were those gold foil stickers with Loving Wife, Mom, and Grandma. It looked beautiful. It was estimated that about 500-600 people came through. Although Aunt Barbara wasn't one of them, you would have been pleased.

Monday was the funeral. What a beautiful service. Father Albert was quite choked up himself. I almost fainted when they closed the casket. They had to bring me a paper bag to breathe into. I didn't want to say good-bye, Mom. I still don't. About 60 cars were in the procession. The pall bearers were William, Gene, Tim and Bob, Alan and Jeff. William and Gene wore their military uniforms. You would have been proud. Leah wrote a poem and read it at the church. We laughed and cried. Lou did the readings. From the church, we took you to the cemetery. You're right by Grandma Christopher! A beautiful spot under the tree.

We then had a very nice luncheon at the church hall. There were about 120 people there.

From there, it was back to the house and you weren't there. It's still hard to believe, Mom. I can't believe it, Mom. I don't want you to be dead. I need you here.

So now it has been one month. We went to the casino up in Windsor for Mother's Day. No use sitting around and sulking with no mom's to celebrate.

Memorial Day weekend at the boat was difficult. I still can't believe you were not there. It just was not the same. I dusted at the trailer for you.

Oh. I didn't tell you about the fountain. Dad bought a fountain and planted flowers around it. It's like a shrine, Mom. Very nice. He really did love you, Mom. It breaks my heart to see him so sad. He misses you.

We received hundreds of sympathy cards. Many masses and contributions.

It's weird. It's like no one wants to talk about it. I guess everyone deals with death in a different way. Dad took your jewelry and put it in the safe deposit box. Hasn't touched your clothes or belongings. He wants to keep things the way they are, I guess. Probably easier.

I visit you often. It's weird. There's just this big mound of dirt. It's like I want to just dig down through it all and hold you again. I want to touch you and hear your voice. It's so hard, Mom. It's so hard.

I don't care about my business. I'm not feeling motivated to do much. I just feel so empty.

Going to go. My hand is getting tired. I love you, Mom. I miss you. I'm sorry you had to die.

Five months earlier . . .

January 2001

I never gave it a thought. I mean, my mom wasn't feeling well and looking back now, it all made sense. She saw a doctor and was told she had bronchitis. The typical western medical practice, she was given a prescription and sent home. Two weeks later, not much better. Back to the doctor. Surprise, surprise. Another prescription. I guess the term "third time's a charm" holds true in the medical community, too. This time, the doctor finally sat up and paid attention and ordered a chest x-ray. Pneumonia—and into the hospital. Still, it had not even entered my mind that it could be anything other than that. Sure, my mom was a smoker for forty years, but she had quit eight years earlier. Thirty-nine dollars at a popular hotel chain, a two hour hypnosis clinic—and she was done. She hadn't touched a cigarette since. I guess I had tucked it into the back of my mind that my mother would never be inflicted with the dreaded disease of cancer. My siblings and I were petrified of it when we were growing up. We didn't know everything, but we knew smoking was bad for you, and thankfully, despite growing up in a home with two smoking parents, none of the four of us ever took up the nasty habit.

But what seemed like a million tests later and consults with a dozen or so doctors, the diagnosed was confirmed: Stage 4 adenoma carcinoma—also known as lung cancer. I didn't know all there was to know about this ugly disease. However, having a sister who used to work in a doctor's office and a hospital, and a brother who is respected in the medical community throughout the world for his research in pulmonary disease, our family was able to cut through the advanced medical terminology enough to know that this was not good.

So began the roller coaster ride of my life.

Most days, it was as if I was moving through life, embodied in a world filled with molasses. My business, up to the time of my mom's illness, was doing really well. I was fortunate enough to have just landed a significant contract for which I only needed to be with the client one or two hours a week.

Days were filled with hospital visits, tests, and doctors at my mom's bedside, filling in charts, offering little hope leading up to the final prognosis. Just prior to my mom's release, the oncologist at the *esteemed* hospital basically said, "Go home and die." And that is what my mother did.

The first day home for my mom was especially heart-wrenching. I will never forget my first morning visit. I woke up early, got myself prepared to be gone for the day, and drove to my parent's house. It was just a short drive, yet long enough for me to grasp the intensity of all that was behind us as a family and the magnitude of what was ahead. As I opened the front door, I could sense the stillness in my parent's home. Our home. It was the house where I lived when I started first grade. The house where I lived when I started clarinet lessons. It was the house where I lived when I had my first kiss and graduated from high school and college and had my first job. I was living there when I became engaged and when my first niece was born. 36 years of memories were born in this house that my dad built. Now, almost overnight, it had become a somber container of fear and uncertainty as to what the days ahead would bring. I said hello to my dad who was reading the paper at the kitchen table. As I had speculated, he hadn't slept well.

I traveled down the hallway to the bedroom. The drapes were drawn shut; the room was only dimly lit as the morning sun hadn't yet fully emerged. The same somber chill I felt when I stepped through the front door was lingering in this room.

My mother's eyes were closed, yet I could sense from her breathing that she was awake. It was one thing for me to learn how to manage the disbelief that had just become a part of my personal journey, yet I couldn't even imagine what must be going on for my mother. Three weeks prior, she had just celebrated her 70th Christmas, complete with the grandchildren she adored, her favorite holiday foods and goodies, and the present-unwrapping marathon that had come to be known as a family tradition.

I softly kissed her forehead and quietly sat on the chair next to her bed. I took her right hand in mine and sat without saying a word. Her hand felt so frail, but I still loved holding it. I always loved my mother's hands. I remember as a little girl being fascinated with the bone structure and the more-often-than-not manicured fingertips. I remember my mom having those soft, cloth gloves, a white pair and a black pair, that covered from her hands to close to her elbows. These were used only for special outfits for special occasions.

When she finally opened her eyes, there were tears streaming down her cheeks. "How are you?" were the only words that I could seem to find in this moment. She spoke softly and it seemed to be difficult for her to look into my eyes. I scooted the chair as close to the bed as it would accommodate. I wanted to hear every word and remember every word. From this day forward, it was impossible to know when one of my mother's words would be her last. And I didn't want to miss capturing all she had to say.

The pain was visible. Her disappointment in the news she had received in the hospital overtook her. I sat there, listening to my mother share her sadness in knowing she would never see her grandchildren marry or experience the joy of becoming a great-grandmother. I listened to her regrets, knowing from the presentation of it all, that she had been processing this in her head long before I came into the room. My heart ached at her anger of it all; her decision to quit smoking seven years earlier was supposed to keep this from happening to her.

And in the next moment of her silence, as I sat next to my dying mother, without even realizing it, I had selfishly slipped into thoughts about my own life. In an instant, it was as if a huge neon sign was screaming in my head, warning me to take heed to the notion that life truly can be fragile and short. No more dress rehearsal, no more some days, no more, well maybe tomorrows. This was it. I found myself feeling as if I needed to leave my thoughts and get out of my head; much like a moment when you realize you might be heading down a dangerous, dark alley and had better turn around. And then there it was—the discontentment that had been hanging around in my life for some time now. And I remember thinking a thought that came through clear as a bell—"I don't ever want to someday be lying on my death bed, shedding tears of regret."

It was in that moment that I knew I had to, timeframe unclear, walk away from my marriage.

The days came and the days went. My sister and dad and I finally got into somewhat of a routine for how we managed my mother's daily care, with her comfort being the priority. She was extremely weak and in pain. Adrenaline kicked in for the three of us and we effortlessly managed to become a pretty good team.

Overwhelm, fear, and exhaustion, wrapped in the ongoing disbelief of it all, I wondered how I was managing to stay so together. As fragile as we can be as human beings, sure enough, strength appears when we need it. And mine was just about to be tested to another limit.

Within less than two weeks from the time we brought my mom home, my husband [at the time] and I received a call late one evening from Robert's dad. His mom had suffered a severe stroke.

The next day, we added hospital visits to the already emotionally heavy days. And somewhere during that time, my mom ended up back in the hospital. A typical day became going to see my mom at the hospital, then to a different hospital to see Robert's mom, and often back to see my mom again. Robert's mom died ten days after her stroke. She never regained full consciousness. Robert and I were with her, just the two of us, when she took her last breath.

The whole process, from the day of diagnosis to the day my mom passed away was 99 days. Out of those 99 days, I was with her 98. My one sister and I were at my parent's house, every day, sharing in what needed to be done to care for my sick mother and support my overwhelmed father. We were all pretty much in disbelief that this was really happening. But it was. I remember the joy when my mom, on St. Patrick's Day, actually dressed herself in her favorite Dublin, Ireland sweater and we celebrated with corned beef sandwiches and green beer from a local deli. A false hope, wondering if it could possibly be that she was getting better. We knew she wasn't.

We did have some fun times during those 99 days. My mom belonged to a civic group and every day one of the members would bring a meal for my mom and dad. We joked with my mom about having her very own meals-on-wheels program. A dear, caring neighbor, every afternoon after she got home from work, brought an all natural concoction filled with vitamins and nutrients. When Sylvia would arrive, we'd announce, "It's happy hour!" When Easter arrived, the entire family, all 15 of us, packed an Easter dinner, complete with a cooler filled with beer and all our favorites that over the years had become family traditions, and piled into her hospital room.

Seventeen days later, my mom was gone.

Never in a million years could I have anticipated the pain and anguish I felt. Hearing the funeral director pound whatever he pounds to lock the coffin shut is a sound I have yet to forget. I was so distraught they thought I was going to faint. I remember my sister frantically telling the funeral director to find a brown paper bag for me to breathe into so I wouldn't pass out.

From that day, well into the summer, I was numb. I walked around feeling like I had just lost a limb. My mother's death was like an amputation. She was there. Then she was gone. Her voice was gone; her touch was gone. Her love was gone. Although I certainly had my share of challenging moments throughout my life in dealing with my mother's somewhat critical nature, I had come to love and accept my mother for who she was. And now more than ever, I could see the importance of that. I was so grateful to have been such an important part of the last three months of her life.

Within eight weeks, I had said good-bye to both of my mothers. My soul was weary and my heart ached. Yet life went on. Spring ended, summer came, and summer went. And sure enough, little by little, I started to feel productive again. I was thankful that I made the choice to attend a grief support group, which was a welcome facilitator to my healing. I was grateful for the support and kindness that I found in my group of kindred spirits.

When September arrived, I was beginning to feel like I might be ready to get back to my business and start making things happen again. September 1st—what a good day to start. And then, eleven days later, just after 9:00 AM, the phone rang and it was a call from my husband. "I know you won't have the radio or television on. Two planes have just crashed into the World Trade Center. They think it might be a terrorist attack."

For the next several days, just as did millions of people around the world, I watched in horror, disbelief, and with some level of concern that there might be additional attacks, anywhere, even Cleveland. I remember watching a news reporter interviewing a college student who lived in Manhattan, just a few miles from the Twin Towers. I found it fascinating that when the reporter asked the co-ed if she was at all afraid once she realized what had happened, she replied, "No, I wasn't afraid because I knew I was at least a couple of miles away." Here I was, 600 miles away, and I was frightened.

The personal impact of September 11, 2001 for each of us could probably be as varied as the pattern of a butterfly or the design of a kaleidoscope. Sure, we talked about it with family and friends and at work and with our neighbors and maybe even with a stranger in line at the grocery store, but only each individual knows what they were really thinking about what the days and years ahead would bring. One thing for certain, is that I believe most people knew, our world was about to be a very different place.

Our own mortality may have come into closer view for some of us. What was happening under the roof that I shared with my husband at the time was a time of personal reflection on what we really believed, not only about life and death, but more significantly, what happens to us after we die. Intimate conversation about the topic clearly revealed, in a way more so than the previous 16 years of our marriage, that we had very different views about this rite of passage.

I did respect Robert's belief and point of view, yet it was so different than mine. I found it difficult to imagine living the rest of my life with someone whose views were so far apart from how I viewed the world. This new reality, combined with the discontentment over the prior few years, and the [temporarily] unforgotten realization I had at my dying mother's bedside, was the piece that made me realize that now was the time I needed to leave.

And so the process began. Divorce. I remember day one of our pre-marriage classes. The priest, almost proudly, announced the current divorce rate. "There are three weddings that day at this church. One of you will make it. Two will not." I was convinced, 100% beyond a shadow of a doubt, that we would be the couple that would make it. Of course at the time, I had no concept of people changing. Up until that point in my life, I assumed that the two of us would continue to be who we were at that time for the rest of our lives. It seemed reasonable to me. In my 27 years of life at the time, I don't remember ever seeing my parents change. I'm sure they did, but through my eyes, not so much. So it never entered my mind that one of us could or would. I moved out the following June and we were divorced on October 10, 2002.

Excited about my new apartment, my plan was to give myself permission to take time off—one year. Time kept moving and I just couldn't get excited about the projects I had been working on when my mom got sick. I was productive in a sense; it just seemed like nothing felt the same as it had before 2001.

During my personal sabbatical, meeting new people, especially men, had little appeal to me. That year was a time of personal reflection. I kept to myself and spent hours reading what seemed like thousands of pages of spiritual, psychology, and relationship books, not to mention the dozens of hours of " meaning of life" tape programs. I was determined to figure this out. I was 42, divorced, and had lost my mother when she was only 70, and a mother-in-law who I loved dearly. I had always thought my mom would live to be at the very least, 90, and I was certain I would be married forever. Within less than a year, a significant portion of my life plans had been shattered.

After about a year, I decided it was time to get back into the game of life. And to start dating. Time to find a new man. How difficult could this be? My former husband was a good man, my dad, brother, male cousins, and uncles were all good men. I saw the world as one filled with good men. This was also the time that internet dating was still fairly new.

So after weeks of bucking the notion, I entered the world of internet dating, kicking and screaming. Even before my divorce, I remember telling a friend, "If you ever hear me mention that I might sign up for one of those internet dating "things," come and take my computer away." But one almost-too-quiet-for-me Saturday evening got the best of me and before I knew it, I was registered. It was an unsettling feeling at best. Just a day or two after, everywhere I went I found myself wondering if this person or that person might have seen me on "the site." I could no longer go to the grocery store without being well-dressed for a potential encounter with one of my matches. Even in business meetings, when I would meet a man for the first time and he would say, "You look familiar," I would shudder to think that maybe he had recognized me from the dot com world.

After just a few days, a friend said to me "You're going to write a book about this." Even though I had already written my first book, which at the time was already published internationally, I said, "No way! I am not doing this to find material for a new book. I'm doing this to find a date!" However, it didn't take much correspondence with men to discover that this might be an experience worth writing about. And then when I actually started to meet these men, it was certain that a book could be around the corner. The concept of combining my comical stories with insights soon came to life.

Although it was not my intent and I didn't have plans to move forward with the idea, I did have enough material to write a book. Many of the men could easily be a chapter. Every time an unusual happening took place, which was almost daily, out would be the material for another chapter. From meeting men who were just totally not a good fit for me, to being called for phone sex, to being offered $5,000 with *no strings attached* (ha!), there was a chapter in it!

First guy out of the gate is Dennis. Dennis is a soldier. Well, National Guard—but he still wears a uniform every other weekend. Dennis was my first sexual experience since leaving my marriage. And he was hot. We had one of those connections you read about in the steamy romance books. We both felt the heat right away. We met; he brought me three roses. We sat at the restaurant and I felt as if I wanted to take him right there. When the restaurant closed, we went across the shopping center parking lot to a bar for a glass of wine. I put my leg on his lap and he played with my foot. I liked it. By then, I'm practically ready to drag him into the ladies room and take him right in the stall. I had never done such a thing, but was always intrigued by what it would be like to be involved in such passion and fun. We closed the bar and went out to the parking lot to say good-night. We stood in the parking lot making out for almost two hours. Although it felt extremely too much like high school, it also felt so good to feel the passion again. And those blue eyes. We finally got in our cars and before we were even out of the parking lot, he called my cell phone and we talked the whole way home.

Soon after that, the military man and I decided we weren't really a good fit and that was fine. I was grateful for having had the fun that I did.

A few weeks later I had the opportunity to connect with Gary—the first of what seemed to be many Gary's. This Gary was a huge Elvis fan. Looking back, perhaps this should have been my first clue to run. I mean, when a guy tells you that he cried for a week when we lost The King, you have to wonder. He was cute enough, actually quite cute in the photo he sent. What got to me about Gary was his voice. He had what I call a melodic voice, one that gives you a sense that he's singing to you; one that makes you want to just lie on the couch and let him do all the talking.

If I hadn't called him from my cell phone in the parking lot, knowing that he had spotted me, I would have turned around when I saw Gary Elvis. Of course, that was not his real name. His name was Gary something. He was so cute in the photo he sent, but now seeing him in person made it clearly evident that the photo he sent was a very, very outdated one at best. And he had an offensive smell. One that hinted he might not have been in contact with a shower for a few days. Not the guy for me.

Then there was (in no particular order and not a complete list, by any means) Lawyer Boy, Rat Bastard Joe, Scottie-the-Hottie, Fly Boy, Pumper Walt, and yes, even a Teeny Weenie Bob.

Having survived all of those, I finally found myself in a new chapter; one I could have called: Beware of the Bachelor Guy. Now let me start by saying, unlike the other chapters, I did not meet this Bachelor Guy via the internet. And I never even had a date with him. So how could he end up in a potential book, and why a whole chapter you might ask? This guy created so much havoc in my head that it just made sense to include him. Let's just say writing about him cost less money than the several therapy sessions I could have used to figure out this man!

I met Bachelor Guy at a charity event: A bachelor and bachelorette auction. A business colleague and I were asked to do a coaching session for the guys and gals who were donating their time and a date for a great cause. A couple of weeks prior to the actual event, all the participants met at a hotel to have their photos taken for the program booklet. Along with the photo, there would be a brief description of each person and what they were offering to the attendee that was lucky enough to have their name pulled from a box.

Our coaching session ended and we headed to the lounge to have a beverage and mingle. I remember exactly where I was sitting and the conversation I was having when I saw him.

In he walked, and BAM—WHOA—went off in my head. "I think I found myself a bachelor," I said [to myself]. This guy was cu-u-u-te. There wasn't any one particular aspect of him that attracted him to me; it was just him. Maybe it was the confidence he exuded as he walked in with his buddy. Maybe it was his hair, his suit, his eyes. I don't know for sure; all I know is that my female antennae kicked in and said, "GO." And as quickly as he walked in, he was gone. (I later came to find out that this kind of behavior was common for him.)

But as fate would have it, we finally connected out in the lobby. It was there that I realized it was his cologne that must have kicked up the antennae. Not only did he smell delicious, we were having a fun conversation. And when I discovered that his date to be auctioned in two weeks included a selection of wine, I was ensnared.

We exchanged business cards and I vaguely remember that one of us said we were going to call. We ended up hanging out for awhile, only to discover that he was not comfortable with the age difference. He still had his sight, and very much so, on being married and having children. I was not the woman to be his wife and a mother at that point in my life. We remained friends and still are today.

And then, several months later, I finally met him! Kelly. The one I thought could actually be my first significant, long-term something. He was sweet, kind, caring, and absolutely delicious. He was a pleasure to be around and he adored me. He was the nicest looking of the men I had dated, for sure. I had more in common with him than previous men. I felt a sense of optimism that ran deeper than with the others.

And then, it seemed that just as quickly as he had come into my life, he left. Just like that…he was gone.

After Kelly, I decided it was time to step away from the dating scene. One on hand, dating was fun. On the other hand, it was not fun at all. I decided I needed to look at navigating this whole single's scene as a skill, and I was in need of some training.

My head, and more importantly, my heart, were far from healed. Kelly's sudden disappearance had left me desolate inside. Nothing, dead, nadda. I can easily say that with Kelly, I actually had my first glimpse into what it feels like to have your heart ripped out of your chest and put into a machine that pulverizes meat. Okay, so that may be a little dramatic. But, it hurt.

So the months came and went, and still, no boyfriend. How hard could this be? Sure, I continued to meet men and have fun, and with many, I thought there was even good potential. Yet more often than not, for one reason or another, the connections were not meant to be.

So I learned to enjoy life as a single woman and in a much different way than I did when I was married. And, through trial and much tribulation, I had gotten to know myself in ways that I probably never would have otherwise. Since being on my own, I had experienced more sadness, disappointment, fear, frustration, and aloneness to last a lifetime. On the other hand, I also had the opportunity to experience more aliveness, bliss, excitement, and fun than I would have had if I stayed in a marriage that wasn't working for me.

Having said all that, there was one area that remained an obstacle for me—the lack of a satisfying outlet for my highly ignited libido. As a single woman, I felt a new sense of arousal and exploration inside me and I had yet to meet the man who could touch me in the way I longed to be touched.

Until Jack…

Trapped in a Fantasy
July 6 and beyond

I know what it's like to crave human comfort like your body craves air, to crave it so badly that you'd sacrifice your dignity to get it.

—Halle Berry, Crashing into Joy

From: Jack
To: Karlee
Sent: Monday, July 12, 2004 7:07 AM
Subject: RE: A card from Karlee

Hey there...

Thanks for the card! I trust you made it back safely.

Things here have been rough. It's 4am and I'm checking email, and then going to bed so I can get up and work tomorrow.

I'll write more when I get the chance...

--Jack

From: Karlee
To: Jack
Sent: Tuesday, July 13, 2004 3:28 PM
Subject: Just a quick hi!

Hi Jack,

Just a quick note to say hello and to hopefully put a bright spot into your rough and busy days!

No need to reply. I clearly understand that you are busy. Yet I figured that your schedule should not keep me from at least popping in to say hi!

Take care,
Karlee

From: Jack
To: Karlee
Sent: Friday, July 16, 2004 8:08 PM
Subject: RE: Just a quick hi!

Hi Karlee!

Thanks for the note. It has been a hectic week so far. The boss has finally left town, and now I can actually get some work done. It's very strange. He's a micromanager, but he focuses on the most trivial of things. We set up the office, ran cables, bought pens, etc, but all of that could have been done with or without him. He didn't want to talk about anything (like what we'll be doing in the coming weeks) but was very big on getting a file cabinet in just the right place. Bizarre.

After hours and hours of trying to put the jacks on the end of computer and phone lines, I hired someone to do it for $100. It saved me three weeks of work, at least...and, I couldn't take it.

So, by Monday things should settle down and I'm looking forward to it. Hooray! How are things with you?

--Jack

From: Karlee
To: Jack
Sent: Saturday, July 17, 2004 11:27 PM
Subject: Greetings from Cleveland!

Hi Jack,

It was great to hear from you. I'm glad to hear you made it through the week with your boss. I sensed there were some tense and frustrating moments and a sense relief that he has gone. Kudos to you for taking matters into your own hands with the telephone lines. I agree; $100 is worth saving three weeks of work! Did you end up going to see a show while he was in town?

Life has been good here. Now of course not nearly as exciting, fun, stimulating, and interesting as the week before and my trip to Las Vegas! I think my computer actually went through "sexy email" withdrawal. Okay, so maybe not my computer; I guess that would be me!

In the meantime, I have managed to keep myself on track with my professional life. My time in Vegas, along with my exploring over the past several months, has finally led me almost to the place I began! Funny how that works. I'm back to focusing on my consulting business. I've always enjoyed coaching and training, so this will be a good fit. I'm actually very excited about this direction. It will definitely give me the flexibility I have grown accustomed to and a schedule that allows me to do the things I enjoy. The possibility of a move is still a part of this picture and I will look at that once I get myself financially re-established in my business. That's one of the great aspects of this business. It can be done from anywhere in the world.

I enjoyed the remainder of my time in Las Vegas. After we spoke on Friday, I met a friend over at the Venetian. After that, I walked down to Treasure Island and the show had just let out. I decided not to wait for the next one and turned around and came back. Saturday morning I arrived at the airport around 9:30 for my 11:30 flight only to discover the plane had been detained in Houston. The departure time had been changed… to 2:15! WOW—was that a long wait. It was almost enough time to go back; but I decided I was best to just stay put. I again got the upgrade to First Class and arrived back home around 10:30 PM.

I've probably written more than you have time to read, so I'll close for now. I have thought of you often. I still have what might be called an "afterglow" of our time together!

 I look forward to hearing from you again!

Karlee

From: Karlee
To: Jack
Sent: Wednesday, July 21, 2004 6:28 PM
Subject: Your very own personals ad . . .

Dear craigslist personals ad reader,

Another personals ad… modified and this time—being sent exclusively to **YOU**!

I will be in Las Vegas August 7-11. I'm looking to have fun with…YOU! We can meet for a bottle of water, dinner, to look at the white tigers, or to have hot, steamy, fantasy-induced sex! I posted an ad, met you, definitely had some exciting sexual experiences and am open to the possibility of more! Still not looking for anything outrageous; just good, hot sex. I am still 5' 2", a size 8 and [I think I still have] great breasts, blonde hair and blue eyes!

Hi Jack!

How are things with you? I am heading out to Las Vegas again in a couple of weeks. Do you have an interest for us to meet? Now, it doesn't have to be just for sex. I would definitely enjoy seeing you again. Of course, if we must have sex, then so be it. I'll start to talk myself into it if I have to! Of course I'm kidding. I'd start walking right now if I knew that's where I'd end up!

We talked about the possibility… and I know sometimes things change. I know they haven't on my end—don't know what you might be thinking. Hey, maybe I should ask… what are you thinking?

Karlee

From: Jack
To: Karlee
Sent: Thursday, July 22, 2004 2:15 AM
Subject: RE: Your very own personals ad …

Hi Karlee!

You're coming back so soon? Great! I would, of course, very much enjoy seeing you again! When exactly are you coming, though? I know things will be hectic for me in mid-to-late August. I believe 16–22nd are the dates that will be hectic. Actually, it could be beyond hectic...I don't know. I had planned to moonlight on a project from that Wednesday through Sunday, but then I found out my boss will be back in town (and presumably wanting to meet) Monday through Friday. I haven't figured out how to deal with that yet. It could be tricky.

I've been working too much anyway, so it'd be nice to have some non-working time, but I have a feeling I'll still be kind of crushed for time. I would like to have more time to hang out with you, but my free time is random these days.

In any event, I would like to see you again. I still get excited thinking about our time together. (Not that it's been all that long, but I still get VERY excited.)

--Jack

----- Original Message -----
From: Karlee
To: Jack
Sent: Friday, July 23, 2004 3:25 PM
Subject: Las Vegas . . . again!

Hi Jack!

Sounds like you will be busy for some time. I hope you have a chance to relax a bit and take a break soon. You deserve it!

It was great to hear from you and even better to know that we're going to be seeing each other again! Now we have to wait more than two weeks. I liked it better when it was only one week. The good news is that I don't have to go through all that goofy anxiety and you can be assured that I won't be getting cold feet about this! My mind (and body) has already kicked in. Of course, I don't think it ever kicked out!

I hadn't originally planned to make two trips in two months. Love those frequent flyer miles!

This trip is different than my last, which might be a bit more complicated as far as us getting together. Part of my reason for the trip is to re-connect with a group of friends/colleagues that will be attending a 7-day seminar at an off Strip property. I am not attending the seminar myself, yet this event gives me an opportunity to see people I have not seen for several years and some that I have seen recently, yet don't get to see that often. We're from all parts of the US, some from Canada and other parts of the world. I, too, will be staying at the same property and sharing a room with a friend who lives in Canada. My friends will be primarily focused on the seminar, which goes from early morning and sometimes into the late evening. So I'll be seeing those I want to see in bits and pieces—possibly on a break or for lunch, or in the morning before the seminar begins, etc.

Aside from all that, I will have plenty of flexibility and availability as far as spending time with you. The complicated piece is really more about where we might spend our time together. One thought is to spend time at your place, if you are comfortable with that. Another would be to spend time at the hotel during the day when my friend is in the seminar. And…she is leaving Tuesday afternoon, and I'll be staying another night, so that opens up another possibility. Between that and your workload…you will most likely have a better idea of what might be feasible.

I look forward to hearing from you!

Karlee

From: Jack
To: Karlee
Sent: Friday, July 23, 2004 3:25 PM
Subject: RE: Las Vegas … again!

Hi Karlee!

Waiting one week is definitely better, although waiting any more than two weeks would be extremely difficult.

As for where we'd spend time together, it's kind of inconvenient to use my place because a) it's a 40 minute drive, each way, and b) it's embarrassingly messy. Besides, the idea of being in the room while your roommate is away is rather exciting, to me at least.

I'm sure we'll find a place, though...that shouldn't be a problem. Whatever time we can grab together will be great, I'm sure!

We can start working on new fantasies...on the other hand, after our first time together, just thinking about being with you again is enough to get me aroused! That's not to say I wouldn't be willing to try anything else you might have in mind. Last time we did my fantasies...I think you should let me know of anything you might want to try!

--Jack

----- Original Message -----
From: Karlee
To: Jack
Sent: Friday, July 23, 2004 9:28 PM
Subject: RE: Las Vegas ... again!

Okay, so who started this anyway? Oh, I guess that was me!

My imagination has gone wild! With all the thoughts I've had since your last email, I need to be in Vegas for at least six weeks.

BUT...because that's not an option, I'll have to regain control and narrow my thinking to a more reasonable amount of thoughts!

I'm not sure about starting fantasy dialogue now, for two reasons: 1. Two weeks of that will probably drive me wild and 2. I want to respect your workload and not take too much time away from what you're doing so you can get a lot done so you have more time when I'm in town!

Anyway, I'll be back soon with some thoughts and ideas!

Karlee

From: Karlee
To: Jack
Sent: Sunday, July 25, 2004 12:36 AM
Subject: Fantasy preview...

Hi Jack,

How are things with you? Are you working this weekend? If I were there, I'd offer a massage to help you relax with your hectic schedule.

I appreciate you for suggesting that we do what I might want to try since we did your fantasies the first time. Like you, I'm excited just thinking about us being together again. AND, I'm still open to the fantasy route! As the saying goes, "If it ain't broke..."

Some thoughts about how we might spend our time together... I still like the idea of the board game; however, if we have limited time, I'm not sure if that makes the most sense. I would also be very happy if we could take a shower together at some point. I know you're not a huge fan of water sports—not sure if showering together falls into that. And, I also like the idea of us repeating anything that was really a turn on for either of us the first time. For example, if you said you loved the Wrong Room fantasy and wanted to do that again, I'd be up for that. Personally, I enjoyed everything. I would be hard-pressed to pick a "what was your favorite part?" Actually, that in and of itself would be very stimulating for me—for us to talk about what we most enjoyed from my visit a few weeks ago. What was your favorite part?

Sunday and Monday are the days I will be sharing a room. That will NOT prohibit us from using the room during the day; it will just make things a little bit trickier as far as timing, etc. As far as evenings, I don't think that will work. It's not like there aren't other rooms in Vegas though! My friend is leaving Tuesday afternoon. I'll have the room to myself (or hopefully with you!) the rest of Tuesday and part of Wednesday.

I decided to go ahead and start a fantasy thread even though I said I wasn't sure that was a good idea. Not knowing how much time we'll actually have to spend together, I was trying to not get too carried away! Anyway, this has a lot of work yet, but I thought you might enjoy the first few paragraphs…

Television Repair Guy

My television isn't working correctly. I call for a service repairman to come to my house. You are scheduled to arrive at 3:00, but finish your previous appointment early and decide to take a chance and arrive at my place at 2:30. I hear a knock on the door and am hesitant to answer because I just got out of the shower and threw on lingerie—a satin two-piece. I look through the peep hole and recognize the logo on your shirt (no, you don't actually have to have a shirt with a logo on it!) from the appliance store and decide it's okay to let you in early, even though I'm not fully dressed.

We introduce ourselves and you're a very friendly guy. I show you the TV and tell you what isn't working properly. I excuse myself so that you can do your job and I can get back to getting ready for the evening. I tell you that I have a formal charity event to attend, and that's why I started getting ready so early. I head back to my bedroom only to discover that part of my shelving unit in my closet has started to come down. Since you seem like such a friendly, accommodating guy, I come back out and ask if I could bother you to help with the shelf. You are more than agreeable and follow me to the closet. I'm still in my satin outfit. I step into the closet a bit and reach up to show you where the screws have come undone. Just as I am ready to step back to get out of your way, you come up behind me to reach over my head to grab hold of the shelf. There's nowhere for me to move. I stand there as you see what adjustment might need to be made to the shelf. Through the light fabric of my lingerie, I can easily feel your body next to mine. I can feel the coolness of your belt buckle as it brushes against the warmth of the skin on my lower back. (To be continued…)

Hope you enjoy!

Karlee

From: Jack
To: Karlee

Sent: Monday, July 26, 2004 10:27 AM
Subject: RE: Fantasy preview...

Hi Karlee,

Things are hectic, as usual. The weekends are the worst for me, right now, and I've sort of dropped off the planet for most of the people I know...sorry if it's taking me a while to get back to you. Busy, busy, busy.

A shower together sounds like a truly excellent idea... although, I don't think that qualifies as "water sports." I agree that it would be fun to talk about what we enjoyed most from your last visit, although there was so much that I enjoyed, it could take two weeks just to cover it all.

Sunday will almost certainly be bad for me, but Monday is a strong possibility, as well as some time on Tuesday afternoon or evening...too soon to know for sure. I suppose it depends on my boss's reaction to the news that I want to adjust my schedule the following week, so that I can moonlight for another job (while he's in town, and before a big project is done).

As for your TV repair fantasy...as soon as you said the TV repair guy arrived 1/2 hour early, I knew it was a fantasy. But, other than that, it's great! To tell you the truth, I would be more than happy just to see you again, to kiss you, to take off your clothes, to feel your breasts in my hands and in my mouth, to see your absolutely perfect sexy pink shaved pussy as you slide your panties down your hips, to feel myself enter you, to feel your fingers run through my hair. All of that was great; I think just being with you again is the main fantasy...anything else is gravy!

--Jack

From: Karlee
To: Jack
Sent: Tuesday, July 27, 2004 12:12 PM
Subject: You're soooooooooooo good...

Dear Jack,

Mmmmmmmm. Mmmmmmmmmm. Perhaps you could hear me moan from here to there while I read your email yesterday. Once again, you turned my arms and legs to mush. And yes, that's a good thing!

My, oh my…since I myself have actually never been much of a gravy person…it's perfectly okay with me that the two of us being together is the main fantasy. I feel much the same way… I will be more than happy just to see you again, to feel you kiss me, for you to take off my clothes (and yours), to feel my breasts in your hands and in your mouth, to open my legs and feel your beautiful cock enter my absolutely perfect sexy pink shaved (I'll add—wet) pussy after I slide my panties down my hips, to feel how you fit perfectly in me and how your absolutely wonderful, skillful, rhythm creates a blissful, floating sensation in me from my head to my toes, to hear you speak my name, and to look into your eyes as we make love and to again run my fingers through your hair…

It's going to be a long two weeks.

Any desires as to just what kind of clothing you would like to take off of me? It brings me pleasure to bring you pleasure…

Karlee

From: Jack
To: Karlee
Sent: Wednesday, July 28, 2004 4:48 AM
Subject: RE: You're soooooooooooo good …

Hi Karlee,

I'm very glad to hear you've turned to mush. I'm a big fan of mush.

>>*It's going to be a lonnnng two weeks.*

It's true…it already IS a lonnnnng two weeks, and yet, it hasn't been two weeks yet. I hope I make it. I'm getting overly excited already!

As far as what kind of clothing I'd like to take off of you...just about anything! You made great choices last time; everything I saw you in (and out of) drove me wild. I don't have any specific ideas, but I definitely trust your tastes!

I'm going to go take a cold shower...then sleep!

--Jack

From: Karlee
To: Jack
Sent: Wednesday, July 28, 2004 10:22PM
Subject: Hi!

Hey there—how's my favorite friendly Las Vegas host today? I'm still mush.

No fantasies to send, and now I know what I'm going to wear. I guess all we need is for the calendar to change!

Remember when you wrote this?

>>For example, I'll give you the information that I'm not turned on by EVERYTHING. Yes, it's true. I'm not particularly titillated by, for example, "water sports" (other than water polo, which fascinates me).

What were you referring to as far as water sports? I'm still trying to figure that one out, now that I know it isn't showering together. Skinny dipping, perhaps? Or maybe there's something else that's often done in the water that I'm not even aware of! Anyway, just a curiosity question.

And here's a "bar talk" curiosity question. What kind of music do you like?

Hope you're doing well, amidst the hectic workload. Hey, I think we're officially at the *less than two weeks* mark! It would be nicer if it was the, "I'll be there in less than two minutes" mark! I know… patience, patience!

Good night,
Karlee

From: Jack
To: Karlee
Sent: Thursday, July 29, 2004 4:28 AM
Subject: RE: Hi!

Your friendly Las Vegas host is overwhelmed with work and eagerly anticipating your return. I guess it's good that I have more than enough to keep me distracted, although if I sit and let my mind wander about seeing you again, I find myself getting unbelievably aroused.

I did think about you today. I thought about you more than once today. In fact, I did more than think about you.

I'm glad you are still mush; I like mush. I'll solidify you when I see you…through a series of pleasurable injections (10 cc's of me into you).

As far as water sports…Hmmm? I'm glad you don't know the reference! Water sports refers to, let's see, how can I say this—releasing bodily fluids on another person. I have nothing against showering or skinny dipping, though.

Regarding music, I like mostly classical; kind of dull in my music tastes. I never developed much of an ear for lyrics, so I've always leaned towards orchestral arrangements. I also like jazz and big band, but I enjoy a weird assortment of songs. It's pretty random. I seem to have limited my music listening to my car these days.

Less than two weeks? Yay! Do you have a list of things you'd like me to do with (or to) you when I see you again? What are you most looking forward to? It's impossible for me to think back on our time together without getting completely excited all over again…you're too sexy, and the whole experience was so much fun and so wonderful. I'm glad we'll get the chance to see each other again. It'll be much easier this time, I think...it's so nice to be able to talk to the person that I shared this great experience with, and expand on it! I remember how excited you made me...and so do you! I don't have to struggle to find the words to adequately explain it, because you were there.

Only two weeks. I can make it!

--Jack

From: Karlee
To: Jack
Sent: Thursday, July 30, 2004 5:13 PM
Subject: Top 100 List...

Hi Jack,

Has anyone ever told you that you could be "habit-forming?" I just can't get enough! And I love the idea that you don't have any calories! Much better (not to mention healthier and more fun) than ice cream, as far as habits go!

So we were both thinking about each other and "more than thinking." I wonder if it was the same time! Of course, I'm making an assumption about what the "more than thinking about you" is referring to!

You asked if I have a list of things I'd like you to do with (or to) me when you see me again? I do have a list...things I'd like to do with you and *to you*!

Since I don't know how many hours we'll have together, I decided I'd better keep my list to just 100!
1. Look into your eyes
2. Run my fingers through your hair
3. Kiss your lips
4. Taste your mouth

5. Nuzzle your neck
6. Nibble your ears
7. Kiss your chest and circle your nipples with my tongue
8. Use my tongue to travel down your stomach
9. Kiss your belly button
10. Take your glorious penis and make love to you with my mouth

#11 - 100 Go to step 1 and repeat steps 1-10

And, what's on your list? Is there anything we did last time that didn't work well for you that you don't want me to do?

As far as what I am most looking forward to...

I am most looking forward to just seeing you again and being open to the possibility of creating the magic and magnificence that we created before, and beyond. I am most looking forward to being with someone who is as turned on by me as I am by him. I am most looking forward to feeling the soft touch of your fingertips and hands on my body. Everywhere. I am most looking forward to hearing our heaving breathing. I am most looking forward to celebrating this incredible experience, one that I have longed for and wondered if I would ever truly experience. I am most looking forward to lying by your side after we make love and just holding hands and talking. I am most looking forward to seeing you and not having to go through the awkwardness of all the stuff I was worried about the first time (like taking my wine to the bathroom with me!). I am most looking forward to me opening the door and just looking at you and having you take me in your arms and pressing your lips to mine and for us to moan with the mere pleasure of the reconnection.

I am so glad you responded to my ad!

Karlee

From: Jack
To: Karlee
Sent: Friday, July 30, 2004 5:25 AM
Subject: RE: Top 100 List...

Hi Karlee,

This was a LONG day for me...so if I suddenly become incoherent, it's due to exhaustion.

As far as the "more than thinking," well, what are you assuming? And what time were you doing more than thinking? Please tell me all about it in detail, and include photographs.

I very much like your list of 100. It's a good list, but I think you missed a few things. Better expand it to 500.

I can't think of anything that we did that didn't work for me last time. I have no complaints. We're very much on the same page as far as what we're looking forward to creating. And as far as you being glad that I responded to your ad—I'm glad, too!

Okay, so here's a thought I had, and I'll just throw it out there because it's crossed my mind a couple of times, but it's kind of out there and I'd understand if you didn't want to do it, but...well...you know. Here's the thought...I would really, really love to have a couple of pictures of you. I mean, all of you. You know, in all of your glory. I think you're so sexy and I still get instantly hard remembering looking at you; but when I'm...more than thinking about you...it would be nice to have that. I realize that's a huge trust thing, and very scary, and I don't know if there's any way that you'd be comfortable with it...maybe if it were just pictures of individual parts...but that would make me happy. Very happy. But, I'd totally understand if you didn't want to do it. I figured it wouldn't be bad to ask, so I am. It wouldn't be bad to say no to my idea, either.

But it wouldn't be bad to say yes!

Just thought I'd throw it out there. So there.

--Jack

From: Karlee
To: Jack
Sent: Sunday, August 1, 2004 2:06 PM

Subject: More than thinking of you...

Hi Jack,

How are you doing today? How was the poker tournament?

I've had a very busy weekend. My brother also came into town and I spent some time with him. My bathroom is about half painted. Not sure if I'll paint today. The weather is beautiful. I getting ready to take my laptop to the park and work on one of my book projects.

I wanted to do this for you yesterday as a "here's something to brighten your hectic workload and weekend," and never found the right time. Today I did! Hope it feels as good for you as it did for me...

I'm sitting in my favorite reading chair looking out the window. I begin to daydream about our first time together. I think about how nervous I was walking to the elevator to go down to meet you. And I remember telling myself, "Just relax, Karlee. Remain calm!" I start to think about us sitting on those chairs in my room and talking. And I smile when I think about you saying that you have an idea. "I think I should kiss your neck." And you did. And I remember finally being able to relax enough to suggest I put my legs on your lap. Oh my, your fingertips shoot what feels like electric currents through my body. And yes, I remember how I noticed that after some time, you move closer and closer to the throbbing beneath my skirt. I'm ready to take you to the bed and kiss you and yet I'm still uncertain.

At this point, I get up from my chair and go to my bedroom. I imagine that you're here, in my bed, naked and sitting up with your back on a pillow, against the headboard. Our eyes meet. I smile at your smile. You've been waiting for me. I stand at the foot of the bed. I take my hands and massage my breasts, wishing you were really here and that my hands were your hands. My right hand moves between my legs. You're getting aroused and I plan to go slow. I lift my shirt over my head. I arch my back and reach behind to unfasten my black lace bra. Oh, how I wish you were behind me unfastening my bra, so that you could cup my breasts from behind and kiss my neck. I climb up on the bed and you reach for me. I move back and say nothing. I put your hands by your side so that you can't touch me. I straddle your lap, and put my breasts in your face so that you can kiss them. My nipples are hard. "These are for you, Jack," I say. I let you kiss, but for just a very quick moment. I'm teasing you and you are starting to breath heavier. I remember how good it feels to hear your heaving breathing, knowing that it's me that is making you feel so good.

I climb back, still looking at you. I'm standing on the floor again at the foot of the bed. I remove my shorts. Your eyes feast on my black, lace boy-cut panties.

Since you're really not here, I lie on my bed, panties still on, my legs spread wide. My vibrator is close to me. I know I'll be using it. I also have with me the red ostrich feather I bought for my doctor fantasy. I take the feather, close my eyes and imagine that the feather is a combination of your fingers and tongue on my body. My arms, my face, my ears and neck, my legs, my breasts, my inner thighs. Now I take off my panties. Every so often I ever so gently let the feather touch my throbbing pussy. I look at the picture of you. "Oh, Jack," I'm thinking. "I can't wait to see you again."

After you and I have a chat (smile), I put your picture down. I reach for my vibrator and tease myself with it at first, imaging that it's really you. I put "you" in me and turn the power on high. I look up at the ceiling and imagine I'm looking at you. I moan. I move to your rhythm. Oh, you're so good. My feet tingle. I cum as I say your name and moan in ecstasy.

After a few moments, I roll over onto my stomach and again talk to the picture of you and think about seeing you again. I get out of bed and head for the shower…

I can stop there…you already know what I look like in the shower…

So there… you have a little bit of what I was doing when I was "more than thinking about you," just about a half an hour ago!

I think my insides have fluttered a million times since we talked on Friday.

See you soon???

A kiss to your lips,
Karlee

From: Karlee
To: Jack
Sent: Monday, August 2, 2004 11:37 AM
Subject: Hi!

Good Morning, Jack!

TGIM! Thank God it's Monday… and we can officially start the one week countdown!

Hope all is well.

Karlee

From: Jack
To: Karlee
Sent: Monday, August 2, 2004 4:47 PM
Subject: RE: Hi!

Hey there,

I was very happy to have these messages from you…it made my Monday!

Your description was…well…it was great. I couldn't help but more than think about you! Twice! You create a very vivid image.

After our talk, I keep thinking about a webcam conversation. I've only ever had one, and it wasn't much of anything, but suddenly that technology seems like the best thing in the world to me.

The poker tournament was fine…a bit frustrating at times, but I met my minimum goal for myself…I made it above the 50% mark. I lasted longer than everyone else I knew playing in the tournament (including a pro player), so I should've taken a side bet. Ah well. I'm not a seasoned gambler, I guess. Didn't win a dime, but I got a free lunch and a couple of free shirts, so I'm happy. I needed the break.

Things have gotten very unsettled this weekend...the other principal person in our Las Vegas office has just resigned. Now I'm waiting to hear what the shakedown will be. I guess there's a chance that everything gets shut down...that would be bad. Stressful.

So, it's especially nice to get your emails, because that reminds me that in a week, I'll be seeing you! That's only 7 days! Yay!

--Jack

From: Karlee
To: Jack
Sent: Monday, August 2, 2004 11:49 PM
Subject: Hello again . . .

Hi Jack,

Sorry to hear the news about the situation with your job. Have you heard anything from your boss yet? I hope everything works out. Those words, (I hope everything works out) to me, do not sound like much encouragement from me to you on such an important issue. If I already knew you for a longer period of time and knew more about the job itself, I'm certain I would be coming up with something more meaningful.

I'm happy to know I made your Monday. I hope I'll be making your "next Monday," too!

More than thinking about me and twice? Wow—I'm blushing! And remember...you're a part of the reason I am able to create that very vivid image!

As far as a webcam visit...Okay, so I'll admit it. I, too, thought about it a few times since our talk on Friday. Although I'm not ready to go shopping yet! Yes, it's exciting to think about on one hand, yet on the other hand…many considerations came up for me. But I do love the idea of *seeing* you more frequently.

Glad to hear the poker tournament gave you a much needed break. Congratulations on reaching at least your minimum goal. And about you lasting longer than everyone else that you knew…my guess is that poker is not the only place you last longer. (Wink, wink.)

Yes, you will be seeing me in LESS THAN 7 days! And in LESS THAN I have on right now!

Good night,
Karlee

From: Jack
To: Karlee
Sent: Tuesday, August 3, 2004 4:47 PM
Subject: RE: Hello again . . .

Hi Karlee,

Thanks. I appreciate the sentiment on your words about my job. I did, finally, hear from my boss, who said he'd speak with the woman on Wednesday and let me know what will happen. He reassured me his commitment to keep the course, which is what I'd expect him to do, but doesn't reassure me too much. I must keep looking at other options to be safe.

Yes, seeing you in less than seven days and in less than what you might be wearing now—that's really good to hear for a number of reasons! I'll be able to touch you. I'll be able to kiss you. I'll be able to slide myself inside you.

--Jack

From: Karlee
To: Jack

Sent: Tuesday, August 3, 2004 1:26 PM
Subject: Hi!

Hi Jack,

I hope you're doing okay, given the stress of the job situation and your workload.

I hadn't planned on writing to you this afternoon; I can't seem to stay focused on my work! And I can't seem to get seeing you again off of my mind! I was supposed to have an appointment this afternoon that would have kept my mind busy and I haven't heard back from the person I was supposed to meet (a graphic designer), so now I'm here in my office thinking of you. And at the rate my mind is going, I have a feeling pretty soon I'm going to be more than thinking of you.

It sounds like you won't know more about the job until tomorrow. Waiting and not knowing can be very stressful. You mentioned other options. I hope there is at least one that sounds exciting to you, should you need to go down that road.

While I'm thinking of it, there is something that I've wanted to mention that I learned last time and would like to share for our next time. I had never used flavored condoms before so I didn't know this at the time. Since I now have...although they are fine for oral sex and I'd like to continue to use them for oral sex, BUT, if we move right from that into intercourse, I think it would work better for me to have you switch to a regular condom. I don't think the flavored ones are lubricated and that's not quite as much fun! Soooo, yet another learning experience for Karlee! I thought I'd mention that now rather than spending valuable time talking about it while we're together! I'd much rather be kissing you than talking about which condoms to use!

Hey, my appointment just called and re-scheduled for tomorrow. I know where I'm going...Mmmmmm! It sure would be more fun if you were here! Come to think of it, I'm beginning to wonder if I sound like a sex maniac to you. This wasn't my lifestyle until I met you! Before you, I had never met anyone who just thinking about him would get me aroused in this way. Now, I'm a person who believes in taking full responsibility for my life and normally I don't blame others. But in this case, if this is a bad thing...I just might have to blame you!!!

That's it for now. I look forward to hearing from you.

Karlee

From: Jack
To: Karlee
Sent: Tuesday, August 3, 2004 4:02 PM
Subject: RE: Hi!

Hi Karlee,

I'm doing okay; thanks for your concern. I'm starting to feel a bit under the weather too...probably not getting enough sleep. I'm going to take it easy to make sure I'm at 100% when you're in town.

Well, I can't say that I'm sorry to hear that you're thinking about me so much. Although, I don't want you to be unable to focus on your work. On the other hand, I'm glad that I'm a pleasant diversion!

Thanks for sharing the piece about the condoms. I think that's fine; I don't mind changing condoms. I haven't always used condoms for oral sex, primarily because the STD risk is extremely low (unless there are visible lesions in or around the mouth) and most of the risk is to the male. I'm a lifelong safe sex fanatic, so I'd not suggest you skip the condoms for oral sex unless you wanted to. But, it's interesting that a lot of people have misconceptions about those risks. Kissing and touching are greater risks (all things not being equal, of course). In any event, I'll switch condoms whenever you like! I'll start right now, if you want...

Your appointment re-scheduled? Where are you going? You don't sound like a sex maniac; you sound like someone who enjoys sex, which sounds like most people to me. I'm looking forward to the time when you sound like a sex maniac! I take full responsibility. But, you have to take full responsibility for turning me into a sex maniac, too.

It's a good thing you don't have a webcam. I'd be on-line all the time looking for you, and naked, and doing a lot more than thinking (and a lot less than working).

As it is, it's hard enough to concentrate (actually, it's hard enough for a lot of things).

--Jack

From: Karlee
To: Jack
Sent: Tuesday, August 3, 2004 11:24 PM
Subject: Feel Better Soon!

Hi Jack,

Oh, no! Let's cancel the "feeling under the weather" part right out! Remember when I wasn't feeling great before I came out last month and I went to see a doctor? You told me the next time you didn't feel well you were going to tell your doctor you were having sex next week and to give you a miracle cure. Hey, it worked for me! (Well, it was antibiotics more so than a miracle cure.) Of course the other thought I had was maybe I'll need to bring my nurse's uniform outfit. Just kidding; I don't have one. Even if I did, it'd be more fun to wear it when you're feeling 100%. Which I guess is what you'll be next week, since you are going to take it easy to make certain you are when I'm in town! Actually, I have another outfit I'd rather wear—it's called a birthday suit. It's really cute—you should see it!

>>Although, I don't want you to be unable to focus on your work. On the other hand, I'm glad that I'm a pleasant diversion!

Yes, a pleasant diversion you are. And it's good. I do some of my most creative and productive work having you as a pleasant diversion!

Your response about condoms reminded me that I was actually in a conversation with a few other women about that very topic not too long ago. (STD's and oral sex vs. kissing, etc.) I'm going to give

131

some more thought to this.

Okay, so what do you think a sex maniac sounds like? If I'm going to turn you into one, I'll need to know what you have in mind! I'm up for the challenge. Of course, that's just using a commonly used phrase. I don't think it would be a challenge at all, once I have the proper guidelines!

Anything new on the job situation today?

Good night,
Karlee

From: Jack
To: Karlee
Sent: Wednesday, August 4, 2004 1:52 AM
Subject: RE: Feel Better Soon!

Hi Karlee!

I feel quite a bit better already. I think I was a bit stressed and run down. I'll go to bed early and take it easy the next couple of days, and I'm sure I'll be fine. The thought of being with you again will be better than 1,000 gallons of chicken soup.

I believe I've seen that birthday suit you mentioned. And it's more than just "really cute." It's unbelievably sexy. It occupies my thoughts. I can't think about that outfit without getting fixated on it...you should wear that all the time! It fits you perfectly! Have I told you lately how sexy your birthday suit is? Every part is spectacular, from head to toe.

I'm not sure, exactly what a sex maniac might sound like. I have ideas that you'd constantly be asking me for sex, sending me erotic photos of yourself, writing your fantasies to me every day...all of that sounds good. The rest of it I probably haven't even imagined yet, but I think I'd probably like all of it!

You're doing that more than thinking all the time without the webcam? Well, me too, actually. A lot more than I have in the past.

A lot. Bordering on too much. It's like my libido has gone through the roof. I flash back to different moments of our time together and it was all so erotic and so exciting and so pleasurable that I never fail to get excited. I can't even write about it. It's tricky.

Tomorrow, supposedly, the boss and the ex-officemate will have a talk about her exit strategy. I suppose one of them will give me the lowdown then. Of course, I'm now wondering how I will (or if I can) bring up the possibility of my doing work for these other people in a couple of weeks for three or four days. I don't want him to worry that I'm looking for another job too, or he may pull the plug. But, maybe he'll need the time to find someone else. If he got a replacement, I think my life might get easier (he wouldn't want to lose me AND her) but maybe not.

Do you remember when I straddled you and touched myself and spurted my cum all over your breasts?

I do.

--Jack

From: Karlee
To: Jack
Sent: Wednesday, August 4, 2004 2:13 PM
Subject: Hi!

Hi Jack,

How are you feeling today? Any news yet from your boss or co-worker?

In regards to all the more than thinking we're each doing…Miss Analysis over here has been back and forth on many areas related to this and us, and the whole thing. AND, I'm also working on letting go of all the "stuff" and just working on staying in the moment. Everything about this feels so good (with the exception of the fact that it's mostly via email rather than in person!) and that's a good thing. Like right now. I just got an email from you and I thought, "Hey, maybe I'll call instead of sending this." And then I think, "No, you'd better not or you might not get anything done for the rest of the day." Yes, just talking to you and hearing your voice could do that to me. And since I'm heading out of town in a few days, I have much I want and need to get done. Now that doesn't mean I won't call, or wouldn't talk to you if you called me; I was just sharing that as a part of explaining the situation. I'm curious though…"Bordering on too much." Too much thinking or too much of the more than thinking or too much of not paying attention to your work?

And, yes, I do remember when you straddled me and touched yourself and spurted your cum all over my breasts. Oh, yes, I do! Feel free to do that again. When you feel good, I feel good.

Karlee

From: Jack
To: Karlee
Sent: Wednesday, August 4, 2004 2:38 PM
Subject: RE: Hi!

Hi Karlee!

I'm feeling much better today, thanks. I should be 100% by tomorrow, I think.

The word from the boss is that he talked to the co-worker and she'll not work next week, work the following week (when he's in town) and then they've got some kind of long term deal.

He asked me if I had any suggestions for replacements for her. I'm not sure how to respond to that question. In the past, when I tried to help hire some underlings (that would've reported to my co-worker) I was told that it was outside my purview and they wouldn't tell me how much they get paid, etc. So, I guess my inclination is to politely stay out of that. I think it'll serve me better. I'm not going to recommend someone for a job that I have no idea what the salary range is…it could be $20K for all I know. So, I know nottttttthing. I'm going to try to talk to her and see if I can find out what's really happening.

Ah well. This is all very uninteresting stuff compared to sex talk. Well, feel free to tell me anything else you'd like to try/try again. When you feel good, I feel good, which makes you feel good. I think we've learned that not only does it not hurt to ask, but it is extremely worthwhile!

--Jack

From: Karlee
To: Jack
Sent: Thursday, August 5, 2004 1:13 AM
Subject: Hello . . .

Hi Jack,

How are you tonight? I was glad to hear that you are thinking you'll be 100% soon! Wow, you're good at everything; even recovering from under the weather! Anything new on the job front since this morning?

I had a good day although I didn't get as much done as I had hoped to, especially in my office. And now it's late—late for me and I'm just getting ready to call it a night. Plus, every once in awhile I remember that I need to start packing for my trip! I'm going to be away a good part of Friday, which means I should try to get a lot done on Thursday, which it is actually already now in Cleveland!.

Yes, I certainly have learned *a lot* since posting that ad! As far as trying new things or doing the same things again…I am limited on positions, and would be open to experiencing even more than what we did last time. Now, don't get me wrong. I totally loved what I (we) experienced. Mmmmm. And, I would be open to knowing if there are other ways that might be extremely pleasurable. A couple of ways I have been curious about, but have never done. One I'm guessing is quite common… I think it would be described as "on the edge of the bed (?)" And I also get quite excited when I think about us being naked and me straddling you on your lap on a chair. Are these Twister positions or real? Do you enjoy doggie style? I've only done that once. It was okay yet somewhat awkward since it was the first time and I wasn't sure exactly what to expect. Telling you this feels a bit awkward (how could anything be awkward at this point, I know!) I feel like I should be embarrassed about all that I haven't experienced, and I know that's not true. I guess I have a lot of catching up to do. And I cannot think of a better person than you to catch up with. You're the best "catcher upper" I could ask for!

Speaking of catching up…now that the week is coming to a close, do you have a better idea of your schedule for next week? What I really want to know is just exactly what time and what day(s) I get to put my hands on you!!!! No pressure; I'm just eager to know! Sooooo eager!

Good Night, Good Looking,
Karlee

From: Jack
To: Karlee
Sent: Thursday, August 5, 2004 1:47 AM
Subject: RE: Hello . . .

Hi Karlee,

Nothing substantially new on the job front. I talked to the soon-to-be-former co-worker as I was running out to work on other things; she told me where she was going and how much she was getting paid. I had wanted to know, and now that she's on the way out, it's good to have that info.

Well, I got your message…I'm sorry I missed you. Busy, busy. I got home about 9:30 PM, which seems too late to call, especially if you're already in bed. I've gotten a lot done in the last couple of hours. I seem to be cranking along. I have a big conference call tomorrow, which will probably have nothing to do with me, but I still have to prepare for that.

I notice every day that you're not around me, too. Like…today! And tomorrow! And the next day! But that'll only be the case for a few more days!

Well, I'm delighted to be your partner in *catching-uppering.* (I made that word up!) As for positions, that's nothing to be embarrassed about. I'm certainly willing to try anything you'd like, but I must say...I've never understood people who think that positions are exotic or wild. Most of them are just acrobatics. The feeling can be different, but only to a limited degree. Man on top, man on top with woman's legs on man's shoulder, doggie style, woman on top, spooning, and what I call the X position (because the bodies form kind of an X)...that's about all I ever do. I've tried a lot more, but, well, I guess it depends on how your bodies are shaped. In a chair would be good...I'm happy to take requests!

As far as my schedule, I think the weekend will be out. Monday afternoon and Tuesday afternoon (and/or maybe Tuesday evening) seem likely. I'm sure I will have time to see you...I'm not sure exactly when, as there's still a lot up in the air, and my schedule flexes a lot. Wednesday may be good, too.

Don't worry...you'll be seeing me. I'm sure it won't be enough, but we'll make the most of it.

I feel like I could pick up exactly where we left off. I'm sure you'll want to spend some time reconnecting, but it'll be interesting to see how we feel with each other. Right now, I feel like I could walk up to your room, pull you close to me, kiss your neck, your ears, run my hands over your body, kiss your lips, take off your clothes, take off my clothes, and put myself inside you, and I think I'd be very happy to do that!

--Jack

From: Karlee
To: Jack
Sent: Thursday, August 5, 2004 12:51 PM
Subject: We're almost there!

Hi Jack,

It won't be long now! Of course it still feels like a lonnnnnng time to wait!

All set for the conference call? Something doesn't sound right; you do the prep work and it doesn't have anything to do with your job. Although, I once had a client and they used to have conference calls for their shareholders and I know the person who spent the most amount of time in the preparation of the script was just a minor part of the whole call. So I guess that happens.

Have you ever given thought to working for yourself? Having been self-employed for almost ten years, I know a lot of people who make their living primarily as writers/authors. I'm sure this concept is not new news to you. I just sense a lot of talent in you and your writing, and you appear to have the commitment to work hard which is what it would take of course, at least at first...

Glad to hear you felt your evening was productive. As far as calling too late, if we're on our cell phones it doesn't matter since I turn mine off when I go to bed, so it doesn't ring anyway.

Thank goodness it will be only a few more days. It's been quite overwhelming (in a good way) the last day or two and I'm sure that will only heighten as time gets closer.

Oh, yes! I remember the X position! Incredible! Mmmmm! Make that Mmmmm times 100.

I am usually more of a giver than a taker. BUT, in this case, I will say that I will take any and all the time I can get!

And don't be so sure about needing time to reconnect. Hey, we can reconnect after we reconnect!!!

Yes, this is certainly much different than the first time, and more time has passed and more emails have been shared. Although I am so looking forward to the sexual reconnection, I am also looking forward to the two of us just having conversation.

The whole picture has me so worked up that it's overwhelming. Other than that, it all sounds good except I think you should run up to my room. Walking will take longer! And, about taking off my clothes…who said I'd be wearing any? ;-)

Karlee

From: Jack
To: Karlee
Sent: Thursday, August 5, 2004 1:28 PM
Subject: RE: We're almost there!

Hi Karlee,

Yes, I know the feeling. It seems like this week has been crawling by. This is the third day this week that I thought (hoped, I guess) it was Friday.

As far as working for myself—thanks for the compliment. When I left my job in NY, I spent a year out here working in a job that I didn't like. After that, I decided to live off of savings and try to do my own thing. I explored a number of ideas, writing a lot, trying to build a couple of ideas into businesses, and looking hard for a job that I thought I might want. I did that for over a year. I used up all of my savings. The last few months before I started this job, I was just looking for anything. I learned a lot in that experience, but I didn't make it happen. I imagine at some point I'll be working for myself, but I didn't succeed this time. I don't think I had enough time or money to get things off the ground, but I put in more effort than I have for any other job, so it was a frustrating time. I suppose my mistake was trying to do too many things at once, but it was good to spend some time figuring out what I think I would like and would not like to do.

I don't really like the idea of freelance writing, because there's too much time spent selling and worrying about the next job. My goal is to get this job under control in the next six months, and then to do it part time while I work on my own stuff. I don't know if that will work out. If not, I'm going to have to find something that has a lot of flexibility. It's tough.

I'm glad that you seem much more positive about seeing me this time than last time!

Hmmm. I hadn't even thought about the reconnecting part. It's not like it's been that long since you were here last, and we've written back and forth a lot. It feels like it's just been a week or so, in some ways, and in others, it feels like an eternity. Hmmm. It certainly would be nice to sweep you up and let my enthusiasm to see you just take its course, but I don't want to be impolite. I'm looking forward to the conversation part too, although maybe conversation would be better after sex, because all that will be on my mind before sex will be touching you.

Not wearing any clothes? Mmmm! Although, I do love the sexy clothes/underwear/lingerie you had. It's like unwrapping a fabulous present (much better than, for example, getting socks for my birthday).

So, here's one thing I wanted to discuss...I seem to remember when we were first together that you were concerned that I "took a long time." I just wanted to remind you that you should never have to worry about me. I enjoy every second that I'm inside you. I really enjoy when you have an orgasm, and I'd be delighted to be with you when you had one, two, three, twelve, or more. If you ever want me to stop, you can tell me. Or, if you really want me to cum, you can tell me; just tell me "It's okay" when I'm sliding in and out of you, and I will let go. I enjoy it all so much; it feels good to "hold back" and I can do it for hours. I got the impression that you were worried I wasn't excited by you, which isn't the case at all.

In fact, I know I mentioned this, but when we finished looking at the spa brochure and you went to take a shower, I was as excited as I've ever been in my life watching you undress. After you slipped off your panties and bra and walked into the bathroom, I peeked around the corner, and took off my shorts. I was so hard and throbbing. I took my cock in my hand and was surprised how hard I was...I was going to leave my shorts on, but I threw off all my clothes instead, and stroked myself as I watched you. I came very close...VERY close to cumming before you had finished the shower...I was so worked up. That would've been a horrible disappointment! But, the point is, I think you're very sexy and I enjoy being inside you every second that I am.

Just in case you couldn't tell!

--Jack

From: Karlee
To: Jack
Sent: Thursday, August 5, 2004 11:42 PM
Subject: Can you hear me now?

Hi Jack,

I'm back to this email I started several hours ago! How was the rest of your evening? I hope you didn't get indigestion from having to rush dinner.

Well, Well, Well, Well…Karlee had phone sex. Yet another new experience for me this evening. Who would have ever thought?! And I have to say—I liked it! A lot actually, and much more than I would have imagined; much nicer than by myself. Now, it still is a bit awkward when I think about it, and once again, I tried something new and survived! What a sexual pioneer I have become! And it looks like you have officially become my guide. I hope you know what you're doing! I wouldn't want to get lost on our trail for days on end and not know where we're going. Wait…sure I would!

And if I had to guess, you're probably going to ask what I liked about it. Here are a few things that come to mind…
1. Hearing your voice
2. Hearing your voice in an excited state
3. Hearing your voice at the same time I was touching myself
4. Hearing you cum when I came—Mmmmm!
5. Hearing you call me "Baby"

Hmmm…hearing, hearing, hearing—I guess it ignites my auditory senses!

Yes, I've spend many a moments in a daze! Last night I was eating dinner and I got up to check something in another room. I came back and walked right past the table, having forgotten that quickly that I had been eating, mainly because my mind had wandered to thoughts of you! My body was probably headed to my bedroom because that's where I often end up when I spend more than three seconds thinking about you.

Believe me; I am giving you compliments every day. Of course, most of them, although connected to your writing, are more about how good you are at doing what you are doing to me!

I can relate to the challenges of freelance. It's pretty much the same way with my consulting business. When I was married, having sporadic assignments wasn't a problem, since there were two incomes. Of course, now is a different story. I'm actually excited about the challenge. I have some lofty goals for next year and am confident that it will all work out. I understand flexibility being important to you. When I was considering taking a job a couple of months back, the thought of giving up my freedom and flexibility was enough to make me figure out how I could make this work!

Speaking of all-nighters…as the plan is for right now, I'm going to check out of the room with my friend and get my own room for Monday and Tuesday nights. I believe I will be more comfortable with that. Although she is totally okay with us using the room, I know myself well enough to know that I probably wouldn't be able to be as relaxed, wondering about what time she'll be back and worrying about the possibility of her needing something in the room, etc. Soooo, that being the case, feel free to put in one or two all-nighters next week. Just thought I'd mention that in case you want to pack your PJ's. Wait a second—what am I thinking? No PJ's would be allowed! That would be a time for me to enjoy your birthday suit! Know that this is of course only if your schedule would allow and if you are comfortable with the idea. However, I will say, the thought of falling asleep next to you and waking up next to you (or on top of you, or in front of you, or behind you, etc.) is, well, let's just say a wonderful thought!

I think I did a pretty good job of demonstrating my comfort level with you tonight on the phone. That was a big stretch for me for sure, and yet not as scary as many of the thoughts prior to my first trip! I still have considerations that tend to come into my mind, although different in nature this time. And no need to worry about feeling impolite. Actually, what less would I expect? As my friendly

Las Vegas host, I think it's in your job description to sweep me up and let your enthusiasm to see me take its course, isn't it?!

I shopped for a couple of new pieces of lingerie this week. I could not believe how turned on I was just at the thought of knowing I was making selections based on what I thought might please you. Much better than buying something sexy and wondering if anyone other than me would see it!

Twelve orgasms?! Oh my! Now that might be something to set my sights on! I'm tempted to ask if you've ever been with a woman who has had 12 orgasms in one night. I'm not sure I want to know! And in case you're curious, I think two has been the most for me. But then that was in my pre-Jack days! I'm pretty sure we can change that. And I'm not implying that two is a bad number, especially when the thought of just being with you feels good. Even if I didn't have any, I'm guessing I would still be smiling!

When I told you the second night we were together that you were the best I have ever had, I meant it. And it just keeps getting better! I'm suddenly sad for anyone who doesn't have at least one opportunity to experience what I have experienced with you.

By the way, I don't think I have told you yet that I think you have the most incredibly sexy eyes. Beautiful. I'm big into eyes and yours are amazing. And I will be seeing them (and the rest of you) very soon!

Good night. Sleep well. I know I will, with lingering thoughts of our time together tonight on the phone.

Mmmmmmm!

Karlee

From: Jack
To: Karlee
Sent: Friday, August 6, 2004 10:51 PM
Subject: RE: Can you hear me now?

Hi Karlee,

I grabbed a pizza, which probably wasn't the healthiest choice, but it sure was tasty.

I liked our phone time, too...though it's not as good as "the real thing," it was nice to hear your voice, too....

I'll definitely stay open to that possibility of a sleepover. It may be tough given the fact that I do a lot of late, late night work, but I'd like to if I can, although you might wake up in the middle of the night with me inside you.

I'm launching into the fun, fun weekend marathon now. But, when it's over, you'll be in town, so it should fly by. Have fun with your sister.

--Jack

From: Karlee
To: Jack
Sent: Friday, August 13, 2004 6:36 PM
Subject: Hi!

Hi Jack,

I hope this email is a welcomed interruption amongst all the work related mail. I know you said you'd be fairly busy again until the beginning of the week. I'll keep this short and for now just say hi, I enjoyed seeing you again, and I look forward to hearing from you when you have the time.

Karlee

From: Jack
To: Karlee
Sent: Thursday, August 19, 2004 12:07 PM
Subject: RE: Hi!

Hi Karlee!

I just wanted to write a quick note and say hi. As busy as I thought I'd be this week, it turns out that I was just wrong—I'm way over extended, but things will be better by Monday. I don't anticipate getting back on email (personal or otherwise) until Monday, which may be a record for me.

I've had a few pieces of good news, but the good news only has meant more work. I got a sponsor for a local TV show, which means that project goes forward. And, once I shower and eat, I start a 4-day marathon of 16-18 hour days on another TV show, after which I come home and do my real job.

But, before I went to sleep last night I managed to squeeze in a few minutes to think (and more than think) of you!

In any event, I'm still here and will write more in a few days!

--Jack

From: Karlee
To: Jack
Sent: Sunday, August 22, 2004 9:49 PM
Subject: Hi!

Hi Jack!

Well… if you are reading this message, it means you survived the horrendous week! Yeah! I hope you get a chance to relax a bit soon.

Congratulations (I think) on the sponsor for the TV show. I sensed you weren't really certain about how happy to be, since it will mean more work. And that's understandable. Might this be something that could eventually replace your "day job?"

I will just say hi for now, as your mailbox is probably quite full if you have not been on email for several days.

Looking forward to hearing from you!

Karlee

From: Jack
To: Karlee
Sent: Monday, August 23, 2004 9:49 PM
Subject: RE: Hi!

Hi Karlee!

Oh, I need to relax. That was a rough week. I'm still trying to
process everything. My meetings for my normal job were
interesting...since starting work several months ago, I've brought up
some issues over and over and over again, mostly relating to the
business strategy. I was supposedly brought on partly because I
have a knowledge of this town, so when they told me things that
seemed to have no chance of succeeding, I'd tell them. I'd be told
either that it was outside the scope of my job or that they'd done
things that way in NYC and they wanted to start with that. About
two or three weeks ago, I gave up. I was tired of trying to convince
them.

Then my co-worker quit. She was there for these meetings last
week, and suddenly my boss was questioning whether his approach
would work. He asked about things that I've been suggesting for
months, and suddenly they concern him, and he wanted solutions. I
think it's too late—at least, as far as I'm concerned. I tried and was
dismissed, and now he wants help. All I could think of was "it's
outside of the scope of your job." I think he burned his bridge with
me. I couldn't get interested in it.

I didn't get to work on any writing in the last week, because I left
work on Wednesday and went over to help out a production
through Sunday. It was a lot more fun than it had been...lots of
work, practically no pay, long hours, but at least it was rewarding.
But, from Monday through Sunday I was doing nothing but work. I
had one proper meal in the last five days; the rest were all grabbed
snacks.

But, it's over now and I can rest my feet and relax.

I've been so busy that I haven't had time to think (or more than think!)

How are you? What's going on? I'm very sorry I didn't have more time to see you this trip...but I was happy for the time I could get with you!

--Jack

From: Karlee
To: Jack
Sent: Monday, August 23, 2004 10:04 PM
Subject: Hi!

Hi Jack,

It was nice to hear from you. I'm glad to hear you made it through the week, although I'm surprised you didn't collapse at some point. Of course, if anyone has endurance... ;-) I'm sorry to hear that your time with your boss was not more favorable. I got the impression when I was in Vegas that things were not going in the best direction. Sounds like that was confirmed last week. I'm glad that the other project felt rewarding even though it was long hours and not much pay.

I enjoyed our time together. Looking back, I wish I would have waited to come out at a time that would have worked better for you. But then I would have missed seeing my friends.

Hope you had a good day!

Good night,
Karlee

From: Karlee
To: Jack

Sent: Tuesday, August 24, 2004 3:40 PM
Subject: Sharing thoughts . . .

Dear Jack,

How are you today? Did you have an opportunity to do anything fun yesterday?

Something has been on my mind for some time now and I have decided to share it. Since I believe that our connection began with taking risks, being vulnerable, and being open to new possibilities (regarding sex and intimacy), intimate sharing should be easy to continue, right? But for me, it's actually been a bit of a struggle. Nothing huge, just something tugging at me.

I'm feeling like I'm in a bit of a quandary as far as our connection goes. A part of me is struggling with just letting it be, telling myself, "Just let things unfold naturally, as they are meant to or not." And another part of me is struggling with the, "This is what I'd like to know" piece.

I realized last night when I was writing to you, that it felt a bit awkward. No fantasies to talk about, no upcoming visits for me to Las Vegas. It was just two people in "normal" dialogue about daily life. And that by no means is a bad thing. Just different than most of our emails up until now.

Although you haven't known me for very long, I think you know me well enough to know that I think a lot! Okay, maybe even too much according to some people. And that's who I am. Who knows, maybe I don't think too much; maybe other people don't think enough. It's like telling someone their eyes are too blue, or their hair is too black, or that they are too tall. I just think a lot.

I have been pondering what took place between us during my last trip to Las Vegas, and since my return. I have experienced a myriad of emotions, both while there, and since returning.

Since returning from Vegas the first time, and now knowing what the outcome was, I periodically think back to the morning I sat down at my computer and typed the craigslist ad. I was trying to get in touch with what exactly I was thinking/hoping the outcome would be. [Regardless, what took place between us, I have no doubt, is and will be one of the most profound experiences I have ever had in my life. Not to mention all the other words like, exciting, wonderful, fulfilling, satisfying, and liberating.] Putting that to the side, and back to my "motive" for placing the craigslist ad… The realization I came to was it was really more about writing the ad and placing the ad. I truly believe I was thinking that I would never really ACT on it! And if I allowed myself to, it would be about me "trying" to "train" myself to have sex and not get emotionally attached. At the time, I found the whole psychology of being able to do that fascinating, and I was thinking that if I did it enough, I could learn how.

What I have come to believe is that I really don't want to learn how. I don't know that I would ever allow myself to move through life with the idea that life is just a series of sexual encounters. I like both the physical and the emotional side of a connection, and for it to be satisfying to me, I now realize that I do desire to have both parts.

So what happened for me is… Our first time together I had no attachment. I went into it with a (relatively) open mind. And I think that was primarily because I hadn't thought ahead to the, "Okay, when this is over, then what?" piece. I never went down that road, probably because I'm guessing, subconsciously, I was thinking I would never really act on it.

And for me, everything the first time was perfect.

BUT…then the emotions kicked in! And it changed. And once I decided to make the second trip, up comes all this STUFF! I found myself thinking of you as more than just "this guy I met through the internet." I started to wonder if you really liked me or if you were just looking at this as sex and your fantasy. I started to think about aspects of what's important to me in relationships and wondered what is important to you. And with all that, it changed the dynamics of our second time together for me. I felt almost more vulnerable than the first time. The first time, I hadn't worried about the "what if I never see him again" since the "deal" was for it to be a casual encounter. But the second time, for me, it was more than that. By that point, I knew I liked you and saw you more than just someone to have sex with.

So, now I'm back home and find myself wondering, now what? Do you have any thoughts about where we go from here? Where would you like to go, if anywhere? Do you think a long distance relationship is feasible? Heck, I don't even know if you are looking for a relationship, with me…or otherwise. You may have a desire to be married and have a family with 12 kids! Or you may have your career as a priority and not have much of an interest in a relationship, period. I know we agreed the first time we were together that we liked each other. Even that can be interpreted different ways. There are a lot of people I like. It doesn't mean I want to have sex with them!

I'm guessing you haven't even thought about this as much as I have, if at all. Studies show that a woman will spend almost an equal amount of time thinking about relationships as a man will spend thinking about his job/career. So, while you were working a million hours last week, guess what I was thinking about? Yep—us! All this wondering. Too bad it doesn't burn calories!

Another piece that is unsettling for me is that I have never allowed myself (or probably even had the opportunity) to be involved with more than one man at a time. I know myself well enough to know that if I am attracted to one person and exploring the possibility of a relationship, I'm not likely to be looking beyond that. I know it's way too soon to know much about our compatibility beyond our sexual compatibility (which if you ask me is pretty compatible—okay, really compatible!). I guess I just thought that if you were looking at this as not much of anything, now would be a good time for me to know that.

Of course if we lived in the same city, I'm guessing the dynamics of all this would be different and probably much easier. Now that I know how wildly turned on I am by thoughts of being with you, I don't know how I could endure seeing you only occasionally. I know there's the possibility of a webcam. I just don't know how satisfying that would really be. You mentioned quite a few travel plans for the remainder of the year. It didn't appear that a trip to Cleveland (and christening the Jacuzzi) was a part of that. And I totally understand that you have a limited amount of time off, and I would never expect you to give up going places you enjoy and doing the things you enjoy doing, plus visiting your parents.

I guess it boils down to a couple of basic questions…what are your thoughts about our connection and, ideally, if anything, what would it look like to you?

Karlee

From: Jack
To: Karlee
Sent: Tuesday, August 24, 2004 7:20 PM
Subject: RE: Sharing thoughts …

Hi Karlee!

Well, I'm glad you're being up front about your feelings.

When I responded to your ad, it was all about the fantasy, and I didn't know if we'd go through with it or not. I liked writing to you and talking to you, but you seemed to have a lot of hesitations (I'm sure you remember that part). I really didn't have any expectation of anything happening…it didn't sink in until the moment when you slipped out of your clothes. Even as we were in your room chatting, I was prepared for you to say, "I can't do this," so I was just seeing what happened and didn't think much about the impact on me. I was excited by the idea from the moment I read your ad, and when I got your email response to my note, I figured I would go through with it. I've never done such a thing before, but I guess the decision was much easier for me.

And, for me, definitely the right decision for many reasons. I guess as far as the "where do we go from here" stuff, I hadn't really thought about it. I mean, I often have tried to fit my personal life in around my professional life, and my professional life has been so crazy lately that my personal life has kind of disappeared…not just in terms of dating, but also with friends. I've had more projects going on than ever before, as opposed to working on one thing for 90 hours a week. I certainly thought (and think) about you, but you're in Cleveland so the reality of that situation kept me from wondering what could happen. The truth of the matter is that even if you were here, I never had the intention of entering into a serious marriage-track relationship...not that I'm opposed to those thoughts, but more that I wasn't thinking about it. I think part of the reason that I never got married is because I'm still not settled professionally, and I've never had enough stability to feel like I could pursue a "serious" relationship.

I suppose I'm highly unusual in that I think about my relationships so little. It's not that I don't enjoy being close to someone; I very much enjoyed being with you on both trips. I guess I never allowed myself to think about other possibilities because a) we're in different towns and b) I have all my energies in locking down my professional life. I don't know if b) ever changes...I feel like I'm behind some schedule that no one has given me, but that I'm getting older and need to find stability and a permanent home and all this other stuff. As much as I like the idea of seeing you at every opportunity, I don't believe I'd be ready to pull back from other things to do that. I don't know though; I haven't thought about it. This started as a sexy idea that surprisingly turned into something great. I've been trying to fit you into my complicated life these days, but hadn't thought about any substantial commitment.

The fact is that I'm not interested in dating a lot of people; perhaps it's my unwillingness to put more into relationships that's kept me single in town. I haven't thought about it. I think I'll have to think more about it.

As for taking trips, I would most definitely like to go to Cleveland and christen your hot tub (among many other surfaces in your home). I just know that between time and money constraints, I'm going to hit the wall with my "real job." Maybe everything will work out. Maybe I'll find another job that does what I hoped this one would: gives me enough to live on, but a great deal of flexibility. I'm finding that there isn't any flexibility and that's what's causing problems. I've not made plans to go home at all, and I haven't been back since last year...but I'd definitely like to see you again.
So, the answer is...I don't know. I don't know what I am able to offer,

or whether it's enough. I'm not sure what you want. I don't know what I want. I know I want you, but I don't know in what ways (other than sexually, to which the answer is "in every way.")

So many things to think about.

--Jack

From: Karlee
To: Jack
Sent: Tuesday, August 24, 2004 11:03 PM
Subject: RE: Sharing thoughts...

You make me smile!

I'll write more tomorrow.

Good night,
Karlee

From: Karlee
To: Jack
Sent: Wednesday, August 25, 2004 3:45 PM
Subject: Hi!

Hi Jack!

How are you today? I started my day with more than thinking of you! It all started last night after I read your email. The "christen your hot tub (among many other surfaces in your home)" and the, "I don't know in what ways (other than sexually, to which the answer is 'in every way')" started a series of those flutter feelings (again) and then this morning, I found myself reliving (in my mind) us in my hotel bathroom during my first visit. Mmmm. Mmmmm. I was going to call you but it was early here which meant it was really early in Las Vegas and I didn't want to wake you. Although who knows, you may not have even been to bed yet!

Anyway, I appreciate you for sharing your thoughts with me regarding my thoughts.

Your answer of "I don't know" is fine. Actually, I don't know if I am really clear on what I want either. The email was probably more about what I didn't want, which was to continue corresponding with a person who has no interest in having any kind of relationship with me, aka, the feeling of being used. I certainly by no means am looking for any kind of commitment.

So maybe for now, it's okay that we don't have all the answers. We can certainly continue with the pieces that we do know. For me, I know I love thinking about our times together and thinking about more times together. I know I enjoy receiving every email I get from you. I know I think you are one of the most intellectual men I have ever connected with and I know now that a man with that aspect is very appealing to me and adds to you arousing me. I know I am grateful for you coming into my life, regardless of in what capacity. I know that although I would certainly prefer that we could look at a more traditional kind of dating relationship, us being in different cities makes that impossible. I know that your professional life is your priority now and I respect that. And, I know that I can easily get wet just thinking about being with you.

By no means do I want to get in the way of your already hectic days. Are you comfortable with the frequency of communication we have now (which is generally an email every day or so) or would it work better for you if I wrote less frequently? I wouldn't ever want you to look at your mailbox and say, "Oh no, not another email." I know that I have much more flexibility and it's easy for me to take time here and there to write. I would prefer to be looked at as, for lack of a better analogy, an asset versus a liability!

I understand you taking a trip to Cleveland isn't feasible right now. Hopefully, some day it will be. I really like the idea of you coming here, for many reasons, including flexibility in what we do and how often [smile goes here], and the selfish part of me likes the idea of you not being able to drive away and go back to work! I will also say that I am willing to take a trip out to Las Vegas ANYTIME (starting tomorrow!) if and when you feel you would have more than just a few hours for us to spend together. Even if it's just a couple of days (and at least one sleepover!) Don't misinterpret; I am grateful for the time we had together on both of my visits. I like the idea of coming out with YOU being the main purpose of my trip. That being the case, a few hours just wouldn't be enough! Now that doesn't mean that I won't end up in Las Vegas again soon for some other purpose, (business or pleasure) in which case I would certainly hope we could get together.

Although it's not a huge priority, I think it's important for you to know that I am interested in eventually being in a monogamous relationship again. I'm not sure that actually being married again is important to me. I do know that I am looking forward to having someone to do things with, such as travel, movies, camping, hiking, walks in the park, going to dinner, cooking dinner, and of course... sex! For now, that just hasn't happened and that's okay. But I also know that realistically, I could meet someone here that would be compatible. I also understand that you could meet someone out there that totally knocks your socks off and makes you forget that you even have a job!

Would you be comfortable giving me your address? There's something I'd like to send to you through the US Mail. No, it's not me and it's not pictures of me!

Can I give you a virtual kiss? xoxox I miss seeing your beautiful eyes. They sparkle.

Karlee

From: Jack
To: Karlee
Sent: Thursday, August 26, 2004 2:12 PM
Subject: RE: Hi!

Hi Karlee!

I was probably asleep. I've been exhausted since the weekend, but not getting as much sleep as I need because I'm backed up with work. I more than thought of you last night, actually. I went to bed because my eyes were so tired I couldn't keep them open. I got into bed and thought I'd be instantly asleep but...well...my mind wandered to happy thoughts and I couldn't sleep.

You can write as often as you like and I'm always happy to hear from you. I never see writing to you as a chore. I don't always get to personal email right away (obviously) so if I'm too busy I'll write later. I'd rather have mail from you than not!

Coming to Cleveland sounds great. It will be a while before I have any kind of free time. I am still pounding away on my book; I guess my part of that process will be done in the next month, with any luck. I'll have to edit and re-write, but the primary content should be done by then (I hope). The other people I work with will want me in late November, but that's only a few days. I'll be gone for a couple of weeks in January. The big obstacle is my job.

I'm not looking for multiple partners, either. I don't plan to pursue any relationships here, but yes, we both know we might meet someone else. As long as we're communicating, I think we'll be fine. I wouldn't suggest that you wait for me if the perfect man shows up on your doorstep...I'd completely understand. I would like to stay in touch and try to find as much time as I can and see what happens. If I get another "day job" my situation might instantly improve. I'd like to come to Cleveland and spend some uninterrupted time with you.

My address is [Las Vegas, NV] Why isn't it pictures of you? I'd REALLY like pictures of you. Oh my, would I. Then again, I might not be able to stop more than thinking! Or a video. Hmmmm.

I'm notoriously bad about mail correspondence, just so you know. Something about printing and licking envelopes...I just never can make that leap.

As for the virtual kiss. How sweet...thank you! You can give me a virtual anything!

--Jack

From: Karlee
To: Jack
Sent: Friday, August 27, 2004 3:40 PM
Subject: Have sex with me today?

Hi Jack,

Good Morning! Wow—I'm still feeling the effects of talking to you last night. Your voice tends to affect me in a certain way at certain times. I am really aroused right now.

After being on the phone with you last night, even as late as it was for me and I was tired, I was still feeling those flutters. And I woke up wishing I had time to stay in bed and more than think of you AND was thinking how nice it would be to be in bed with you, even if only by phone. Via the telephone, does any "one way" turn you on than another? For example, would it be just as exciting for you if you told me what you were going to do to me, as if I was telling you what I was going to do to you, or if you are telling me what you are doing to yourself? If not, I would love to try the, "you telling me what you would like to do to me." Operators are standing by! Of course I am making an assumption that you have an interest in doing that again. If not, I trust you will tell me. And by all means, I would still prefer the real thing. Until we can create that again, I remain open to other options!

Are you working this weekend? The bathroom I thought I had finished, I decided is not finished. I wasn't happy with some of the painting near the ceiling, so I still have some touch up work to do on that. With summer coming to a quick close here, being outdoors will be a priority as well.

Okay, great! Perhaps you can take my virtual hands and my virtual mouth with you when you take your next shower. And you can imagine them all over your body. I think I want to christen my shower, too! Although the Jacuzzi is my priority, I love the idea of having sex with you in my shower. (Heck, I love the idea of having sex with you just about anywhere—and now!) The idea of all that slippery soap and the water pouring over our bodies is Mmmm Mmmm! I felt a time restraint while we were in the shower in Las

Vegas, so if you don't mind…I'd like to put that on the list as well!

Karlee
xoxxo

From: Jack
To: Karlee
Sent: Friday, August 27, 2004 5:07 PM
Subject: RE: Have sex with me today?

Hi Karlee!

Hmmm…I know the feeling. I was heavily aroused last night too, and again this morning. It went away for a while, but then I read your email and it's back.

I'd be "up" for the telephone experience again…I enjoyed it a lot more than I thought I would. I wasn't sure if you liked it. Granted, it's nowhere close to the real thing, but it's quite a bit nicer than just lying alone in bed. That's why I am so fixated on the whole web camera idea…it seems like it would be the next best thing to being with you. I'm mostly visually stimulated, like most men.

I think both ways are extremely sexy. Because I'm so accommodating, I'll try both ways!

Sadly, I am working again this weekend, as every weekend. It's the only block of time I can have meetings and work on my non-job projects. I have a big meeting late Sunday with some TV people, and I've got another few chapters to crank out before then, plus meetings with my co-author. It'd be nice to have a day or two to not do anything. I'm going to take it easy until tonight (that's why I've got more time to write to you!)

Good luck with your bathroom painting by the way.

I like what you have on your list. Hmmmm….I don't mind. Sign me up! Now you've got my mind wandering again.

--Jack

From: Karlee
To: Jack
Sent: Saturday, August 28, 2004 3:08 PM
Subject: Hi!

Hey Sexy,

For now, I just wanted to say hi, I'm thinking **of** you, thinking **about** you, and wishing I was **in** you. Of course, the anatomically correct reference would be wishing you were in me, but that didn't flow as well! Either way, I trust you'll get my point!

Hope you're having a good day. I have a bit of a headache at the moment; I'll write more soon.

Karlee
xoxxo

From: Karlee
To: Jack
Sent: Sunday, August 29, 2004 5:53 PM
Subject: Hi!

Hi Jack,

How are you today? Hope things are going well with the writing and other projects/meetings this weekend.

A rainy, rainy day here. No outdoor activities today.

Boy did we have fun this morning in my bed! Yes! You and me—in my imagination, of course. I had slept in my favorite lime green Myrtle Beach T-shirt (with no panties). I took it off to get into the shower. But then I decided to make my bed first. Then I decided to just crawl back into bed since I was still tired. As soon as I crawled in and turned on my side, my mind was instantly back to the Wrong

Room Fantasy…and the sensations I felt when you crawled in next to me, and then you moving close to my back side. Gosh, that night in Vegas was soooooooo good!

Anyway, I really am trying to see if I can come up with other things to write about other than having sex with you. That just seems to be where my mind goes first!

The bathroom painting is still calling my name. I need to have someone here for the last piece. Because of the tub, it's almost impossible to steady the ladder enough for me to reach the corners above the tub enough so that I can paint near the ceiling without making a mess. If I was taller, this probably wouldn't be a challenge.

Take care,
Karlee

From: Jack
To: Karlee
Sent: Monday, August 30, 2004 9:16 PM
Subject: RE: Hi!

Hi Karlee,

Things are going well—thanks. I've got a meeting set up for a week from tomorrow about getting some money. I've got another meeting tomorrow and I have to have another phone conference tomorrow also to see if I can get one deal in place. My boss is coming back Tuesday night for a few days to indoctrinate the replacement for my co-worker who quit.

It must be nice to have rainy days. We had a couple of rainy days a few weeks ago, and it was great. I miss weather.

Mmmm. Yes, you and I had fun late at night this weekend here, too! We enjoyed reliving a lot of our times together... Don't ever feel like you need to apologize for writing so much about having sex with me. I like the way you think!

--Jack

From: Karlee
To: Jack
Sent: Tuesday, August 31, 2004 8:29 PM
Subject: Any good news today?

Hi Jack,

I hope you're doing okay. Sounds like another busy, busy day for you. And the boss is coming again—yikes!

I wish I could just blink my eyes like Barbara Eden in I Dream of Jeannie and have your entire job *stuff* in place. How was the phone conference today? A positive outcome, I hope.

You miss weather? I miss you.

Speaking of weather, we're quickly moving into fall here. I have a sweatshirt on right now. You remember sweatshirts, don't you? You probably haven't had much of a need for them since your move to Las Vegas.

Guess I'll just have to let my mind wander as a way to relax. I know what that means...Mmmmmm.

Good luck with the boss.

Karlee

From: Jack
To: Karlee
Sent: Wednesday, September 1, 2004 3:07 PM
Subject: RE: Any good news today?

Hi Karlee!

The boss is here...I have met the new co-worker, and...it'll be interesting to see what happens. I'm sitting in my office now, they're talking, and she continually talks over him. I also learned that a major competitor for our business in Las Vegas has just been purchased by a much larger corporation. My boss and co-worker were trying to spin things in a positive light, but I can't imagine how this doesn't further hurt the company.

They wanted me to go to a show with them tonight, but I can't muster the enthusiasm. I just want to go home and sleep.

It's too bad you don't have Genie powers. That would be very helpful. I'd have a tough time fitting in only three wishes, though. How come Larry Hagman got unlimited wishes on that show? The conference was fine; no positive or negative outcomes—just more meetings in a few weeks.

When I think about you, I usually don't focus on one or two moments. I let my mind run through all of our times together, like a film montage (an unbelievably hot sex film montage).

--Jack

From: Jack
To: Karlee
Sent: Friday, September 3, 2004 12:34 AM
Subject: RE: Any good news today?

Hi Karlee,

Well, the boss left. It's a very stressful thing. He's a very nice guy, fortunately, but...well...every time we talk, I get more scared and frustrated. They never did their research before launching in Vegas. There was a major merger, that I believe could very well cripple his business plan, but he was trying to spin it as a positive. I spoke to the new woman in the office, and she has a number of concerns, too. I think the boss needs to come up with plans and back up plans; but then I remind myself that it isn't my job, and I go back to my desk.

Then I stare at the screen.

Oh well.

I've been so busy I haven't had time to do laundry. I've got to write something tonight and finish a proposal, so I guess I won't do it until tomorrow. The good news is that I'll be running around naked! I'm sure that will lead to many fun times, which will all involve thinking (and more than that) of you.

How's Cleveland? Any new client leads? Did you get your ceiling painted? Any new and exciting fantasies or thoughts about things?

--Jack

From: Karlee
To: Jack
Sent: Friday, September 3, 2004 12:18 PM
Subject: Hi!

Hi Jack,

I just re-read your email and now see Friday is laundry day. Oh well; I guess even if I would have reached you last night, I could have imagined you were naked. Perhaps I'll have better luck today!

I remember being in job/employment situations in the past that were so stressful and draining for me. I can relate to the agony of the day in and day out of an unsatisfying job. Again, not having known you for that long and not knowing your job background, (you could send your resume!), it makes it difficult to throw out a bunch of ideas. I want to help; I feel I'm limited on suggestions. Are you at a place where it makes sense to consider a "non-professional" type job just as a temporary means of making money and still giving you flexibility? I have no idea what your salary requirements are…what about a part-time job in casino? I know you said some of the positions require some kind of card. I would think that perhaps not all of them do; the positions that are not directly connected to gaming, such as the restaurant and hotel parts to the casinos, perhaps? With all of the production shows on the Strip, I would think there would be something out there.

Is moving back to Chicago and living with your parents an option? I'm guessing that this would not be your first choice! I understand you are already feeling like you should be more settled at this point in your life. And my belief, personally, is that it's okay not to be! My theory is that Life doesn't always unfold in ways we think it should or in the ways that society leads us to believe it should. And sometimes one has to take a few steps back to move ahead. I know looking for a new job when you're miserable can affect the outcome. And it also sometimes causes people to accept something when it's not really what they want.

Anyway, amidst all this strain you're experiencing, I'm sending a virtual hug! Maybe that will make it a tiny bit better.

The bathroom is officially finished and all back together. Looks very nice. Not perfect by my perfectionism standards, but definitely a good job! I plan to paint my office eventually; perhaps a winter project.

As far as new and exciting fantasies or thoughts about things—Oh, yes—always! (And ALL WAYS!) Not new fantasies per se, other than thoughts of how much fun it would be (will be) to be with you again. I cleaned the Jacuzzi yesterday and that in itself is stimulating. Not the cleaning part; thoughts about the possibility of you actually being in it. Ooops, I mean you and me in it! Of course, now that I think about it, just you in it with me watching you...that could be fun. Perhaps a reversed Bathroom Fantasy! Gosh, as I sat here for a few moments and thought about that, I really like that idea. By the way, I appreciate the offer to bring the champagne; however, I think it would be best if I implement a "no glass at the pool" rule. Something about shattered glass and naked bodies just doesn't mix! Of course that does not prohibit us from sipping champagne in another room while we take off each other's clothes to get ready for the christening!

Here's a new thought that gives me the flutters—thinking about the way you lowered the straps of the camisole I was wearing when you came to the hotel the night I had already been asleep. Mmmmm!

The doctor fantasy still occasionally pops into my head. I think the stimulating aspect of that for me is feeling vulnerable, yet knowing

I'm safe. Does the thought of you shaving me do anything for you? I'm not 100% sure about that, but it did enter my mind, with a slight level of eroticism to it. You'd have to promise me that you have a very steady hand! Ouch!

I'll be heading up to the lake tomorrow. It's my sister's birthday and my brother is also coming up with his two kids. Any plans for you for the weekend? I hope you have a chance to get out and do something fun!

Take care,
Karlee

From: Jack
To: Karlee
Sent: Friday, September 3, 2004 2:15 PM
Subject: RE: Hi!

Hi Karlee,

Well, given my expenses (like my overpriced apartment) I can't imagine a part-time job cutting it. I just had a phone interview with a company—a direct competitor to where I'm working now. The difference is, they've been in business for a while, they have a full staff, and they have money. It's full time, too, and involves managing two or three other people, so it probably won't work out. I have no idea what the salary is, but I guess my feeling is that if I'm going to be stuck without freedom, I should make a bit more money. On the other hand, I might ask them to do the work remotely, and see what they say...nothing to lose, certainly.

I have had the offer to go back with the parents, but I can't imagine that would be the answer. I believe it's harder to find anything from there than it is from here, and I wouldn't be able to work on my other projects from there either. The sad fact is this job IS a step back. I make less money than I have in many years (more than being unemployed, though). I have less control. I have less impact. It won't lead anywhere.

I appreciate your well wishes. The fact is that the job isn't a constant source of stress...it's really just a worry. The worry is more based on the fact that I'm afraid I'll just blow it off, because everything else I'm doing in my life has more meaning to me. I'm a guy who likes to work: I've never been in a job before where I couldn't stay focused. I feel like it's a lost cause, so if I'm ever presented the choice between my job and ANYTHING that's remotely interesting, I choose anything. What am I doing?

Well, I guess I won't be able to concentrate now. I'd be "up" for the reverse bathroom fantasy...I'm surprised you would be, but if you like the idea, I like the idea! And, I like lowering your straps!

I love the doctor fantasy. As for shaving...I think my reaction is the same as yours...I'd be worried about shaving you. Having my hands that close to your beautiful pussy would probably get them trembling....

--Jack

From: Karlee
To: Jack
Sent: Saturday, September 4, 2004 3:21 PM
Subject: I desire you . . .

Hi Jack,

I'm off to the lake in a few minutes. Just wanted to say that I am really, really, really missing you and your body right at the moment. I could really use some "more than thinking of you" time. Have to get on the road, though. I just might have to get that webcam!

Have a nice weekend.

Karlee

From: Jack
To: Karlee
Sent: Monday, September 6, 2004 11:14 PM

Subject: RE: I desire you...

Hi Karlee,

I hope you enjoyed your lake adventure. I've been working hard all weekend, and today. I forgot today was Monday, but it worked out okay because it's Labor Day anyway. I figured it out after I tried making some calls that didn't get picked up.

I got your gift...thank you very much! I haven't had time for leisure reading, but I will put that on the top of my stack. It looks like a good book!

I hope you had fun!

--Jack

From: Karlee
To: Jack
Sent: Tuesday, September 7, 2004 2:00 PM
Subject: Good Luck!

Hi Jack,

The weekend at the lake was nice. Great weather, finally! I'm sorry you were working, although I remember you said you would be.

Glad the package arrived. I know you don't have much leisure time to read...just in case you ever do.

Good luck today (and the rest of the week) with the Poker Tournament. I see you winning a big part of the $50,000!

Have fun!

Karlee

From: Jack

To: Karlee
Sent: Tuesday, September 7, 2004 7:07 PM
Subject: RE: Good Luck!

Hi Karlee,

Today hasn't been good so far...I had a big money meeting on my
video project and...the guys didn't show up. It wouldn't have been a
big deal, except that I was stuck in traffic and ready to drive my car
into a wall. I left an hour early, and still wound up being late.

Back to work...I'll write more later.

--Jack

From: Karlee
To: Jack
Sent: Tuesday, September 7, 2004 10:34 PM
Subject: Hope your day got better!

Hi Jack,

Oh, my. I'm sorry to hear this. Have you heard from them yet to
find out why they didn't show? Will they re-schedule?

Sounds like you definitely need to come to Karlee's Healing Center.
It's actually another name for my Jacuzzi. See, for your birthday, it's a
Party Center. When you've had a bad day or week at the office, it
becomes Karlee's Healing Center and if you want to be a "bad boy"
we throw a bag of sand in the middle and call it Fantasy Island! Of
course, with you, there is no such thing as bad. You are all good.
And I mean, really good!

Tonight I did something really out of the box for me. I had signed
up to be in the Community Band and tonight was the first practice of
the season. I played clarinet in grade school through high school;
really haven't played much since. I went to the music store this
morning and bought a new reed and wiped off my instrument and
away I went. Actually, for not having played for 25+ years...I did

okay—not too bad. It was fairly easy for me to follow the music—I just couldn't remember how to play many of the notes! By the end of the evening, I was actually able to keep up for a measure or two! I'm not 100% certain that I will go back. I might go and get a notes chart and see if that helps. And, of course practice would help, too!

In the meantime, imagine my virtual "anything" being sent to help with the rough day you had. Your choice...

Karlee
xoxox

From: Karlee
To: Jack
Sent: Thursday, September 9, 2004 3:48 PM
Subject: Hi!

Hi Jack,

Hope all is well. How's the Poker Tournament going?

Karlee

From: Jack
To: Karlee
Sent: Saturday, September 11, 2004 4:30 PM
Subject: RE: Hi!

Hey there,

The tournament went from 8am until 1am, and it was a half hour trip to get there each way. I used the opportunity to try and make some business connections, and some of that seemed to pay off. I'll know in the coming weeks. I of course fell behind on everything else, so now I've got a busy stretch coming up.

I'm still looking around for jobs, as always, but I don't seem to have enough hours in the day. I'd do writing/searching after 17 hours of poker, and got very little sleep. I keep trying to sleep in, but I haven't been able to do it yet. I look forward to some unrestricted sleep. I think I'll need to inaugurate your Jacuzzi and then follow it up with twelve hours of sleep.

I'm full of good ideas!

--Jack

From: Karlee
To: Jack
Sent: Monday, September 13, 2004 1:59 PM
Subject: Hi!

Hi Jack,

I hope all is well. Sounds like the poker tournament kept you busy. Any big winnings?

Inaugurating the Jacuzzi followed by twelve hours of sleep? This comment almost sounds like you're ready to make the trip; you can't possibly wait three or four months to get 12 hours of sleep! I'm guessing that's not really the case. The invitation still stands and I'm ready for you! I could really enjoy the X position right now. Mmmmmmm! Or any position, now that I think about it! I do like that X though!

I know you're full of good ideas! And, hey, I have a few, too. But I think yours are better. I don't know what they are, but I'm guessing they're better!

Karlee

From: Jack
To: Karlee
Sent: Tuesday, September 14, 2004 2:45 AM
Subject: RE: Hi!

Hi Karlee,

Well, it was very interesting. I used the opportunity to make a few contacts, which has led to a Big Meeting for money tomorrow. We'll see. I'm angling for corporate sponsorship of my TV project, or maybe a job. Who knows? I got the meeting; we'll see where it goes.

I played in a few tournaments. I did well (six places shy of the money) in one, one place out of the money in another, and absolutely stinky in a third (I was one of the first thirty people out). My fourth tournament I was paid a whopping $15 profit. I played three times in poker rooms and have come out substantially ahead each of those times, so I must have learned something.

We make a good X.

Good ideas? If that was true, you'd have a webcam already! Not that I've been around all week to use it. But, soon. Maybe I'll win a poker tournament that will have a first prize trip to Cleveland. Mmmm.

--Jack

From: Karlee
To: Jack
Sent: Tuesday, September 14, 2004 11:43 AM
Subject: Hi!

Hi Jack,

Now, I don't know what has more appeal to you—poker—or sex with me. BUT, just for future reference…all I know is that if you had been in Cleveland last week for that same number of days, I would have gladly given you $15!!! Heck, I would have even doubled, or quadrupled it! I'm teasing you of course. I would never want to keep you from doing things you enjoy and poker appears to be one of them.

I know someday all this will be behind you and you'll be on to something more fulfilling and satisfying.

Speaking of fulfilling and satisfying…it doesn't look like you'll be here for my birthday. I'm sad; I know how much I enjoy being in my birthday suit with you!

I hope all goes well with your meeting today. Sounds promising.

Karlee

From: Jack
To: Karlee
Sent: Tuesday, September 15, 2004 4:20 AM
Subject: RE: Hi!

Well, NOW you tell me. Sex and $15...and I wouldn't have had to look at any bad cards, too. Actually, it was fun and may have opened up a few interesting doors (as the door on my job seems to be quickly slamming shut).

When is your birthday? I suppose telling me won't help, because I'm terrible with remembering dates. I forget everyone's birthday, including my own. I don't know why. I can remember other numbers. Perhaps if I had a photo of you in your birthday suit, I could attach it to my calendar, and then I'd be sure to remember.

The meeting seemed to go much better than I expected. I have to try not to sound surprised whenever anyone agrees to help me on this. The money may end up being 1/2 to 1/3rd of what I need, if it happens, but it's a huge step in the right direction. It's also a big nail in the coffin of my real job. More importantly, the meeting led to another possible project, which I'm highly motivated to work on. I just need more hours in the day.

Thanks for the call; I'm sorry I missed you. I must have been eating. I seem to have a problem with my cell phone where it won't charge even when it's plugged in, so I'll have to get that fixed soon. I'll give you a call soon and say hi.

--Jack

From: Karlee
To: Jack
Sent: Wednesday, September 15, 2004 6:34 PM
Subject: Calendar reminder . . . just for you!

(Picture attached.)

OKAY, here's the answer to your question.

I can't believe I did this. A few words of, "I promise you won't regret it," would be nice!

Me

From: Jack
To: Karlee
Sent: Thursday, September 16, 2004 4:13 AM
Subject: RE: Calendar reminder . . . just for you!

WOW!

This is hands down the best email I've ever gotten in my entire life. I was not expecting this, not at all, and I was checking my email before going to bed after a long day. If it wasn't 4 AM your time, I'd be calling you right now, so you could hear me breathing heavy. Oh, baby. So sexy. I got so hard so fast that I literally felt dizzy. It's a good thing I was lying down.

I can promise you that you won't regret it. I'm putting it in my secret file. You're safe and sound there and by far the most important item in there now is my picture of you!

Did I mention wow? I'm filled with the same warm, tingling, nervous excitement that I felt on our first night together. I love your breasts; they're so perfect, and they photograph so well! Your skin looks soft and silky and I remember how your breasts felt in my hands and in my mouth. Mmmm.

Needless to say, I am more than thinking of you.

I think the only way you could regret sending me this is if it makes me hop on a plane and show up at your doorstep. This turns me on more than I think I can describe in words; it's the nicest thing anyone has ever sent me! And it's not even my birthday!

Wow...you're so sexy. You made my day, my week, my month, my year...

--Jack

From: Karlee
To: Jack
Sent: Thursday, September 16, 2004 1:57 PM
Subject: Mmmmmmmm!

Hi Jack,

WOW! too!

Your enthusiasm, sincerity, and excitement about my email now has me all worked up! You'll laugh when I tell you the story (a good phone story—too long for email) about what took place yesterday morning as I was doing the photo shoot! Thank you for not complaining about the shot. I was afraid you'd make a comment about it just being "partial," or no head, or no . . . other body parts. I think you know me well enough now to know how frightening (in a good kind of way) this was for me. Perhaps not quite as scary as the Las Vegas venture, but almost up there!

>>I think the only way you could regret sending me this is if it makes me hop on a plane and show up at your doorstep.

Why would I regret THAT? Actually, nothing would be more exciting and make me happier. I think about that every day, especially when I look at the Jacuzzi (or bed, or couch, or chair, wall, or floor, or ceiling, or washer, or dryer, or refrigerator...okay, maybe not the refrigerator!). Aside from your own personal calendar reminder, the picture is also a way of reminding you of what's waiting for you when you get here! And of course, the rest of the picture is here, too!

Okay, back to the not-as-exciting stuff… What's happening with work? Any more good news this week?

I definitely need to buy a new computer. This one is doing weird things and I can't afford to wait until this one goes before having something else in place. I went to buy a computer yesterday and picked one out and they were out of stock. That's probably a good thing. I think I should do a bit more research. Do you have an opinion about brands? I'm going to get another laptop. And yes, I actually did look at the webcams while I was there. It doesn't make sense for me to even attempt that until I get a new computer. And even once I get a new computer, I'm still not sure about it, but hey, I never thought I'd do the photo, so who knows. I surprise myself every day! How boring I must have been before I met you!

I think I need to go and more than think of you! The flutters are in full gear, even just writing to you!

xoxox

From: Jack
To: Karlee
Sent: Thursday, September 16, 2004 4:36 PM
Subject: RE: Mmmmmmm!

Hi Karlee,

Well, believe me; I can't describe my level of enthusiasm. You'll just have to try to imagine it, and then take my word for it that I'm ten times more enthusiastic than that!

Believe me; I want the rest of the picture! And the Jacuzzi…and the washer…and the kitchen table…

Nope, no good news. I'm slowing to a crawl at work. My boss comes back again in two weeks, and I guess we'll have to talk about some serious issues. Actually, I keep looking at the photo you sent me, and I can't seem to stop thinking (and more than thinking) about you. It's pretty amazing.

I would've thought the photo would've been scarier to do than a webcam, but either way, I support you in your activities 100%!!! Any time you want to send me additional body parts, I will be absolutely more than delighted to receive them! Eventually, I can assemble them into a collage of you! On the other hand, I think there's a good chance that I'd more than think of you so many times in such a short period of time that...I don't know. I wonder what happens. I'm about to shatter some kind of world record, I think.

You have flutters in full gear? Me, too!

--Jack

From: Jack
To: Karlee
Sent: Friday, September 17, 2004 3:43 AM
Subject: Happy Birthday!

(Photo attached.)

From: Karlee
To: Jack
Sent: Friday, September 17, 2004 10:56 AM
Subject: RE: Happy Birthday!

Hi Jack!

WOW!

Now I understand a bit of how you must have felt when you opened the email with the picture of me. My whole body went "mushy" and in about two seconds I noticed I was breathing heavy.

Wow! Thank you for the wonderful present and the song! This will definitely be the best part of my day, I'm sure. Unless of course you're on a plane on your way here!

Wow! I've already made a copy and I'm looking at it now and I think

I'll take it to bed. Mmmm—Mmmmm!

If the photo of me resulted in this, I wonder what I can come up with so that you don't forget Christmas!

I, too, am so glad I met you! This will be a fun birthday present to remember...and I'll also be looking forward to the "real" present when I see you.

Soooooon, I hope.

Karlee
xoxo

From: Karlee
To: Jack
Sent: Friday, September 17, 2004 11:31 AM
Subject: Photo Report!

Well, you don't taste as good on paper as you do in real life...yet it sure was more fun—even if just with a picture. My imagination was in full force. I could actually feel your hair on my tongue as I kissed your upper thighs on my way to your beautiful cock.
MMmmm—thanks again for remembering my birthday!

Soooo, now I only need 199 more orgasms until next September 17 for my "healthy 200"!!!!!!!!!

See, I knew you'd be a good for my health. That's probably why I have my doctor fantasy with you!

xoxo

From: Karlee
To: Jack
Sent: Friday, September 17, 2004 2:54 PM
Subject: Photo Report!

I REALLY like the picture!

198 to go…(they better count even if you're by yourself!)

Karlee

From: Jack
To: Karlee
Sent: Friday, September 17, 2004 6:52 PM
Subject: Photo Report!

I'm glad you REALLY like the picture! I REALLY, REALLY like yours, too!

198 to go...I'm way ahead of you...I've barely been able to stop to eat/sleep/work.

I'll be healthy for the next few years, I'm sure.

--Jack

From: Karlee
To: Jack
Sent: Friday, September 18, 2004 7:08 PM
Subject: Hi!

Hi Jack,

Hope you are doing well. I'm having a busy family birthday weekend here. I will write more soon. Just wanted to say hi and although I haven't had time to be with you (your picture) in bed today, I did think about it. Many, many times.

Off to dinner with my brother and a friend.

Wish you were here.

Karlee

From: Jack
To: Karlee
Sent: Friday, September 20, 2004 8:18 PM
Subject: RE: Hi!

Hi Karlee,

I'm sorry I missed your call. It just gets busier and busier around here for me. I haven't had a moment to even more than think about you!

I hope you had fun with your family on your birthday...I bet if I'd been there, we would have had even more fun (although, a different kind of fun).

--Jack

From: Jack
To: Karlee
Sent: Friday, September 21, 2004 3:50 AM
Subject: RE: Hi!

Hi Karlee,

Another long day, but now I'm finally able to get back on my own laptop and lie down for a while. I've been staring at your photo...you're so sexy; I can hardly stand it. I start breathing heavy whenever I see your photo. It reminds me of our times together and how excited you make me. You certainly have a knack for making me excited...

See why I thought the webcam might be a good idea? Maybe now you'll have a better idea of why I thought it might be...nice (to say the least).

The only problem with the photo you sent is that now I want to see more of you. But other than that, you've boosted my "more than thinking about you" sessions to new record levels.

I had fun making the photo for you, too. But, you could probably tell that from the photo. I've never done anything like that before, either. See, we're both in exciting new territory!

Any word on your possible November dates? My boss is in town a week from Tuesday and I hope to have more information then.

Now, I'm going to stop typing because I have to take off my underwear and stroke my cock until I cum while looking at your photo. I'm breathing heavy again, and I can't seem to stop myself.

--Jack

From: Karlee
To: Jack
Sent: Tuesday, September 21, 2004 7:38 PM
Subject: Still here...

Hi Jack,

I hope you are doing well. Of course you are doing well. I just remembered that you've got your special "stay healthy" plan in place!

It was fun, fun, fun to read your email this morning! I'm glad you're enjoying my picture. I too have had a lot going on and haven't had as much actual time "with you" as when I first got the picture. I made a color copy and it is either on my bed or on my nightstand at all times! (Except of course when it's on my body!)

I had a nice weekend with my family. (And yes, it would have been another kind of fun if you were here! Mmm—Mmm!) It's rare that my two sisters, me, and my brother are all together at the same time, since once sister and my brother live out of town. Do you ever long for having brother(s) and/or sister(s)? I can't imagine growing up as an only child. I get along really well with my siblings. We are all very different. Sometimes it's hard to believe we were all raised under the same roof! Do you ever think about having children of your own? Boy, I'm full of curiosity tonight!

I did get more information about the seminar in November. Now I just have to decide if I want to make the financial investment to attend. (Deciding if I want to see you is the easy part!) I was told the seats are almost filled (he takes only a small number) so I know I need to decide soon.

I would love to know more about your other projects. You've talked a little bit about the book and your writing. I really have an interest in learning more about what else you are involved in and enjoy.

Big news here! I bought a webcam! Now, before you go and get all worked up…I ended up buying a new computer yesterday. So, now that I have a computer that should operate properly, I thought I would go ahead. I don't have it hooked up yet. And I wonder about the time difference…it seems that often at the time you email me, I'm asleep! I'm still not 100% sure I can do the webcam thing. Actually, I'm not even sure if I'm 50% sure! But I thought I'd at least let you know…

On that note…

Good night!
Karlee

From: Jack
To: Karlee
Sent: Wednesday, September 22, 2004 12:42 PM
Subject: RE: Still here . . .

Hi Karlee!

When I was a child, I used to want brothers and/or sisters. I figure that nowadays it's probably too late. The need to share a room and clothes…well…that part never particularly appealed to me. How can one think with someone else in the room? More importantly…how can one more than think?

I suppose it's good that you are different from your siblings…if you were exactly the same, what fun would that be? What would you have to argue about? Isn't that why you have brothers and sisters?

Let me know about the seminar. I hope you make it. It would be great to see you.

Well, I'm sure you could do the webcam thing just to say hello...and that would be fun in and of itself. It would be nice if I could get my own webcam working on my laptop, so I could be in bed too...the last time I had it plugged in, it was on my desktop. But, when you get set up, I guarantee I'll figure out a way to make it work!

As for the time difference, I'm sure we can work it out.

See how accommodating I am?

--Jack

From: Karlee
To: Jack
Sent: Thursday, September 23, 2004 10:40 AM
Subject: Hi!

Hi Jack,

How are you today? What's happening with work and the projects this week?

Not too much new here. Eagerly awaiting my software so that I can get my new computer up and running. I thought I lost this one again yesterday, but it seems to be okay for now. Probably a virus and I'm still glad I bought a new one. This one isn't that old, but it just hasn't performed for me the way it should. (Unlike you—who performs very well for me!!!)

I pretty much have decided that I am NOT going to attend the seminar in November in Las Vegas. BUT...I might be making a trip out in October. A friend is taking her son for his 21st birthday and she asked me if I wanted to join them. So that's a possibility. If I made the trip, would your workload allow for us to spend any "uninterrupted" time together? A couple of days, perhaps? Now a couple of weeks would be better...but hey, at this point, I'll keep my requests to a reasonable level, even though I know you are accommodating! :-)

I had fun with you last night! After I called you, I climbed into bed with your photo and the Wrong Room fantasy! I wonder what aliens would think if they had landed in my room and found me talking to a picture of a penis! I will say, you responded very well to my conversation! I should probably have the photo laminated; wonder what the people at the office supply place would think of that! Noooo, I think I have some laminating sheets here in my office that will do just fine.

Karlee
xoxox

From: Karlee
To: Jack
Sent: Tuesday, September 28, 2004 10:53 AM
Subject: Hi!

Hi Jack,

How's my "World's Best Lover"? (I saw that on a magnet yesterday and thought of you!)

You must be extra busy on top of your extra busy! I think your boss comes to town today. Not sure if I should say good luck, have fun, or oh no! Anyway, I think you'll be looking forward to seeing what's left of your efforts with this job, and that could be a good thing.

Not much new here. I don't have my new computer hooked up yet and that's on my list of things to do today.

Karlee

From: Jack
To: Karlee
Sent: Tuesday, September 28, 2004 3:30 PM

Subject: RE: Hi!

Hey there!

Can we get a Co-World's-Best Lover award? I think you should get an award, too.

It's sunny and warm (88) but it was raining. I'm at my office. My boss didn't show up until about noon. My co-worker and I haven't had a word with him yet. He leaves tomorrow. This is a crucial meeting as far as I'm concerned.

I almost didn't come into work today. I have so much else to do. Other projects have taken off, to some extent, even though there's as of yet not a dime in them for me. I've been trying to follow up on other leads and get things done, and this job is just a distraction (Okay, it's a distraction AND my only source of income). I've now got four people trying to tell me I should quit and start playing poker full time (fortunately, none of those people are my boss).

I'm trying to finish the book ghostwriting by the end of this week. In the meantime, I thought I'd make the most of my time and write to you.

Good luck hooking up the computer. It shouldn't be too bad, but...well...good luck anyway.

--Jack

From: Karlee
To: Jack
Sent: Wednesday, September 29, 2004 9:25 PM
Subject: Awards and more . . .

Hi Jack,

Of course I'll share the award with you! And thank you for the compliment. I was surprised and you put a big smile on my face and a Mmmmmm on my lips. I wish we could start working on some other awards, too…perhaps one for most hours spent in a Jacuzzi!

Sooooooo, what was the outcome of the time with the boss? Any glimmers of hope or is it all downhill from here? As far as professional poker—if it allows you for some travel time, I'm all for it! Of course I understand that it's probably not as easy as just that. Many other considerations, I'm sure.

I took my new laptop to Starbuck's today thinking I could do some work. It was so noisy (for my noise level anyway) and I left after about 15 minutes. Thought that a change of scenery would be good. As much as I like working here, it's good for me to get out, too.

Good luck this week on finishing the ghostwriting project.

Good night!
Karlee
xoxo

From: Jack
To: Karlee
Sent: Thursday, September 30, 2004 12:42 PM
Subject: RE: Awards and more . . .

Hi Karlee!

Welllllll....the meeting with the boss was Not Good. More wheel spinning, no decisions made, no direction. I made the almost certainly big mistake of telling my co-worker that there was nothing for me in this job any more. That may or may not get back to the boss; I'm not sure.

We discussed the same things we've discussed the last several times he's been here. His response: spend another month gathering info, and then we'll talk about what changes we might need to do. Except, we have all the info and we have had it for a long time. He wouldn't even listen to "what if" scenarios.

Now I decide if I outright quit now or find another job first.

No fun.

--Jack

From: Karlee
To: Jack
Sent: Thursday, September 30, 2004 7:44 PM
Subject: More than thinking of you . . .

Hi Jack,

Wow. A lot to consider regarding your job. I'm sorry that the time with your boss was not more favorable, although I have to say I'm not surprised. (I think I was saying the same thing last time he was in town!) I'm not sure what to say other than the traditional, "I'm sure it will all work out," which seems rather hollow. Of course, I believe it really will, but I'm not the one making a potentially life-altering decision.

If it makes you feel any better, you can know that I have been feeling a heightened sexual charge today and am planning a nice "more than thinking of you" session before I go to sleep. I should probably re-phrase that; it's not like I need a planning session per se! Since the evenings are getting chilly here, the thought of taking a warm bath in my Jacuzzi sounds good. And I probably won't be able to resist imagining that the water jets are your tongue on me. Mmmmm! And of course, as ALWAYS, having the real you here would be better.

Good night!
Karlee

From: Jack
To: Karlee
Sent: Friday, October 1, 2004 12:11 PM
Subject: RE: More than thinking of you . . .

Hi Karlee!

I tried to call you yesterday a few times but I assume you were on the phone; I got kicked immediately to voicemail. I would've left a message, but it would have been something along the lines of "I'm sitting here naked on my bed..." and, well, I wouldn't have wanted you to get into an accident if you were driving or something.

I'll try to reach you again soon. I'd rather be in your Jacuzzi right now than working on what I have to work on.

--Jack

From: Karlee
To: Jack
Sent: Saturday, October 2, 2004 1:48 PM
Subject: RE: More than thinking of you ...

Hi Jack,

I'm sorry I missed talking to you on Thursday. If your call goes right into voicemail it's because my phone is off. See, so you can call anytime and leave a heavy breathing message! If I'm driving and it's too much, I'll just pull off the road!

Well, I'm officially on my new computer. I had someone come out to check to make certain everything was hooked up correctly and to remove all the junk that's often on a new system that isn't needed, etc. I've never paid anyone to do that before but thought it might make sense since I had so many problems with my other system.

Do you like caramel apples? I was out yesterday because it was a picture perfect weather day and stopped at this place that is known for great caramel apples. I bought one and sat on the grass overlooking a big valley and was thinking how fun it would have been if you were with me. Of course, they sell just regular apples, too, so it's not mandatory that you eat a caramel apple. What about clam bakes? I'm going to one today. I'm not particularly crazy about clams, but it's a neighborhood event and it gives me an opportunity to be social. I live in a condo development where I believe I am the second youngest person. Most of the people are 55+. But, it's still good for me to get out.

You were hoping to have the writing project done this week. Did you hit your target? Are the other projects ongoing or do they have target ending dates/timeframes as well?

See you soon! (Of course, I don't know when I'll see you, but it is fun to write it!)

Karlee

From: Karlee
To: Jack
Sent: Tuesday, October 5, 2004 10:02 PM
Subject: Anybody home?
(Attached photo of me in the Jacuzzi—"There's room for two/you!")

Hi Jack,

Now that I have your attention…I hope all is okay. It's usually not quite this long in between hearing from you!

xoxox

From: Jack
To: Karlee
Sent: Wednesday, October 6, 2004 3:53 AM
Subject: RE: Anybody home?

WOW! Hi beautiful. Your photo made my otherwise horrible day.

So, things have been strenuous for me. Disaster hit. My main computer got hit by a virus. Actually, it was a really nasty combination of worm, virus, malware, and spyware. It seized control of my web browser and reset it to a different page. I tried the usual stuff to fix the problem, and nothing worked. It was the worst virus problem I've ever had. It was in memory, attached to legitimate programs, and hidden in 39 places on my hard drive. I couldn't send anything or go to many sites.

I spent four hours yesterday and 18 hours today trying to fix the problem. Eighteen hours. Eesh. All that, and at the end of the day, I'm back to where I was a few days ago. It took eight pieces of software and about 35 reboots of my computer.

But, the good news is that after all that, I got onto my newly cleaned machine and found your picture waiting for me! Hubba, hubba! I didn't even notice there was an attachment at first, so it was an even bigger surprise! In a display of no self control whatsoever, I instantly pulled off all of my clothes and threw them on the floor and more than thought of you while I looked at your photo. Mmmm. I forgot all about my problems and thought only about you. It was...good.

I need to go to Cleveland.

--Jack

From: Karlee
To: Jack
Sent: Thursday, October 7, 2004 1:40 AM
Subject: Hi!

Hi Jack,

Well, now you went and made my day...it's been a long time since a man has said hi beautiful to me! That might just deserve another picture. No, better not start that!

Wow—I am exhausted just reading about your computer problems. With all the challenges I had a few weeks back...I had to reboot many-a-times, but not 35! I would have been very frustrated, to say the least. You must have a lot of patience. I'm glad you got everything back together and I'm glad I was "there" to put at least a bright spot into your horrible day.

>> I need to go to Cleveland.

Why are you telling me this? I already KNOW you need to go to Cleveland. I go to the airport every day and wait by the gate that comes from Las Vegas, but you're not there! Just think what kind of calendar reminders I could send to help you count down the days!!! Actually, I was just thinking that I'm getting close to knowing how long I can go without seeing you. There was about five weeks in between our first and second meeting and now it has been seven weeks, but hey, who's counting? I guess I am! But only when I look at your pictures and think about you crawling into bed with me in the Wrong Room fantasy or only when I think about you touching my legs when I had them up on your lap on the first night and "we" were trying to get me to calm down and relax, and only when I think about all the other wonderful moments…but other than that, I hardly think about it.

I'm off to bed. I went to Columbus today to see my nephew who is here on leave from the Navy.

Good night! (Gosh, I just had a flash of how nice that would be to say that to you in person—nuzzle up to your neck and give you a gentle kiss before you fall asleep for that 12 hours you had talked about!)

Karlee

From: Karlee
To: Jack
Sent: Monday, October 11, 2004 4:05 PM
Subject: Hi!

Hi Jack,

How was your weekend? Did you enjoy the movie screening on Saturday? How are you feeling? Better, I hope.

Not too much new here since Friday. I had a nice weekend. Somewhat quiet, but nice. Spent part of yesterday getting a few things ready to sell on eBay. I don't do that a lot, but had a few things that made sense to put them on the site. It just takes time as far as taking photos, writing a description, etc. We'll see.

This morning I got up at 5:30 to take my other nephew to the airport to go back to North Carolina. He'll be home again for a 30 day leave later this month. I'm just glad he's back from Iraq. We're actually very lucky. He was driving a Hummer and just totally as a fluke veered and missed driving over a bomb. Unfortunately though, the bomb detonated and hit the Hummer behind the one he was driving and killed the driver, who was a friend of my nephew's. How awful.

I was just in my room looking at your pictures. I've got the flutters today!

Looking forward to hearing from you.

Karlee

From: Jack
To: Karlee
Sent: Tuesday, October 12, 2004 1:36 AM
Subject: RE: Hi!

Hi Karlee,

I'm glad you got to spend time with your nephew. I'm sure he's happy to be home for a while.

The movie screening was nice...it was good to do SOMETHING besides work. I'm running dry. I'll have the book draft done by Friday, and then my boss comes back to town next Thursday and Friday.

The big project they were working on hasn't launched yet. Supposedly, it'll be around October 24-30. It was supposed to be October 1. That is, after it was pushed back four or five times. Until that's done, they can't begin working on the technical stuff or the Vegas project. That means they're at least three months away, but much more than that, I'm willing to bet.

It'd be nice to make some money. That's what I've decided. I'm doing some projects I enjoy, but not for money. I'd like to be doing one thing and get paid for it.

I guess I'll get back to work on that now.

Too bad we can't get paid to look at the pictures we have of each other. I'd be rich!

--Jack

From: Karlee
To: Jack
Sent: Wednesday, October 13, 2004 1:01 AM
Subject: Hi!

Hi Jack,

I'm glad to hear you enjoyed the movie on Saturday. And you deserve to have something fun to do besides work.

Today I feel a somewhat renewed sense of direction. Although I usually say, "I'm not lost, I'm exploring!" That at least sheds a more positive light on the situation. It just seems that the passion has gone out for me in a few areas of my life since my divorce and the death of my mom. BUT...onward and upward! I was washing my outside windows yesterday and finally admitted something that has been tugging at me that I just didn't want to acknowledge: I'm really not that happy here. I was referring to my condo. It's a beautiful place and a nice neighborhood; I just don't think it fits who I am right now. Where I'll go from here, I don't know. It's exciting to think about the million plus places that could be options!

Hmmmm? I hope you can get here soon. I would hate to leave this place never having christened the Jacuzzi! What a tragedy!

How about a trip to Cleveland? Is that more appealing? I know, I know. It doesn't pay anything. Well, perhaps not money, but I certainly think I would be able to compensate you for your time and effort! Ya know, they say that sexual activity really helps when one has shut down with their job. Really, it's in all the latest magazines, and on TV, and, and, and…hey, I'm trying! Maybe we need some new fantasies to lift your spirits regarding the job. With you not feeling well last week, I wondered about a nurse… And, yes, I'm still holding out for my doctor fantasy!

By the way, are you okay with me sending you cards? I know you said you weren't much on sending mail. I've always been a big fan of cards. I guess I'm a bit curious as to whether or not they are received joyfully, rather than, "Oh no, now what is this woman sending me?!" Do you like the attention or is it beyond what is comfortable for you given our non-traditional relationship? What about the xoxox? I sign a lot of my correspondence that way; just comes as a natural way of showing my affection.

Good night, Sexy,
Karlee
xoxox

From: Jack
To: Karlee
Sent: Tuesday, October 12, 2004 11:51 PM
Subject: RE: Hi!

Hi Karlee!

I've been trying to kick-start myself. I have a phone interview later this week for a job that I applied for online. I didn't remember applying, so I wrote to them and asked for the posting. Then, I found it. I don't even know where it is...seems unlikely that I'll get it, but it's worth a shot.

Every day brings the renewed possibility that I'll be out of a job and have all kinds of free time, but sadly, not yet. When are you planning to move? Where will you go? What will you do? I'd hate for your Jacuzzi to be un-christened, too...I'm thinking about a solution for that...

Ah yes, fantasies! I should think more about them. Nurse is a good one, though I like your doctor fantasy a lot. I need to spend more time fantasizing. It's much less fun working than it is fantasizing.

The cards are nice and I enjoy them, though as I told you, I'm horrible with traditional correspondence. Of course, every time I get a card from you, I have the fleeting notion that inside there might be a naked picture of you, and that always gets my heart racing. I guess that's because I've always associated getting cards with birthdays...

Good night to you, too, Sexier!

--Jack

From: Karlee
To: Jack
Sent: Wednesday, October 13, 2004 4:22 PM
Subject: Hi!

Hi Jack!

Why do you think it seems unlikely that you'll get that job? I am a firm believer in the power of affirming what it is we want in life. Why do you think I spend so much time looking at your pictures? Just this morning, I stared at your "birthday present" photo for so long, it was as if I could feel you in my mouth. So, you're not here (yet), but I believe if I stare long enough, you'll show up. If not you, another man with the same body part will. I prefer it be you, but I know enough to know that as much as I think about being in my Jacuzzi with (you) a man, it will happen. Same thing can work with a job. I just know in my own life that using affirmations and visualizing what I want works! It doesn't always work in the time I'd like it to (or you'd have already been here) and in the same way, but if I stick with it, something similar shows up. Anyway, that's the end of the lecture! And about not knowing where that job is...what if it's in Ohio!

Now trust me, I'm all for you having free time, but I'm not sure I am in favor of you getting fired! Yes, you may have free time, but it also brings another set of circumstances that may not be that pleasant. So we'll keep our fingers crossed that you find another job that is

FANTASTIC and that pays you what you are worth for your brilliant mind. And one that also allows you the flexibility to work on your other projects. And, (MOST importantly) one where they won't need you to start right away so that you'll have time to take a trip to Cleveland to make love to me and let me make love to you! Or just sex, if you prefer to look at it that way! But, I was reading the Wrong Room fantasy again this morning and to me, that is more than sex!

(I seem a little feisty today, don't I?!!!)

I have no plans yet as to where I might go. There are some other pieces that I need to get into place before I would start the process. I will most likely head to the west. I know I've talked about Las Vegas before. It would probably be a good idea for me to visit other places that I might consider, just to be certain there isn't a place I think I would like even more (with the exception of you being there). Sedona, AZ, perhaps. I love parts of California, but it just seems so far away, even though it's not much beyond Vegas. I don't see myself moving right away, but I know I will move, even if just to another place in the area. It might take me six months or more to make up my mind, etc. I see myself getting serious about my books again. This morning I was interviewed for my collaborative book project which will be out in early 2005. I've been working on two additional books, but up until now, not with much seriousness. The one I plan to start working on more diligently. At this point, my consulting will continue to be my primary source of income. I'm very grateful to have picked up three substantial corporate clients and a request for some freelance work. So that feels like it's falling into place. I enjoy the seminar work, too.

I'm glad you're thinking about a solution for my un-christened Jacuzzi!

Karlee

From: Jack
To: Karlee
Sent: Wednesday, October 13, 2004 4:06 PM
Subject: RE: Hi!

Hi Karlee,

I agree with positive thinking and visualization. But, it's not a job I really want. It's a job. It might have some interesting elements, but the description was kind of vague and I applied to it on a whim. It involves knowing a lot about wireless service providers, and I don't care about cell phones. But, I like the company and thought it might be a good in. As for where it is...it turns out it's in Washington State....somewhere.

I like when you're feisty! Feisty can be good! I remember exactly how good, too.

I've been enjoying all of the non-job work I've been doing. It's just a matter of getting paid to do it. Writing is great...I know I have the discipline to do it, it's just a question of whether people would want to read what I write. As for where to move, Arizona is great. I like it a lot there. I don't know that I'd recommend anyone move to Vegas these days (whether I'm here or not)...housing has become insanely expensive. In fact, when my lease is up, I think I'll be leaving town. Cost of living isn't too bad, except for gas, but I'd never be able to afford a home here, and it's getting noticeably more crowded. Traffic is as bad (if not worse) than New York City at times. If my boss ever laid down the ultimatum that I had to be in the office every day, I think I'd quit on the spot. Mid-sized towns seem like the way to go. It's too bad there aren't suburbs around here...it'd be nice to be in driving range of restaurants, but the cost of homes and condos have gone up several hundred percent in the last couple of years.

Well, last night I was looking at your photos and thinking about you. I was reliving our first night together. I imagined you in your sexy little outfit, rubbing your legs, slowly trying to move my hand further and further up your skirt. I was nervous...I knew you were nervous too, and I didn't want to make you uncomfortable. I wanted to touch you, and I thought I'd be slow and gentle, and maybe you wouldn't object. Then I think about standing behind you, going over your little brochure, and the moment that you said you were going to take a shower. It still makes my heart race. Watching you, standing in front of me, slowly taking off all of your clothes...it has to be the sexiest moment of my life. I could feel my heart beating in my chest so hard that I was sure you could hear it across the room.

When you entered the shower, I took off my pants and shoes and socks and leaned in to watch you for a while. My cock was so hard it was throbbing up and down. I pulled it out and began to stroke myself, then decided I should take off my clothes, so I threw off my shirt and kicked off my boxer shorts. I was so excited I almost came just watching you...I've never been that excited before.

Anyway, I more than thought of you last night. Twice. It was very late and I was very tired, but I could feel you with me. I practically screamed when I came; I hope I didn't wake up my neighbors.

--Jack

From: Karlee
To: Jack
Sent: Thursday, October 14, 2004 3:22 PM
Subject: Hi!

Hi Jack,

How was the interview? Anything exciting?

I hope you slept well. I took a hot shower, hit the pillow, and I was out. Unfortunately, I awoke from my sweet sleep to a dream (nightmare?). I was on a cruise ship and it turned over and eventually sunk. Rather than putting on a life jacket, etc. I was spending time looking at a magazine and by the time I decided to get off, the ship was totally underwater and everyone was gone. That's when I woke up. Bizarre. I'll have to look in my dream book to see what the heck that's supposed to mean. I enjoyed our time on the phone, even though I missed not hearing the "Oh Baby." (I guess I notice things like that!)

Hmmmm! I love imagining you rubbing my legs, slowly trying to move your hand further and further up my skirt. You were nervous? I didn't realize that. What were you nervous about?

Karlee

From: Karlee
To: Jack
Sent: Tuesday, October 19, 2004 3:35 PM
Subject: It's cold outside but I'm hot in here...

Hi Jack,

How's my favorite Las Vegas lover? Okay, my only Las Vegas lover. Okay, my only lover!

I am so horny today that of course it would be natural that I'd be thinking about you, and more than thinking about you, and be writing to you. It all started this morning when I stepped into my Jacuzzi to shave. I was thinking about how fun it would be if you were there to kiss me—being freshly shaven. Then I went into the shower and had an image of you being in there with me. I imagined you sitting on one of the small seats and me straddling you. I would be close, very close to your cock, but you would not be in me—yet! I was taking my time, washing your hair and letting you kiss my breasts as I did so. The warm water felt really nice. I'm not exactly sure where we went from there, but it was probably something like turning the water off, quickly drying each other off, and you carrying me to the bed.

What's new? How was the interview last week? Is your boss still coming to town this week?

I'm going to go. Time to go look at your picture again and imagine you here for a little afternoon delight! Mmmmmmmmm!

xoxox

From: Jack
To: Karlee
Sent: Wednesday, October 20, 2004 4:17 PM
Subject: RE: It's cold outside but I'm hot in here...

Hi Karlee,

I'm okay. I turned in my first draft of the book; they're now working on selling it (after making some additions that are, frankly, not good).

I have an interview lined up in Portland. I talked to someone at the company on Monday and they tried to get me to come out Tuesday and return Wednesday, but my boss is in town Thursday and Friday, so I pushed it to next week. I have no idea what the salary is; if it's great, I think I take the job on the spot. If it's about the same or a little bit more, I have to think hard about it. It's doing basically the same work I'm doing now, but stable with growth possibilities. My job will hit a wall sooner or later, and I'm not comfortable taking advantage of the situation.

So, we'll see.

HMM! What you wrote about being horny... Now I won't be able to help thinking about you...and more than thinking about you. That sounds very nice. Mmm.

Looking at your picture and imagining you here for a little afternoon delight...that sounds good to me, too. It's nice and cool and rainy here today...a good day to lie around naked!

--Jack

From: Karlee
To: Jack
Sent: Friday, October 22, 2004 1:32 AM
Subject: Thinking of you . . .

Hi Jack,

Just a quick note to let you know I'm thinking about you (actually, just that at that moment, not the more than!) and hoping that the time with your boss is going okay. I'd ask if there are any new developments, but I'm guessing I already know the answer. Hey, you never know—perhaps he came to town with a business plan!

Congratulations on the book draft. I hope they sell it for millions and you get 50%. Remember, I'm an optimist! I'm guessing it will probably be some time before you know what will really happen.

It sounds like the trip to Portland will be interesting. I hope the outcome is good for you, no matter how it turns out!

Good night,
Karlee

From: Jack
To: Karlee
Sent: Tuesday, October 26, 2004 4:44 PM
Subject: I'm back

Hi Karlee,

How goes it? I got your message; I returned very late last night from my job interview. It was a long trip, but it was nice to get out of Vegas for a while. I had some spectacular seafood, too.

The interview itself was a bit odd. I met seven people individually, 45 minutes per meeting. At the end, the human resources person gave me an idea about the salary; it's roughly half of what I had in my mind to take the job. It's too bad, but on the other hand, I think everyone was working very hard (like 60+ hours per week, minimum). I'd have to give up everything, so it has got to pay reasonably well. We'll see...I expect they'll call me, but you never know. I did like the town, though.

Everything is, as usual, up in the air. Sorry I've been slow getting back to you. I expect things will calm down considerably at some point.

How are things going with you? Any news on the consulting front? Are you looking at employment type jobs? Any leads?

--Jack

From: Karlee
To: Jack
Sent: Tuesday, October 26, 2004 8:04 PM
Subject: Hi!

Hi Jack,

I hope all is well. Did you go to Portland yet? Any other new developments regarding a new job? What's happening with the current job? I know—questions, questions!

I'm sensing a more infrequent communication on your part and am wondering if you are still interested in staying connected. I know you've got a lot going on and I'm really trying to be patient. I'm pretty sure I am more involved in the *us* thing than you are. And that's okay. You made it very clear to me that a relationship was not at the top of your priority list! I'm thinking it might be time for me to move on. I don't want to, yet I am finding it more difficult not seeing you. I'm really beginning to wonder if the time and space will ever allow you to come to Cleveland, and the last time I said something about me coming out there, you weren't overly encouraging to the idea. I remember the last time I shared what was on my mind, you were appreciative of me sharing my thoughts and feelings and I hope they are welcomed again. I just know the situation is weighing heavily on me and you can't know that if I don't tell you!

xoKarlee

From: Jack
To: Karlee
Sent: Friday, October 29, 2004 12:39 PM
Subject: RE: Hi!

Hi Karlee!

Well, I would think that, at some point, I would be able to come to Cleveland, but I have no idea when. If you have these concerns (and you've hinted at them in the past, too), then I totally understand your wanting to move on. It's an odd situation because we are so far apart, but also I had no expectation of things going further than (or as far as) they went. If you have needs that aren't being met, I'm really sorry about that...I certainly don't want to be a source for concern or frustration. But I'm struggling to get my professional life in order and that seems like it will be the case for—who knows how long? I'm always hopeful that things will come together, but they never seem to. Even if they do, I wonder what the best case scenario is. I see you a couple of times per year?

I haven't given it much thought because I haven't given much thought to a relationship at this point; I want to have my job settled first. Everything else is just getting crammed into the cracks in my life. I understand how that would not be enough for you, but that's always been the case. I haven't been looking for a relationship (with you or anyone else) because it's not on the top of my list. I guess I see our relationship as unique...but because we're apart, it's not really boyfriend/girlfriend. Sort of lovers and friends.

I definitely don't want to be a source of unhappiness in your life. If you feel like you have to move on, I understand. If you feel like you're waiting for me in some respects, you shouldn't feel that way. Quite honestly, if you lived next door to me, you wouldn't see me much more often. I don't see my friends in town more than once or twice per month these days.

I guess this isn't the inspirational positive email you may have been hoping for, but I don't want you to be confused about where I stand. Since you've brought this up before, I think maybe you already know what you want to do, and that's fine. I don't want to lose touch with you (in any sense!) but I'm not able to give more.

Again, this is strange, because I never felt like we were in any kind of traditional relationship, so I've not worried about the fact that I haven't made time to keep up a certain level of communication. But it seems clear to me that you need more, and I don't want to hold you back from being happy.

So, that's my thoughts. I hope they're not too distressing...

I don't think this should be something that weighs heavily on you...since it does, it seems like it must be time to move on. I think you deserve a situation where you don't have heavy weights on you, and I want you to find it.

--Jack

From: Karlee
To: Jack
Sent: Monday, November 1, 2004 2:16 PM
Subject: Hi!

Hi Jack,

I hope you are doing well and that you had a nice weekend. Did you do anything fun for Halloween? A friend and I dressed up and went out, but there were very few people dressed up. I think the most fun we had was laughing at each other in our costumes. She went as a French maid and I was a sexy Santa. Black fishnet stockings, black boots, and a long, blonde hair wig! It had been several years since I dressed up for Halloween and now I know why!

I had a bit of a sore throat over the weekend and yesterday it got really bad. I've been in bed most of the day and a good part of yesterday. While I was up earlier, I went to change my voicemail messages on my home and business line and discovered I have laryngitis! Good news is that my throat isn't as sore. I might have to call my sister and ask her to deliver some mint chocolate chip ice cream—ya know, it's always good to soothe a sore throat!

Any news from the Portland group on the job? The interview process sounded quite extensive. All those people! I'm glad you were able to enjoy some good seafood while there.

I'm glad I sent the email I did last week. Although a different response from you may have been more desirable, it was not what I would have called distressing. I was thinking I would need to move on if you were going to tell me that things would be different some day, soon, hang in there, a few more weeks, months, etc. I knew that was a scenario I was not interested in enduring. Knowing where you stand and that our connection will most likely be what it has been, I would like to "stay" vs. move on. I, too, prefer to keep in touch (in many ways!) and do enjoy having you in my life. What I will do though, is free up my mind to allow for a more traditional relationship to come into my life. It is important for me to have a boyfriend in the sense of frequent physical contact, as well as the everyday kinds of things like dinner, traveling, movies, etc. I believe I gave up a lot when I left my husband. It's important to me that I value myself enough to not settle for another relationship that is lacking what I desire. Now granted, if I thought the other pieces of a relationship with you might come together, I would be more willing to be patient, knowing just how fulfilling it is for me to be with you. You telling me that even if I lived next door, it wouldn't be much different makes the reality of things very clear! Unfortunately, really, really, really, phenomenal sex once or twice a year is not going to be enough for me. However, if you are willing to leave the door open as lovers and friends, I'm open to that, too. I pray that I will eventually find a man who is as skilled a lover as you are, and turns me on as much, and thoughts of being with him gives me the flutters the way you do, and thinking about him makes me wet like thoughts of you do… Until then, how about I hook up my webcam?

Looking forward to hearing from you.

Karlee

From: Jack
To: Karlee
Sent: Tuesday, November 2, 2004 3:01 PM
Subject: RE: Hi!

Hi Karlee,

I didn't do anything for Halloween other than work. I've been working or playing poker, and that's about it. And, playing poker lately has been more work than anything else. But, I think it will pay off some day (just not lately). I'm glad you had a fun time…how come you didn't send me pictures of you as a sexy Santa? I'd ask to sit on your lap, but I wouldn't want to squish you.

I'm a big fan of mint chocolate chip, so I envy you (other than the sore throat). I've been doing most of my communicating lately via email, so laryngitis wouldn't slow me down much, but I can imagine it's no fun. At least it's a good excuse to hang up on telemarketers.

No news at all from Portland. I wrote to two people and nothing. That, to me, is the universal symbol for "we hired someone else and can't be bothered to write back." I'm not terribly upset, because the money wasn't even close to what I'd want. Portland was nice, though.

I certainly wouldn't want to hold you back from finding what you want. I think part of the reason I've never pursued getting married is that I'm still working on getting my own life in order, and that's proving to be a much more difficult and time consuming task than I'd hoped.

I'm always ready for the webcam! In fact, I'm ready right now!! At least, until I have to go to a meeting in a few minutes...

--Jack

From: Karlee
To: Jack
Sent: Tuesday, November 2, 2004 8:21 PM
Subject: Ask and ye shall receive . . .

Hi Jack,

Actually, I did have my friend take a couple of pictures "for Jack." And as far as you sitting on my lap, there's no better way I can think of that I'd like to be squished! After all, I know you've been a really good boy this year—on July 6, 8, and a day in August for sure, so it's only fair that you should be able to sit on Santa's lap and tell her what you want!!!

I'll write more soon. Still not feeling that great and heading to bed.

xoxox

From: Karlee
To: Jack
Sent: Tuesday, November 2, 2004 8:43 PM
Subject: Photos too large . . .

Hi Jack,

Okay, I've tried to send the photos several times and I keep getting a
Delivery Failure Notification. They must be too big. I'll re-size and
try again tomorrow. For now, I need to get to bed.

Karlee

From: Jack
To: Karlee
Sent: Wednesday, November 3, 2004 7:57 PM
Subject: RE: Photos too large . . .

HUBBA HUBBA! I got one (very large) photo. The Delivery Failure
is because this email account gets filled up and the attachment
overflowed my inbox.

I'd go trick or treating at your house any time!

Ho ho ho...

--Jack

From: Karlee
To: Jack
Sent: Thursday, November 4, 2004 7:01 AM
Subject: Here's another Halloween idea . . .

Hi Jack,

Of course you can trick or treat at my house any time. BUT, since
you've already seen the Santa outfit, I say next time, I'll be a dish of
mint chocolate chip ice cream...

No need for you to bring a spoon—and—you can provide the toppings!

Does your schedule allow for a webcam visit in the next day or two?

Karlee

From: Jack
To: Karlee
Sent: Thursday, November 4, 2004 10:39 AM
Subject: RE: Here's another Halloween idea . . .

Hi Karlee,

Excellent...then I'll be a giant tongue. My buds get all tingly thinking about it.

I'm working from home and don't have to be anywhere until about 6pm my time, although I'll have to exercise in there somewhere. Do you have Yahoo Messenger? I can turn it on if you're going to be on. I think I gave you my ID when we talked last time.

Let me know...I'd definitely be up for trying it!

-- Jack

From: Karlee
To: Jack
Sent: Thursday, November 4, 2004 2:50 PM
Subject: RE: Here's another Halloween idea . . .

Hi Jack,

A giant tongue...I didn't even think of that! I like how you think!

Will you be around in about a half an hour for a webcam visit? That's assuming I can figure this out!

"See" you soon!

Karlee

From: Jack
To: Karlee
Sent: Thursday, November 4, 2004 2:54 PM
Subject: RE: Here's another Halloween idea . . .

I'm around...I added you to my list...I'll look for you at 2:30 my time.

--Jack

From: Karlee
To: Jack
Sent: Sunday, November 7, 2004 5:36 PM
Subject: Hi!

Hi Jack,

I hope you had a good weekend. Mine was quiet; they usually are. I'm still not feeling 100%. I did continue with the painting of my office today. Got quite a bit done. I hadn't planned on starting this project until the winter months. I had ordered (and are now installed) new blinds and wanted to paint around the windows before they were installed. I remember you offering to help with the painting when you came for your visit. See, now if you're able to make the trip, there'll be no painting to do and we'll have more time for sex! Now it's just sex, waffles, and the Jacuzzi!

Well, what did you think of our (first) webcam visit? Once again, I have to say—I enjoyed it much more than I thought I would. I was delightfully reminded of how cute you are to me and how "sparkly" your eyes are! It was almost like being there with you. (Yeah, right!) But, definitely better than just the phone. I hope your keyboard made it through. I'm not sure about the typing, watching, touching, etc. We'll have to work on that. I have a speaker phone in my office—do you? It would be great if we could talk hands free. Of course, here I am assuming we're going to do this again. Maybe you didn't even like it and won't want to. I mean, after all, you've seen my sexiest bras now. What more could there be?

Any poker tournaments coming up?

I think my marketing materials are now complete. I might have to modify as I go along, but all-in-all, I'm happy with what I have.

Karlee
xoxox

From: Jack
To: Karlee
Sent: Monday, November 8, 2004 2:01 PM
Subject: RE: Hi!

Hi there...

I hope you feel better soon. I had a busier than usual weekend. I decided that I absolutely needed to make time to clean; I haven't been able to make the time before. I didn't really have the time this weekend either, but I jumped in and got a lot done. It seems like I'm eternally waiting to hear from a dozen people about a dozen things, and I can't get call backs quickly enough. So I looked for some other jobs, but nothing leaps out. I have a bad feeling that the jobs I usually get are gone until the beginning of next year...no one hires after Halloween because Thanksgiving is so close, then Christmas, and people are distracted. Nonetheless, it would be nice to get a word back.

I was also pleasantly surprised at how much I enjoyed the web visit! I'm sure we can come up with something as far as talking hands free. The bad news is that I don't have it and the phone is difficult to use. One of these days I'll look into the voice component of this thing. Supposedly it can be set up to use your computer as a phone at the same time. I do have a microphone...

I've been too busy to play much poker lately, but while I was working this morning I played on-line. I did fantastically well; I was

in 1st place going into the last 25 slots (out of 900). I played a hand
where I knew I was beaten, but I called anyway because...I'm not
sure why. I guess I got greedy. If I'd won the hand, I do believe I
would have been unstoppable to win the tournament. On the other
hand, it was only for a few dollars.

Congratulations on the new marketing materials. I'd love to see
them. I'm not in the market for a coach right now, but it would still
be fun to see them. Hey! Wait a minute! Maybe having a coach on
hand would be extremely beneficial. Wow—why I hadn't thought
of that earlier.....

--Jack

From: Jack
To: Karlee
Sent: Monday, November 15, 2004 10:08 AM
Subject: RE: Hi!

Hey there,

I got your messages, but it's been a busy week and it will continue to
be for me. I have three places I need to be tonight, and I have to
figure out how to get to all three. My co-worker leaves for NYC
tomorrow, I think, and my boss will want to have a teleconference
on Wednesday or Thursday. I will be unavailable because I'm
working on this project with the out-of-town folks from Wed-Sun.
It's an exciting time (in a very busy and frustrating way).

Did you enjoy Atlantic City? I've only been twice. There is a good
sandwich shop there. It's a different vibe from Vegas, although they
do have slot machines.

I probably won't have much time to write this week. I have to get
everything done I'd normally get done in the week and weekend by
Wednesday, and that seems unlikely to happen. I need a nap.

--Jack

From: Karlee
To: Jack
Sent: Thursday, November 18, 2004 11:18 AM
Subject: Hi!

Hi Jack,

I hope you're having (or had, depending on when you read this) a good time with your project. How did the rest of the week turn out? What did you hear from your boss while they were in New York? Any promising changes?

I did enjoy my trip to Atlantic City. Thanks for asking. It was fun to be away and great to see my friend. She had comps so we stayed at the new Borgata which is a very nice property. I left here around 12:30 in the afternoon and had not planned to drive the whole way. But I was awake and alert and ended up in the AC area around 10:00pm with no room booked, and I wasn't meeting my friend until Sunday. After a few phone calls, the only thing I could find that was reasonable was one of the Boardwalk properties at $200 a night. And not that great of a room at that. But I guess it was better than sleeping in my car! And because it was getting late, I really didn't want to turn around and head back to the highway to find something less expensive. Anyway, aside from that, I enjoyed my short visit and was glad to return home Monday evening.

I thought about you A LOT while I was in AC. Once inside a casino, you really don't know if you're in Vegas or any other place. So of course being inside a casino was reminiscent of Las Vegas which always reminds me of you! And...the shower in the room would have been perfect for us! The countertop would not have worked as well though! So, needless to say, I was quite aroused while there and all the way home.

I was wondering...how would you feel about me converting our email conversations to somewhat of a book format and sending some query letters to erotica publishers and see if anyone is interested? I know we talked briefly once about writing fantasies, but I wasn't really serious about it at the time. For some reason, I have kept our emails, and every once in awhile I go back and read them. They really make quite a good story. Now just because I feel that way doesn't mean a publisher will. I would want to change names, etc.—any reference that would clearly identify us! And we would have to come up with an ending. (Just for the book, not for real, please!) I'm not looking to add to what your already have on your plate. Your part would really be just giving input to pieces you might not want included, and perhaps helping with a way to put an ending to it. I'm not sure how serious I really am about the idea, but I thought I'd run it by you.

You wrote…*I need a nap.*

I write…I have pillows!

I hope we can "visit" again soon.

Karlee
xoxox

From: Jack
To: Karlee
Sent: Sunday, November 21, 2004 11:54 PM
Subject: RE: Hi!

Hi Karlee!

I'm exhausted…a very, very long week for me. It's 11:50pm on Sunday night. I just got home and I smell like cigarette smoke, and I've been up since 6am; that's been my schedule since Wednesday. The week went well, though.

Atlantic City sounds like fun. I want to see the Borgata one of these days.

Hmm…let me think about the book idea for a bit. I'm not sure how I feel. Let me mull it around, and get some sleep and then I'll be able to think more clearly!

I hope we can "visit" again soon, too.

--Jack

From: Karlee
To: Jack
Sent: Monday, November 22, 2004 6:46 AM
Subject: Book project . . .

Hi Jack,

It was good to hear from you. Glad you made it through the week.

Before you spend time thinking about my book project idea, I wanted
you to know I have re-thought the idea myself and don't think it's a
good idea. I didn't want you to spend a lot of time and then have me
tell you that later. The more I thought about it, although I don't
think it's a bad idea, I just don't think it makes sense for me to put
the time into making this into a project. I really need to use my time
to build my business. And although the book could land some
exciting opportunity, it could take months, etc. Hope you didn't
spend too much time thinking about it. And now that you don't need
to, I give you permission to think about me instead!

The office painting job is going slowly; I worked on it again
yesterday. On Saturday, I had my dad take down a credenza that I
really didn't need. My office furniture is a bit big for a room this size,
so it feels good to have one less piece of furniture in here.

Karlee

From: Jack
To: Karlee
Sent: Tuesday, November 23, 2004 12:09 PM
Subject: RE: Book project . . .

Hi Karlee,

That's good about the book. Given the amount of time I have these
days (none) it seems like it'd be a bit much. I can't keep up with my

current projects, and things seem to be getting more hectic for me.

I'll keep plugging away for the rest of this week and weekend, and hope to have some news by the beginning of December, and maybe I can get some free time before (or after) Christmas.

I haven't been sleeping more than five hours a night, and I'm getting concerned that it will become a permanent condition. If I weren't tired all the time, it wouldn't be a worry, but I always feel ready to sleep.

On top of my other projects, I had a couple of minor inconveniences crop up.

Someone backed into my car this weekend and broke my tail light. It's mostly cosmetic, but I don't particularly want to get pulled over for a busted tail light. My cell phone also broke: the little antenna came off. This is a problem, because I get no reception anywhere (including my home) without the antenna. I replaced one a few months ago, and between that and the bad battery life, I think I need to go buy a new one. Maybe I'll get a camera phone! What could I do with that?

Do you have plans for Thanksgiving? Are you going to see your family?

I hope to have a bit more time to write this week...unless I fall asleep for a few days. That'd be nice too. I'm sure I'd have plenty of good dreams about you.

--Jack

From: Karlee
To: Jack
Sent: Tuesday, November 23, 2004 8:44 PM
Subject: Hi!

Hi Jack,

Oh, my...I wish I could just take you in my arms and hold you close to my breasts and run my fingers through your hair and just let you fall asleep until you wake up. Perhaps that would bring on more than five hours. Especially if that was preceded by an hour or two of passionate lovemaking and perhaps a fantasy for you! Sounds like you definitely could use some time at Karlee's Healing Center!

The car and cell phone certainly could never have come at all or perhaps at a time when there weren't these other things for you to think about. I spent $400 on Friday putting four new tires on my car. Guess it's a part of life; not one of the more enjoyable aspects though. Let me know when you get your new phone. I'd love for us to chat via the web cam again soon. As far as the photo phones...I have one and I don't even know all is does as far as the photos. I think you can send them, but you might have to have a special service on the phone to do that. I don't think I'm signed up for that.

As far as Thanksgiving...I'll be at my dad's. This will be the first holiday meal we're having there since my mom passed away. My brother will come up from Columbus and he's going to be in charge of the turkey and mashed potatoes. My sister will bring sweet potatoes, a green bean casserole, and rolls. I'm making a cranberry salad, the stuffing, and pies. I going to make two pumpkin pies—and a cherry for my nephew who was in Iraq. It's his favorite and I think he deserves it! (By the way, if you were going to be here, I'd make your favorite pie!). All that food will be more than enough for our small group. What will you do? I know what you're probably going to tell me—work. I do hope you have somewhere to go to at least enjoy a nice meal. With you being an only child, what do your parents do when you're not there? Are your grandparents still living?

Speaking of holidays—what about Christmas and New Year's? You'd look really cute with a bow tied around you and under my tree! Ringing in the New Year (in bed) with you sounds wonderful! Do you still ever think about coming to Cleveland? If not, any feasibility of me coming to Vegas? I mean, I know I can come to Vegas anytime. Any of the casinos would love to have me, I'm sure! But I mean me coming out and us spending some time together? Please let me know if I bring this up too often. I by no means want to add to the pressure you currently have or be looked at as a pest—and I want you to know I would love to see you again! (And feel you, and touch you, and taste you, and hear your heavy breathing, and…I think that just about covers all the senses!)

Good night.

Karlee
xoxox

From: Jack
To: Karlee
Sent: Monday, November 29, 2004 11:52 AM
Subject: RE: Hi!

Hi Karlee!

I'm still alive… Thanksgiving provided very little respite for me, although I did have a night with an uninterrupted 10 hours of sleep, and that was good. I'd like to do that every day. I hope you had a happy Thanksgiving!

I've been trying hard to find a different job, and working hard on getting a particular meeting about a writing project. The fellow I need to speak with is one of the hardest people to reach that I've ever dealt with. I might get a chance in mid to late December.

Anything else new? How goes it with you? Did you enjoy Thanksgiving?

-- Jack

From: Karlee
To: Jack
Sent: Thursday, December 2, 2004 10:19 AM
Subject: Hi!

Hi Jack,

Congratulations on getting 10 hours of sleep during the Thanksgiving holiday. We enjoyed our Thanksgiving. A small group at my dad's and thankful that my nephew was with us and arrived back from Iraq alive and well.

How's the job search going? Any poker tournaments coming up?

I've been spending some time "trying" to interact with men and explore possible relationships. I'm meeting some interesting people; no one exciting or compatible by any stretch of the imagination. I met a guy and we had what seemed to be a nice connection and things were going fairly well until he told me the age he posted on the dating site was incorrect. So instead of being 50, I found out he was 56! Not that being 56 is the worst thing in the world...I just don't sense that things will go far, if anywhere. So that being said, you are still my first choice for New Year's Eve!

Did you get a new cell phone yet? I called yesterday but didn't leave a message just in case they don't go anywhere or you can't retrieve them.

Are you still planning to be able to go to...(I can't remember where—it's a ski resort) in January? I sensed it was for some sort of work, but I'm not sure. Is this making sense? You talked about it a bit when I was out in August.

Going to close. I have a friend flying in from New York today. She's coming to Cleveland for a convention of some sort and will stay with me tonight and then tomorrow I'll take her downtown to where the event is being held. I'm looking forward to spending time with her.

Hope to talk to you soon!

Karlee

From: Jack
To: Karlee
Sent: Thursday, December 2, 2004 1:41 PM
Subject: RE: Hi!

Hi Karlee,

Aieeee! I need to clone myself to keep up with things these days. Apparently there's some interest in a book project, which means a lot of writing back and forth. Some friends of mine are going to ski in LakeTahoe, renting a huge house with a pool table, and they want me to come...but I can't. I just don't have time. And, my boss is coming back on the 20th of December. He had asked me to have everything done (!) by then. I still don't know what's going on; I have no idea if he's settled on a business plan. All I know is that the changes that have been suggested will take at LEAST three months for the tech guys to do, so, I'm finding it hard to be motivated to enter all these pieces of data.

No big poker tournaments; I don't have enough of a bankroll to enter any big ones anyway. The job search continues, although I'm not expecting any responses for the rest of the year. Unless it's a seasonal job, I've never had anyone get back to me between Thanksgiving and New Year's...too many parties, I guess. In any event, I keep looking.

I'm glad I'm on top of the list for New Year's Eve! I don't understand why people would lie. That'd put me off completely, and it happens frequently on-line. People lie about their age, their height, their appearance, their education...do they think someone won't find out? If the rationale is that if he'd put he was 56, you might not give him a chance, I'd think he'd realize that misrepresenting yourself isn't the best way to start a new relationship. I just don't get it.

The ski trip is at the end of January...I'd like to go; it all depends on what happens with my job. I can't imagine I'll still be at the same job. It's going to be tough. It's a good opportunity for networking, but I won't have any time left for vacation. I'll see what happens.

I'm hoping to resolve a lot of my work issues by the 21st; although I'm worried they may not be resolved for the better.

I still want to find time to christen that hot tub.

Have fun with your friend.

--Jack

From: Karlee
To: Jack
Sent: Sunday, December 5, 2004 5:26 PM
Subject: Hi!

Hi Jack!

Cloning yourself? This is **the best** idea I have heard in a long time! Please—put me down for at least two, or as many as you can spare!!!!!

Another book project? I hope it's something you'll enjoy. Of course I don't think you'd be considering it if you didn't think you would. Another poker book?

A trip to Tahoe sounds wonderful for you. I'm sorry you had to say no.

Well, you made it to December with your job. When I saw you in August, I really wondered if you would. I agree with your thinking on it being quiet as far as interviews during the holiday. It's like the whole country shuts down for the whole month of December. Christmas has definitely become a season instead of a one day holiday.

I keep forgetting to ask you if you received the Santa photos I sent you via the US Mail. (?)

I had a great time with my friend. I picked her up Thursday at the airport. We went to dinner and she spent the night here. Then I took her downtown on Friday for her conference. She called this morning and she was done at 10:30. So I went back downtown and picked her up and we came back here and I got to spend a couple of more hours with her before I took her to the airport at 2:00 PM. I've known her for about five years but had never spent that much time with her, one-on-one. She left me inspired and more excited about my consulting work and writing.

So happy to hear that you're still thinking about christening the hot tub. This is probably even better news than the cloning, since I know the hot tub is probably more realistic! Believe me; I think about it a lot. Not the hot tub so much, but just about seeing you again! And how about this…I received a voucher in the mail from the Borgata for a free hotel night! It's good until the 17th of January. I was surprised, since I didn't play that much. It might have been since I was a new My Borgata member. See, you could come to Cleveland, and after we get tired of the Jacuzzi (????!!!!) we could go to Atlantic City! (And christen whatever we want there!)

Any time for a webcam or telephone chat this week?

Karlee
xoxox

From: Jack
To: Karlee
Sent: Monday, December 6, 2004 10:03 AM
Subject: RE: Hi!

Hi Karlee!

Two of me? Wow. What would you do with two of me? I can only imagine.

Yes, another poker book. And, probably, another deal where I'd be a ghostwriter or assumed peripheral writer. It'd be less creative but more informative. It'd also be (I'm pretty sure) very simple to do. I'm becoming quite the little well-read poker expert (although I have a pile of books I haven't had time to open).

Great news about the consulting and the writing! That seems to be something you're passionate about, so you should keep after it.

I'd like to chat, but I don't know when I'll have some free and clear time. I've been multitasking and trying to get things done, but it would definitely be nice. Unfortunately, the best times for me are usually late at night, but this week (through Sunday) is likely to be one of my worst.

You know, until next week, probably.

--Jack

From: Karlee
To: Jack
Sent: Tuesday, December 7, 2004 12:14 PM
Subject: Hi!

Hi Jack,

I hope you're doing well today. I don't even know what to say anymore about all you've got going on. I wish I had a magic wand that I could wave and everything in your life would be "normal." But ah, who's to say what normal is? I could really go on from a philosophical point, and although I'm sure you would find it fascinating (Ha!), it's not like you have time to read about my philosophies on life.

Quitting seems to be what I think many people would do. Rationalization often comes easy in situations like this. I think the important thing here is that you recognize this and that it bothers you. Some people go through their entire life justifying behavior that you and I would look at as less than acceptable, but because we have a conscious, it bothers us. We know it's not who we really want to be. Sometimes we just have to accept the situation as it is in order to move beyond it. I know for me, whenever I find myself complaining about a situation, it stays. Once I let go, it seems to take care of itself.

So yes, winning a big poker tournament sounds like a good way to go.

Here's one of those virtual kisses…

Karlee
xoxoxox

221

From: Jack
To: Karlee
Sent: Monday, December 13, 2004 9:37 AM
Subject: RE: Hi!

Hey there,

Well, if all goes well I should have a meeting today and I'm hoping strongly that it leads to something. It's been a rough week and it doesn't feel like I got much done. I didn't sleep last night (must be anxious about my meeting).

I'll let you know if anything exciting develops...I'm guessing it won't since it's our first face-to-face meeting, but I'm uncharacteristically hopeful.

I heard that my resume had been given to a company and that they had me as the "top candidate" and were going to offer it to me sight unseen, but instead they went with an intern at this company. They aren't happy with the intern. I still don't know who passed on my resume or what the company was, but I was told by someone who knows the person who knows the person. Very odd. I was very close to getting a job that I don't remember applying for.

How are you? Any new and exciting developments?

--Jack

From: Karlee
To: Jack
Sent: Monday, December 13, 2004 8:18 PM
Subject: Hi!

Hi Jack,

Did you have your meeting today? How did it go?

The news of someone being ready to hire you "sight unseen" should seem that you're close to something!

Well, winter officially hit Cleveland, Ohio today! We had (only) our second snow of the season, but a big one. Some areas had commuters with two to over three hours of commute time getting home. I went to the mall and came out to about three inches of snow on my car in just a short time. Although it was definitely pretty (and good packing snow for snowball fights or snowmen), I was instantly reminded of why I was considering that move to Las Vegas earlier this year! Of course having lived in Cleveland all of my life...it's not like this snow is a big surprise!

I am looking forward to the end of the year. This has been one of the most trying years of my life. Meeting you and having such a positive experience in Las Vegas and since certainly added many positives. So thank you for that! I have always been a big fan of the New Year—I love turning the page to January on a new calendar and starting with a clean slate. And as far as I'm concerned, 2005 cannot get here soon enough!

Onward and upward, as the saying goes!

Hope to talk to you soon.

Good night,
Karlee

From: Jack
To: Karlee
Sent: Thursday, December 16, 2004 10:32 AM
Subject: RE: Hi!

Hi Karlee,

It's been crazy here. I'm still not sure what to make of my meeting on Monday. It was interesting and informative, but I don't know where the guy stands, and I doubt that he'd be able to focus enough to get that ball rolling. I also have the possibility of another film project, but that may be a struggle, too.

I have my meeting with my boss on Monday, but a recruiter wants to talk to me on Monday about contract jobs.

Sorry I missed your call. I've been going all day and fairly late into night trying to get opportunities lined up; there's a major poker tournament in town so a lot of the people I need to speak to are here for that.

It's the time of year when people talk but no one makes a decision. Jobs, deals, contracts...they talk about deadlines, but no one wants to do anything until after the 1st. It's maddening. I should be used to it, but I always have hope that someone will actually make a decision this time of year.

Enjoy the snow...I had to turn my air conditioning on because it's cold at night and hot during the day. I'd rather be in snow—believe me.

As soon as I see a break in the clouds, I'll give you a call...

--Jack

From: Karlee
To: Jack
Sent: Tuesday, December 21, 2004 11:10 AM
Subject: Hi!

Hi Jack,

Well...how was dinner with the boss? Any optimistic outcomes? I know, I know...what am I thinking?!

Congratulations on the writing project. It sounds like a good opportunity. Eeeee gads, please don't tell me I'm going to have to watch reality TV to see your work. But nonetheless, I'm excited for you and the opportunity no matter what it is. If it sounds good to you, then that's great! Seven projects, huh? Well, seven is a lucky number for many people. Perhaps this will be the project that propels you to something magnificent!

Christmas will be very quiet this year. My oldest sister lives in Wisconsin and won't be making the trip. My other sister is going to Florida to be with her son. So, that leaves me and my dad. I think the plan is that we're going to drive down to Columbus for Christmas day. My brother will have his kids and it will be fun. We decided it didn't make sense to make a big turkey dinner (we did that for Thanksgiving) for just three adults. I think I'm going to make a pan of lasagna which will be way beyond our traditions of the past!

So no, I haven't left for any exciting ventures! I've had invitations to Wisconsin, Florida, and Reno, Nevada. But sadly enough, no invitation to go to Las Vegas (other than from the Flamingo Hilton!) to spend Christmas or New Year's in bed with you.

What are your plans for the holidays? Lots of snow here...

Karlee

From: Jack
To: Karlee
Sent: Tuesday, December 21, 2004 3:16 PM
Subject: RE: Hi!

Hi there!

I'm sorry you won't get to see your sister. But hey, that's one less gift to give!

I will be very Grincherdly this year...I have had no time for anything. If I can get my draft in on time, I plan to fly out to see my parents for the holiday. I haven't seen them in a year.

I think there's still an outside chance that some other things will change soon that will make my life easier in the short run. We'll see...no one seems to do anything during the holidays.

I'll write more in the next couple of days. My new phone has been a disaster...same service, weird problems. It drops calls constantly, and it's hard to hear. I like the gizmos, but it's not nearly as good as far as speaking goes. I'm not sure what to do...I think my return period has already expired.

If I don't talk to you before then, have a Merry Christmas!

--Jack

From: Karlee
To: Jack
Sent: Wednesday, December 22, 2004 10:01 AM
Subject: Ho! Ho!

Hi Jack,

Glad to hear you might have the opportunity to visit your parents. Dress warm. We're getting hit again with snow. They're predicting up to 18 inches here by sometime tomorrow.

Did a package from me show up? I mailed one Friday by US Priority Mail. It should have been there Monday. I was going to send it signature required, but if you weren't home when it arrived, that would have required a trip to the post office for you. I didn't want to add to all you have on your plate.

Merry Christmas to you, too!

Karlee
xoxox

From: Karlee
To: Jack
Sent: Wednesday, December 29, 2004 8:35 AM
Subject: Carnac says: "The answer is...7 days."

The question is...what is the absolute most number of days Karlee can go without writing to Jack?!!!

How are you? How was your Christmas? Did you make it to

Chicago? Maybe you're still in Chicago. All I know for sure is you're not here. I checked everywhere to make certain Santa didn't hide you someplace I didn't look. Oh, wrong holiday.

My Christmas was quiet, as I had expected. I did enjoy the day at my brother's.

This has been a quiet week as well. I love the last week of the year. I find myself tying up loose ends, finishing little projects, and getting organized for the new year.

I had some friends (that I used to teach with) over for lunch yesterday. There are five of us and we have been getting together several times a year for many years now. They've become such special friends and it's so nice when we're together.

Last week the "move" bug bit me again. After contemplating the thought, I decided I would just let it sit for awhile and see if it goes away! I still think it makes sense for me to get a bit more re-established professionally before I uproot. I don't know; perhaps that's just a stalling technique to compensate for the uncertainty and some fear that comes up when I think about moving.

Hope you're doing well and I look forward to hearing from you.

xoxxo

From: Jack
To: Karlee
Sent: Monday, January 3, 2005 9:31 AM
Subject: RE: Carnac says: "The answer is . . . 7 days."

Hi Karlee!

I'm back from Chicago and mostly caught up from work that couldn't be done there. I'm glad this was another holiday weekend or I might have been sunk.

My Christmas was good. I spent the day playing with the dog and watching my parent's new TV.

The move bug, huh? I have the same feelings. I'm not sure how much more Vegas I can take. It seems like the big thing keeping me here is poker. How strange. I found myself missing things after being in Chicago, like weather and human kindness. But given the problems I had prior to last year, I think I'd want to have something established before moving. Despite the rosy reports I've heard about the economy, I've seen no first-hand evidence of it.

I'm fine otherwise, other than being hungry (and not just for food if you know what I mean!). Sorry I was out of touch, but now I'm plugged in.

--Jack

From: Karlee
To: Jack
Sent: Monday, January 3, 2005 11:15 AM
Subject: Yeah! You're back!

Hi Jack,

It was great to hear from you!

Okay, so here's a wild idea. How about you move here with me? I'm not sure how accessible poker is, but I can supply the weather and human kindness! Hey, I took a HUGE chance with you once—I'll try it again! Plus, think of all the exercise you'd get and the calories you'd burn!

Did my package arrive? The one with a naked picture of me used as a Christmas package tag?

Off to the Post Office.

Karlee

From: Jack
To: Karlee
Sent: Monday, January 3, 2005 11:11 AM
Subject: RE: Carnac says: "The answer is . . . 7 days."

Hey! I love the gift! I got all excited reading your well-crafted and professionally laminated card. Your ad and my response...just reading it filled me with happy thoughts.

Mmmm...

--Jack

From: Jack
To: Karlee
Sent: Wednesday, January 5, 2005 9:11 AM
Subject: RE: Thinking of you . . .

Hey there,

It was great talking to you, too. I've been doing a lot of research on this procedure and various dentists and costs. Dental insurance for individuals, it seems, is stupid crazy expensive.

I had a strange writing offer today...not sure If I can take it. Lots of pros and cons. I'd have to quit my "real job" but I'd be locked into a project for a year and a half. I believe in the project, but not sure about the success of it. I'd make the same salary I make now, minus benefits. No chance for promotion, and I'd be shutting the door to other possibilities. I'm trying to weigh the pros and cons.

I have a feeling I won't be able to talk, chew, or eat much for three or four days after the procedure, but I'm sure I'll be able to use the computer!

--Jack

From: Karlee
To: Jack

Sent: Tuesday, January 4, 2005 7:10 PM
Subject: Thinking of you . . .

Hi Jack,

Hope things are going a little better for you today—or even a lot better! It was so good to talk with you yesterday.

Karlee

From: Karlee
To: Jack
Sent: Wednesday, January 5, 2005 2:33 PM
Subject: Hi!

Hi Jack,

Wow! Congratulations on the writing offer. How is the decision-making process coming along? I agree that there appears to be some pros and cons. Letting go of your current job could definitely be a plus, since you dislike it so much. On the other hand, no insurance and no room to grow might not be so good.

Looks like it's dentist week for both of us. I had an 8:45AM appointment today and was there for more than three hours. I think I told you I had been having some pain in my jaw and sensitivity in one of my teeth. The reason it took so long was that it took three shots of Novocain to get me numb! I will tell you though, I used our time together as a relaxation technique when the endodontist was doing the drilling, etc. Every time I'd feel my neck tensing up, I'd bring up an image of us in my hotel room. Seeing you ever-so-gently tapping and touching my legs while they were on your lap seemed to be the most soothing and helped me to relax. I think the other images would have been too much for this procedure! (Other than the one time I spent a few minutes thinking about you kissing me while I was on the bathroom countertop.) Sooooo, I give you full permission to take any images you'd like with you to the dentist on Friday. And if you create new ones, that's fine, too!

I'm meeting a colleague on Friday. She called me and said she wanted to talk about some possible professional opportunities for me.

Karlee

From: Jack
To: Karlee
Sent: Wednesday, January 5, 2005 10:59 PM
Subject: RE: Hi!

Hi Karlee!

I still haven't made any decision yet. I'm talking to the guy with the money tomorrow. It's going to be tough. My gut tells me it's probably not the best idea in the world. It'd be interesting and I'd like it, but still...I have doubts.

Of course, I found out today that I may not have a job after 60 days. Even so, it doesn't greatly affect my thinking about this writing project. Apparently my boss is losing money hand over fist and he wants to re-evaluate the business plan in a couple of weeks. To protect himself, he's exercising an option in our contracts where he can give us 60 days notice. He said he'd like to call that off before the 60 days, but "another couple of weeks could be problems." He hoped me and my co-worker wouldn't look for other work. Right.

I guess I'm glad you thought of me for relaxation at the dentist's office, although I'd hate to think that you would start to associate me with intense pain and suffering. I hope my painkillers work. I'm not looking forward to the process. Bleh.

Now I've got to finish up some other work. Busy, busy.

--Jack

From: Karlee
To: Jack
Sent: Thursday, January 6, 2005 9:09 PM
Subject: Good Luck and Feel Better Soon!

Hi Jack,

Wow—I was surprised to hear the news about your job. Not that I never expected it. I guess just not now. When you said they launched the site in Hawaii, I thought things would start to get better before they got worse.

How was your conversation with the new writing project guy? Sounds like you had already decided it might not be a good choice. Having doubts is probably not a good sign. But not always of course!

Associate you with pain and suffering? Quite the opposite. I often use thoughts (and images!) of you to escape unpleasant thoughts that creep in from time to time. Of course there is the suffering I experience every day when I don't get to see your beautiful eyes, or touch you, or feel your hands and lips on me, or feel you inside of me. Other than that, it's not too bad!

I hope your painkillers work, too! I don't envy you. If you feel up to it, let me know how it went. I will be thinking of you and hoping the process is not too painful and uncomfortable.

Take good care of yourself.

Karlee
xoxxo

From: Jack
To: Karlee
Sent: Monday, January 10, 2005 9:58 AM
Subject: RE: Good Luck and Feel Better Soon!

Hi Karlee,

The procedure took 4.5 hours. The painkillers worked well, for the most part, but there were four spots where it was not pleasant, but I managed not to scream. The bad part was that near the end, the Novocain had worn off in one of the quadrants of my mouth...that hurt. I can't imagine what the most painful spots would have been like without Novocain. It sure left me feeling drained. And not the good kind of drained, either.

--Jack

From: Jack
To: Karlee
Sent: Tuesday, January 11, 2005 2:49 PM
Subject: RE: Good Luck and Feel Better Soon!

Hi Karlee!

I got your packet in the mail today! Very nice...I look forward to reading your suggestions! I don't think I've even ever seen a booklet for a tour...it looks like more fun than I imagined. Pretty swanky. I'll definitely think about it.

I wrote a letter of inquiry to an agent the other day. He wrote back quickly and sounded interested which surprises me...he promises to contact me by the end of the week. With any luck, he'll take me on and maybe I can do my own thing. If that's the case, I'm definitely signing up for More Fun! Other than that, I continue the bleak job search process. I couldn't log into my email account, which meant I couldn't apply for a job I was interested in. Ah well, at least my gums are doing better.

What's new in Clevelandia?

--Jack

From: Karlee
To: Jack
Sent: Wednesday, January 12, 2005 9:05 AM
Subject: Hi!

Hi Jack,

I was glad to hear that you survived the dental procedure! 4.5 hours—yikes! Glad they finished before the Novocain totally wore off. Hope you're feeling better every day.

Exciting news about the agent. Congratulations. This sounds very promising. I hope you do indeed hear from him as he promised and that it turns out great! And...if one expressed interest, that means there are others out there that probably would as well.

I'm glad you found the travel booklets appealing. I actually stopped at a travel agency and picked up several, but I didn't want to overwhelm you by sending one for every place in the world! I though what I sent would be a good starting point. And I have to say that I see no better way for you to start a More Fun program! I'd be happy to be your very own personal program director.

I'm really enjoying my pet fish! I thought for sure I lost him over the weekend. I was changing his fish bowl in my utility room and he jumped out of the net and landed UNDER THE WASHING MACHINE!!! Of course it's heavy and I didn't want to just yank it out in case he was near one of the four corners of the machine. By the time I inched it out, he was just lying there, not looking good at all. I finally managed to get him into the bowl and he looked bad. All day, I kept expecting to see him floating at the top of his bowl. But, low and behold, by Sunday morning he was good as new! Now I remember why I had been so hesitant about getting a pet in the first place.

Or having kids!

Karlee

From: Karlee
To: Jack
Sent: Thursday, January 13, 2005 1:14 PM
Subject: Hi!

Hi Jack,

Hope you're doing well today. How are the gums? Ready for any heavy duty kissing yet?!!!

I had another great meeting this morning with another colleague. Things are starting to pick up!

When's the big teleconference with the boss?

Any news yet from **your new agent**? (That's my think positive spin on this!)

That's enough questions from me for today…

I'm off to meet a friend for wings!

Karlee

From: Jack
To: Karlee
Sent: Thursday, January 13, 2005 2:01 PM
Subject: RE: Hi!

Hi Karlee!

I'm just about ready for kissing...gums are doing better. I need to figure out how to use my fancy expensive electric toothbrush without drooling toothpaste all over myself. They feel healthier and don't bleed anymore, so that's good.

Great that things are starting to pick up! We'll be able to sail around the world with all the business you'll have.

The big teleconference was today. It was okay, but not great. So, we'll see. I don't really care. I can't afford to lose the income, but I'm not sad about the job going away...it'll free up more time.

No news from the agent yet. Tomorrow, I hope. But I'll follow up next week in any event.

Oh, I miss wings. Healthy eating is so much work. I haven't had anything unhealthy in weeks. It's like being on a deserted island, with no dessert.

--Jack

From: Karlee
To: Jack
Sent: Friday, January 14, 2005 11:02 AM
Subject: Hi!

Hi Jack,

How are you today? The wings were good and I enjoyed the time with my friend. Wow—sounds like you've been doing great with your new eating plan. I haven't asked because [some] people are funny about that topic. Sometimes they just don't want anyone asking, "How are you doing?" I can relate to that. It could make one feel like they *should* be doing something, and if they're not, it adds more pressure. I've kicked up my workout sessions too because after the holidays my clothes were not fitting the same!

So is your job officially going to end or is the boss still hanging on to any remote signs of hope? When will he actually pull the plug? I'm sorry the conference call wasn't great.

I hope you hear good news from the agent today!

Karlee

From: Jack
To: Karlee
Sent: Friday, January 14, 2005 2:18 PM
Subject: RE: Hi!

Hi Karlee,

I'm glad to hear business ideas are flowing. I've been getting a bunch of writing projects lately, although none are particularly lucrative...at least it's something I love to do and it's better than my current job.

I believe that my boss is trying to act like there are signs of hope, though my only hope is to hang on as long as I can. I can't imagine he'd make the decision to move forward, but he does not have a history of good decision making, so maybe he will.

The agent contacted me...he says he's interested and wants a sample chapter.

Now I need to find time to do that.

I need a nap.

--Jack

From: Jack
To: Karlee
Sent: Sunday, January 16, 2005 6:08 PM
Subject: RE: Hi!

Hi Karlee,

I'm taking a breather before heading out to buy some food, then doing more work tonight. It keeps piling on. I'm feeling very good about passing on that one book project; the back-up writer has been contacting me, trying to find out why I passed. She's got many of the same concerns, the difference being that she's probably going to do it, and it'll be big problems for her.

Talking to her made me very glad I passed.

Anyway, I got your card yesterday...thank you! I'm glad to hear you're more than thinking about me...I haven't been thinking much about more than thinking, but I'll have to start. That note helps! Very nice, thanks...

Don't work too hard...I need to take that advice myself.

--Jack

From: Karlee
To: Jack
Sent: Monday, January 17, 2005 11:41 AM
Subject: Hi!

Hi Jack,

I hope your weekend was good. How's the chapter for the agent coming along? When does he expect you to have it to him and did he give you any indication how long it would take for him to make a decision?

I have two meetings this week regarding two consulting projects. I'll be talking with someone later today to learn more.

A package arrived from FedEx today with my new business cards, etc. reflecting my new name. I'm actually doing pretty well at remembering to sign my new name on credit card purchases, etc.

Any chance to think about the trip idea? I'm guessing you're waiting to have more clarity on your current job situation, writing projects, etc. to see what your workload will allow. I just don't want to wait too long to book something and find out the availability is crumby or all the good deals are gone. For me, ideally, the end of February. or first part of March would work well, but I certainly have some flexibility. I was thinking perhaps three or maybe four nights? And if it doesn't work out to go someplace like the Caribbean, a cruise, or Cancun, I'm certainly open to other options for us to see each other.

I'm glad you liked the card. Sorry to hear that you haven't been thinking much about more than thinking. Mmm? Perhaps some outside stimulation would help to get you started. Maybe it's time for me to set up my camera again! You haven't run out of fantasies, have you? That would definitely be a sign of working way too hard.

Karlee

From: Jack
To: Karlee

Sent: Monday, January 17, 2005 2:13 PM
Subject: RE: Hi!

Hi Karlee,

I'm fortunately working without any spoken deadlines; I want to get it to him as soon as I can, though, and I'm guessing he'll decide whether he likes the project (or me) within a couple of weeks at the most. I think I finished up another project. Next week I'm going to Utah, and by then I should have heard back from my boss, so I guess by February 1st I'll know a lot more about my life. At least, I hope I will...things rarely work out that neatly. If you're looking to go on vacation in Feb/March, it might be hard for me to come along, and I wouldn't want you to miss out on your own trip. We could shoot for Cleveland, maybe, once I have some answers.

Yes, I think it's time for you to set up your camera again and provide some outside stimulation! I would hate to forget how to more than think of you.

It doesn't seem possible, but I wouldn't want to take the chance!

--Jack

From: Karlee
To: Jack
Sent: Thursday, January 20, 2005 5:13 PM
Subject: Hi!

Hi Jack,

It definitely sounds like yesterday was busy for you, and somewhat exciting?!

When do you leave for Utah? I hope you have a really great trip.

Karlee

From: Jack

To: Karlee
Sent: Monday, January 31, 2005 8:14 AM
Subject: RE: Hi!

Hi Karlee,

I'm back, at last. I got sick and managed not to fall apart until I was on the last leg of my trip home. It was exciting and fun, even though I spent most of my time schmoozing and networking. I now get to start the long process of writing to the people I spoke with.

Of course, I got an email from my job just before leaving. No word on what they're going to do, but they wanted me to pack up and ship two of our office computers to them. I didn't have time, so I'll do it today. There were several concerned emails in the days between wondering why I hadn't written back.

Ah well.

I need to get some cold medicine. I woke up early and I'm still exhausted.

How are you doing?

--Jack

From: Karlee
To: Jack
Sent: Monday, January 31, 2005 12:23 PM
Subject: Welcome Home!

Hi Jack,

I was happy to hear from you. Glad to hear you had a good trip. Did you do a lot of skiing? Sounds like you made a lot of new contacts. Anything exciting or extremely optimistic?

I had a good week. I spent a good part of it working on ideas for the new program I want to implement.

Vegas [the fish] is doing well. And he/she should be—I bought an aquarium! I transferred him from a small, vase-like container that held probably less than a quart of water to a five gallon aquarium. A lot more swimming room for sure! I thought about adding a fish or two, but I really want to keep it simple.

Well, it's official—my office is completely painted—finally. There were a couple of times I had planned to finish and got distracted. I finally got tired of looking at half painted walls and finished it yesterday. I must say, it looks pretty good. I had to put two coats on a couple of the walls. I didn't like how the one wall turned out so I went to the store and bought just a quart of paint. I was warned it might not match exactly since the formula is a bit different for quarts versus gallons. But the woman seemed pretty certain it would be okay. Well, it wasn't! It didn't match…so I had to go back and buy a gallon anyway.

Sounds like you still have a job! Were you able to get the computers packed and shipped? Guess that could be another sign that they're getting ready to close down the operation.

Any word from the agent?

I'm sorry to hear you came down with a cold. I hope you feel better soon.

Karlee

From: Karlee
To: Jack
Sent: Thursday, February 10, 2005 11:25 AM
Subject: Hi Jack, just a quick question . . .

Are you still alive??!!!!!!!! I hope so, of course. Just thought I'd pop in for a quick hello. I'm assuming you are busy beyond busy.

I look forward to hearing from you when you get the chance and just wanted you to know that you were on my mind.

Thinking of you,
Karlee

From: Jack
To: Karlee
Sent: Thursday, February 10, 2005 7:25 PM
Subject: RE: Hi Jack, just a quick question . . .

Hi Karlee,

Yep, I'm alive. I've been sick for more than a week, and I'm just getting back on my feet. I've got more to do than I can, and I've got to figure out where I'm going to go and what I'm going to do on top of all of it.

Thanks for thinking of me! I'll write more when I get my head above water. It's crazy. I hope all is well with you, though!

Don't get the flu.

--Jack

From: Karlee
To: Jack
Sent: Sunday, February 13, 2005 6:54 PM
Subject: A Valentine's Day Package for You!

(Photo attached – Naked breasts with bow around my neck.)

Hi Jack,

I hope you're feeling 100% by now. Sounds like the flu really knocked you down. Based on your comment about deciding where to go and what to do...I'm guessing that means your job is no longer (?). I know you said you'd write more when you had the chance so I won't ask a million questions right now!

I don't know when your lease is up, but if you need a place to stay until you figure out what to do next, you are welcome here! I know

Cleveland may not be at the top of your list, and I don't have a swimming pool, but the rent is free and there are a few amenities here that I don't think you'd find at most places! Like the one in the photo attached!

Happy Valentine's Day!

Karlee
xoxox

From: Jack
To: Karlee
Sent: Tuesday, February 15, 2005 12:19 AM
Subject: RE: A Valentine's Day Package for You!

Hi Karlee!

I'm finally taking a breather. Whew. Everything has been so complicated and I haven't had a chance to do...well...anything, really.

Anyway, I got sick as a dog. 102 degree fever for many days and too weak to get out of bed for several days after that. A bad flu that hit my respiratory system. I'm finally up and around, but I couldn't get things done. I have a proposal I need to write ASAP and send, but I'm so behind in everything else that I couldn't touch it. I need to get to work on it and get it out the door.

On top of all that's going on and not going on, I've had no social life. I'm in solitary, constantly buried under piles of things that are overdue. I have leads that might eventually hopefully lead to a temporary bit of income, maybe. I need to solve my job situation, but I get nowhere on that. If everything goes as well as it could, I'll have three more months of income. It's stressful.

All that aside, it was good to hear from you. I got your cards today too, thanks! Of course, as nice as the cards were, your email definitely made my...year! Without a doubt, that's the absolute best Valentine's Day card/message/gift that I've ever received! Wow! I didn't see that coming, and it made me smile. In fact, it made me more than smile. And more than think. It was a powerful reaction, let me tell you...between being overwhelmed and sick for so long, I've not even had a sexy thought in a long time. It was like all of my focus went from everything else to you...I suddenly let myself remember our unbelievably sexy times together, and it flowed through me like electricity. I actually felt woozy (fortunately, I was sitting down at the time). I sat here for a few seconds and couldn't control myself...I pulled off my pants and pulled down my underwear and began touching myself while I looked at your picture.

I'm not sure what the reasons are, but I don't think I've ever had a more explosive orgasm, at least by myself. (I remember the Wrong Room fantasy as being one of the more explosive orgasms in my life.) I practically screamed and I was moaning so loudly. I kept cumming and cumming and cumming...it was like a fountain. Then, I collapsed back in my chair and thought nice thoughts about you.

So, thank you for that! It was nice to feel something other than overwhelmed anxious panic!

As for the rest of your note...thank you for your offer about Cleveland. Believe me, I will consider it. At the very least, I am thinking hard about coming for a visit. The job duties will be done soon (if they're extended a month, I can't imagine they will go longer than that). The contracts will have to be resolved soon, and the proposal needs to get finished. But in the meantime, I may disappear for a while, buried by my projects. I'll try to be better at keeping in touch.

I hope all is well with you. I'd like to know what's happening...only good things, I hope!

Happy Valentine's Day, and thanks for making mine unforgettable!

--Jack

From: Karlee
To: Jack
Sent: Wednesday, February 16, 2005 12:07 PM

Subject: Hi!

Hi there, Sexy,

It was so good to hear from you. I'm sorry you were so sick and glad you're back on your feet.

Your job is still there; I can't believe it! Just like the Eveready Bunny—it keeps going and going. I know that's a good thing from the financial aspect, but other than that—I know you'll be glad to have that behind you. It appears that your boss finally listened to you. Too bad it's most likely too late. If he would have listened in the first place...

Congratulations on the film! Although I have to say, I don't remember you mentioning too much about a film in the past, so I'm not exactly sure what that is all about, but it sure sounds like a good thing! How could the remuneration be nothing? That doesn't seem possible!

I'm sorry to hear that you have had no social life. A friend of mine once reminded me that "we come into this world alone (unless you're a twin!) and leave alone," but I still believe it's our nature as human beings to have some interaction with other people. I hope the piles of projects dwindle down to a more reasonable and manageable load for you so that you can have some fun. And soon!

As far as my world, hmmm, so much of it is not easily explained without a lot of writing. I'll give you a couple of Cliff Notes versions.

I have a new web site! It still needs some work, but I'm really excited with the design of the banner. Paying to have a new site created "forced" me to spend [more] time getting clear on what it is I really want to do. So that was a good thing. I'm meeting with an ad agency guy next week to talk about personal branding. I want him to help me create some sort of concise marketing campaign so that I can get busy again.

I'm glad you liked your Valentine's Day message. I actually took two pictures and chickened out on sending the other one. Ya know, some parts of a woman's anatomy just don't photograph as well as the breasts! I'm happy to know that I was the source of more favorable feelings than what you've been having for a long time. I'd like to be your number one choice for more favorable feelings! As far as the explosive orgasms and electricity, (I get tingly just writing it), I can relate. As far as the reasons, a part of it for me is I have a feeling that the experience we had in Las Vegas has been locked into my subconscious and that a part of that is triggered when I self-pleasure.

It just seems to make it easy to bring back all the incredibly wonderful feelings associated with our time together. That's mostly good. But, for me, sometimes I'm sad because we're not together for me to be able to recreate it on a daily basis, or even weekly or monthly!

I'm keeping my fingers crossed that it works out for you to come to Cleveland soon. I miss you!

Take good care of yourself and good luck with your projects.
Karlee
xoxxo

From: Jack
To: Karlee
Sent: Monday, February 21, 2005 2:38 PM
Subject: RE: Hi!

Hi Karlee!

Yes, being sick is no fun. Especially when you don't have time to be sick.

Dental work is crazy expensive. My teeth are healed, I suppose, though I have to go back for a checkup in April. I can tell some big differences, but we'll see. They want to do a bunch of other work, but I have neither the time nor the money to do anything that isn't immediately threatening. A root canal isn't fun, although I must say my dental experience was much better than my last one a few years ago...everything seems less painful.

I loved my Valentine's Day message! Why chicken out on the other one?! I'm sure you know that no matter how worried you were about the other photograph, I would have LOVED it. Hmmm. I'm not even sure what it was, but I love looking at all parts of your anatomy. Mmmm.

I'm working on a trip. I have feelers out there that may get me on the road, and that's my first-choice stop!

--Jack

From: Karlee
To: Jack
Date: Wednesday, February 23, 2005 5:00 PM
Subject: Valentine's Day Part II

Hi Jack,

I don't know why I do things for you that I normally would never do! This is by far one of the most outrageous steps I've taken so far! I hope I'm not making a fool of myself for sending this photo. And I hope you definitely still have room in your encrypted folder for this one!

Hey, it's your turn to send another photo!

I'm sorry we didn't get much of a chance to chat on Monday; I sensed I caught you at a bad time, and yet it sure was good to hear your voice.

Good night,
Karlee

From: Jack
To: Karlee
Sent: Thursday, February 24, 2005 2:49 PM
Subject: RE: Valentine's Day Part II

Hi Karlee!

WOW! Why didn't you like that photo? It's great! Very sexy. Mmm. Don't worry...it's in the encrypted folder and you're absolutely not making a fool out of yourself. I might, given my reaction....

I'll send you a photo as soon as I'm able to. Things are difficult and time consuming with the wind-up of this job...it's going to come to a head today.

I hope to find out if I'll be paid for the remainder of my contract or not, and then decide whether to fight or not. It's been a huge time drain last week and this week...I'm more than fed up.

Excellent picture! Now THAT's a valentine!

--Jack

From: Karlee
To: Jack
Sent: Thursday, March 3, 2005 8:00 PM
Subject: Hi!

Hi Jack,

How are you? And the job? It's past March 1st...I am wondering about the outcome.

Hope you are doing okay.

Karlee
xoxoxo

From: Jack
To: Karlee
Sent: Thursday, March 3, 2005 10:50 PM
Subject: RE: Hi!

Hi Karlee,

I'm holding up. My last official day is actually March 5th, though that's a Saturday, so it's technically tomorrow. My co-worker's father died. I admit that it's a bit suspicious; she was given an absolute deadline to complete some work, and she never did. Ten minutes before we were supposed to all have a conference call, she called me and told me, then emailed the boss.

The end result is that I get the lovely task of closing up the office this week and all that hassle. I decided that I'd be happy to make a phone call to have things done, but it turns out to be more work than that. Tomorrow I'm going in to coordinate some movers to get equipment from the office to the UPS store, then paying them to box it up and ship it off. The boss wants me to forward mail, etc, too...but my co-worker has the mailbox key. It's all a pain and I've got other things to worry about (like finding a new job). Still, I'm trying to go out on the "high road" if I can.

Stressful times.

How go your adventures? Is the business booming? What else is up? How are you doing?

--Jack

From: Karlee
To: Jack
Sent: Sunday, March 6, 2005 5:58 PM
Subject: Hello . . .

Hi Jack,

I was happy to hear from you. Heck—I'm always happy to hear from you!

So now what comes next for you regarding a job?

I'm doing okay. Business is not booming (yet), but I am happy to say that I took some steps last week that will keep things moving in the right direction. There will be a lot to do, which will be a good thing. I've had more than enough weeks with little on my calendar.

It's been good for me to be out a bit more. I was starting to wonder if I would ever adjust to my new life as a single woman. Even though it has been almost three years since the divorce, there are still parts of my life that are unsettled. At least staying busy helps to keep my mind off of the pieces that have yet to fall into place. I stopped at my ex-husband's house tonight to pick up some mail and I think his girlfriend may have moved in with him. Her car was in the garage; that could be a pretty good indication. It's strange; for some reason I think that helped me to see the finality in this. Of course, one might think that I would have realized it was final when I signed the papers three years ago!

On that note, I'll say good night!

Karlee

From: Karlee
To: Jack
Sent: Wednesday, March 23, 2005 11:04 AM
Subject: Thinking of you . . .

Hi Jack,

Just a quick note to say hi and tell you how good it was to hear your voice yesterday. I'm sorry things aren't better for you yet. I was hoping you had found a fabulous job and that you were busy getting settled in with that.

What's the best way for me to support you during this rough time? I'm happy to send an email every day, even if you are not able to respond, if that would brighten your day. Or do you prefer I leave you alone until things are more settled? Perhaps a photo of me in bed more than thinking of you. NO! Sorry, that's not an option. (You're welcome to come here and watch, though!) And of course, you can always take the virtual hugs and kisses.

Let me know if there's anything I can do.

Love,
Karlee
xoxox

From: Jack
To: Karlee
Sent: Thursday, March 24, 2005 3:18 AM
Subject: RE: Thinking of you . . .

Hi Karlee,

Thanks for the nice note. I too wish I had a fabulous job and was busy with that.

But, what can you do? It's extremely stressful.

>>*What's the best way for me to support you during this rough time?*

I'm rarely even on email lately; but thanks for the offer of the daily notes! I'm trying to work my way through this. I'm not thinking about much else.

YES, YES, YES to the photo! Oh...oh well.. I got all excited there for a minute. Of course, if I was there, I'm sure I wouldn't be just watching for very long...

I appreciate your support. Sorry I'm not more chipper. But it's good to hear from you and I'll be in touch soon...literally, I hope.

--Jack

From: Jack
To: Karlee
Sent: Wednesday, March 30, 2005 4:09 PM
Subject: RE: Thinking of you ...

Hi Karlee,

I'm taking a little breather and wanted to send you a note. I got your card—thanks for that.

It's been stressful...not much sleep for me.

So, now I can sit and wait a couple of days, not answer the phone, and try to focus on important things like getting a job. I'm waiting to hear back from a literary agent, too, and that's looming overhead. Have you ever crossed that threshold where any news—even bad news—is better than not knowing? I'm there.

So, that's it. I'm still in hiding...still stressed...not at all optimistic, but at least I'm moving forward.

I hope all's well. I'll let you know if I hear anything.

--Jack

From: Karlee
To: Jack
Sent: Wednesday, March 30, 2005 8:19 PM
Subject: Hello . . .

Hi Jack,

I was happy to hear from you and glad you were taking a breather. (I wish you were breathing on me!)

I have been thinking about you every day and hoping that the week would bring something positive.

>> *Have you ever crossed that threshold where any news—even bad news—is better than not knowing? I'm there.*

Yes, unknowingness sometimes gets to me. I think it's because I am so analytical by nature. I spend time thinking and want to know the outcome as soon as possible! Perhaps some would call that being impatient; I don't always see it that way. And I think based on all you're dealing with it would make sense to want some kind of news so that you can deal with it and move on.

I've been fighting an upper respiratory bug and totally lost my voice today. I need to get to bed and see if I can kick the laryngitis.

Know that I am sending good thoughts your way. Please take good care of yourself; you're important to me. I wish I could give you a hug.

xoxox

From: Karlee
To: Jack
Sent: Monday, April 18, 2005 11:58 AM
Subject: Greetings from Cleveland!

Hi Jack,

It sure was good to talk with you yesterday, even if just for a short time. I hope the rest of your production work went well.

I bought a new bike! (the peddle kind—not a motorcycle!) A couple of weeks ago, I took my old bike into a bike shop to see about having a tune-up, etc. I hadn't been on it for probably over four years and wanted to have it checked before I went for a ride. Well, by the time I would have paid for the tune-up and all the other things they were suggesting, I decided a better way to go would be to buy a new one. The one I had was a good bike, but not really ideal for the type of riding I plan to do. So I shopped around a bit and brought the new one home Friday evening. I love it. I've been out twice—about 11 miles each time and it's a great ride. I live close enough to our Metroparks that I ride right from my condo down to the park. I have to ride on a couple of streets that are less than ideal for riding, but I still think that's better than taking it apart to get it into my car, etc. I plan to do a lot of riding this summer, so I'm glad I made the decision to get a better bike. We have been having [finally] some good weather for being outdoors.

I've also been spending a lot of time reading about menopause! I

know—not a topic I'm sure most men want to even hear mentioned.
I started to notice some changes and decided to be pro-active and
really find out what this is all about. Most women seem to grow up
with not really understanding what it is...just that it's BAD...
according to our mothers, grandmothers, aunts, etc. I have found a
couple of really good books that do a great job of explaining the
hormone loss that women (and men) experience and options for what
to do about it. I'm currently reading one by Suzanne Somers that
actually has me excited about the change! She has some very
favorable and optimistic stories to share. I'm grateful that my libido
has not been affected. (Of course, it's hard to tell for sure since I
haven't had sex since the last time I was with you.) I do know I still
want it—with you!

Sending a big hug,
Karlee
xoxox

From: Jack
To: Karlee
Sent: Tuesday, April 19, 2005 11:50 AM
Subject: RE: Greetings from Cleveland!

Hi Karlee!

I got your card (about the shower)...who knew that the big card
companies would make cards just for us?!

The production was fine. I got along well with one of the executive
producers, and was asked to play a lot of "after show" poker, for
money. We'd also play for money during the day in the green room,
while waiting for people to get through hair and makeup and
promotional stuff.

The bike sounds like fun. I haven't ridden a bike in years. I used to
bike to school every day, and that was it for me. Out here, there
would be interesting places to ride, but it's already too hot. I miss
the snow. It'll be 120 here in no time. I've got to get out of Vegas
soon. It almost hit 90 the other day. I'm ready to leave this town. I

need to move to Alaska or something. I've never been a huge outdoor guy, but did enjoy the wilderness during spring and fall. Out here, it's just dirt.

I'm glad you're looking forward to menopause! I must admit, I have not read any books on menopause, but I don't hear very much about the "pros." I suppose the aspect I've heard the most about is the hot flashes...I can remember a couple of VERY hot flashes you've given me, though, so I could see how menopause could be tremendously positive! Hooray!

I agree completely! Your libido has not been affected. I am the grateful recipient of that!

Anyway, I'll keep you posted. Feel better! It was good to talk to you, albeit briefly.

--Jack

From: Karlee
To: Jack
Sent: Tuesday, April 26, 2005 6:30 PM
Subject: You're sexy . . .

Hi Jack,

Thanks for the note.

For months I've been saying that you need to get out of Vegas. I'll put some snow in the freezer and save it for you. But you'll have to act fast. It's almost gone again.

See you soon! (Even if it's just in the pictures of you I look at every day!)

I know, I know, I know, I know, I know. Oh, how I know that the real thing is better. Believe me, I want the real thing. There are days when my body physically aches for your touch. I don't know what to do anymore. On one hand I try to be patient, etc. On the other hand…I'd rather have the other hand on you! Are you on your way yet?

Karlee
xoxox

From: Karlee
To: Jack
Sent: Thursday, May 5, 2005 1:58 PM
Subject: Hi!

Hi Jack,

How are you? Sooooo…any good news, bad news, no news? I keep thinking one day I'll get an email from you with the subject line reading: Great News!

I hope you'll consider this great news…I'm coming to Vegas! A friend twisted my arm. Well, really…she didn't have to twist—I always love the idea of a trip to Vegas. We considered a few other destinations, but when it came down to what was important to each of us for a short trip, Las Vegas made the most sense.

I arrive on Sunday, May 29, for three nights. I hope your schedule will allow for us to spend some time together.

I love my new bike. I don't know about being a Lance Armstrong, but I did ride 16 miles yesterday. Not bad, considering that was only my fourth time out (the weather had been really crumby for outdoor activities for about two weeks). I'm determined to kick my sluggish metabolism back into place.

I'm still sending good thoughts your way and hoping things are improving.

Karlee
xoxox

From: Jack
To: Karlee
Sent: Monday, May 9, 2005 2:08 AM
Subject: RE: Hi!

Hi Karlee!

No good news yet! I did speak to a company about a position that I
might like a lot, though it would require a move to Florida. I'm not
too keen on that idea, but it'd be a great job. I'm not at all
optimistic that I'll get called back on the job, because I'm clearly not
qualified for what they want, but maybe I'll get lucky.

The position required a couple of changes, which might not be
approved on their end, so I'm waiting to hear back. I've been
waiting on a bunch of other projects, too, and hope to hear back
something this week or next. Work, wait, more work, more wait,
repeat. Every few months, I get a "no." It keeps me busy.

You're coming to Vegas? Excellent! Why wouldn't that be great
news!?

I'll do my best to free up as much time as I can for those days. Of
course, knowing my luck, I'll get called for an out-of-state interview,
and then won't get the job. But, that seems unlikely.

Is the friend you're traveling with the same one you met up with
here before, or is this a friend from home? Is she the one who took
those pictures? I owe her one if she is!

I haven't had the time or energy to exercise at all in the last few
months...very bad. 16 miles on your bike is very impressive! I'm sure
your metabolism will kick into high gear at that rate. Maybe you
should bike out to Vegas.

Congratulations on the seminar work. Money is good, I've heard,
and flexibility is great. Although, I'm burning out on flexibility,
personally. I have to work so hard to keep projects coming in that
it's wearing me out. A regular 9-to-5 job is much easier, though
usually less fulfilling. Clearly, winning the lottery is my best option.

Thank you for the good thoughts...I appreciate that, and I send good thoughts back! We're both hoping for something good to hit. The last couple of weeks seem to be showing movement in the right direction, and a couple of interesting doors have either opened, or not slammed shut yet, which is encouraging. I'm a bit anxious, and trying to keep all the doors open in case one works out, but there's a lot of waiting. Patience isn't my greatest virtue.

Time to gear up my fantasization efforts, I think. I haven't been thinking enough about fantasies lately. I still seem to get a great deal of pleasure recalling the Wrong Room and shower fantasies.

Mmmmm...

Do you have any? Send them along!

--Jack

From: Karlee
To: Jack
Sent: Monday, May 9, 2005 4:32 PM
Subject: Hi!

Hi Jack,

Hope things are going well for you today.

Aside from moving to a state you're not that keen on, the job in Florida sounds optimistic. What type of position is it? They would be lucky to have you.

The friend I'm traveling with is this a friend from home. We've been friends since 5th grade! And noooooooo...she did not take those pictures! I took those pictures all by myself! I chuckled at the idea that you thought someone took those, but I guess anything's possible. Did someone take the picture of the photo you sent to me?

I was actually thinking of setting a very lofty goal for myself regarding the bike. I hadn't thought quite as big as cycling out to Vegas, though. I wonder if AAA would do a TripTik for me. I did 13 miles today; 17 on Saturday. Ten is probably a more reasonable amount. The last couple of miles aren't as much fun, but I guess that's a part of the challenge.

That's okay about the patience. I have been on the receiving end of some of your other qualities and as far as I'm concerned, they far outweigh patience!

Most of the fantasizing that I've been doing the past several months has to do with you coming to Cleveland. Just normal stuff, like me picking you up at the airport, us in the Jacuzzi, us in bed, us having breakfast in bed, me having you for breakfast in bed, you having me for breakfast in bed, us lying naked on the couch watching a movie, us taking a walk in the park (okay, so every once in awhile a non-sexual thought comes in!), us in the Jacuzzi again, us cooking a meal together, us in the shower, the absolute world's best oral sex, in the shower or otherwise…

I'm so excited at the thought of seeing you again, and touching you, and feeling you next to me, inside me, on top of me (or any combination thereof), I really don't care what we do. Well, that's not totally true. But in a way, it is.

Karlee
xoxox

From: Jack
To: Karlee
Sent: Sunday, May 15, 2005 4:31 PM
Subject: Hey there

Hi Karlee,

Well, things seem to be moving, at least a bit.

I submitted a proposal and now have an agent working on selling another project I created. He said he's taking it to 12 publishers this week. I think his efforts will be worthwhile. At least, I hope they will.

I have a teleconference about a job on Monday. I don't think I have a prayer to get it, but I'm doing all kinds of research (more than for any other job I've applied for in my life, actually) so we'll see if hard work pays off.

I'm still trying to push other projects forward. I got the galleys for my current book and am fixing a number of small errors. It has to be done this week, so I'll be working on that for quite a while. Every page, every comma, every word...this is the last chance to make corrections. There are a lot.

Any news on your end? Are you still coming to town? What's been happening?

--Jack

From: Karlee
To: Jack
Sent: Sunday, May 15, 2005 8:03 PM
Subject: RE: Hey there

Hi Jack,

I will keep my fingers crossed that your teleconference goes well on Monday. I do hope your hard work on the research pays off.

And, another project going to 12 publishers this week...wow—that sounds good as well. I know it's too soon to get overly excited, but it seems to be a step in the right direction.

Yes, yes, yes, I'm still coming to town! In less than two weeks...and I am very excited about seeing you. Do you have any better sense of what will be going on for you and what day(s) (and/or nights) you will be available for me to devour you? Okay, maybe not devour, but at least nibble. Mmmmmm!

Good luck again on the teleconference. I will be sending good thoughts!

Good night,
Karlee
xoxox

From: Jack
To: Karlee
Sent: Monday, May 16, 2005 2:04 PM
Subject: RE: Hey there

Hi Karlee,

Unfortunately, the teleconference has been put off for one week. This is very distressing for me, since on top of everything else, I need that to happen to be able to figure out what my schedule will be. This is the second time this company has cancelled a scheduled meeting. And as much as I want to work with them, I've got a 3-strikes policy with being blown off for meetings. This is strike two.

I hope to hear something by Monday, but I have a bad feeling they'll put me off again, or not make any decisions. I'm taking all of this as being not a good sign, but I'll keep you posted.

I'm in the thick of proofreading now. Unfortunately, I'm in the galley phase, where we have to write directly on the original manuscript, so I can't get other people's eyes on it. I'm getting tired of re-reading the same stuff over and over again.

I'll let you know of any updates. I look forward to seeing you!

--Jack

From: Karlee
To: Jack
Sent: Monday, May 23, 2005 7:34 PM
Subject: Hi!

Hi Jack,

How are you? Did you have your teleconference today? If so, I hope it went well. I hope you didn't have to implement your three strikes policy.

Are you ready for me?!! I'm looking forward to the trip, for many reasons. Seeing you is just about at the top. Okay, maybe at the top! I'm not sure what to expect, since we haven't been dialoging as much, and our recent emails are much different than the pre-arrival emails we were sharing last year! Maybe that's a good thing; I'm actually able to concentrate this week. But when I think about seeing you again... Mmm—Mmm—Mmmmmm...the flutters kick in!

I'll be in Schaumburg on Wednesday, then Naperville on Thursday and Friday. Saturday I have a wedding to attend and then we head out on Sunday. So I have been working on getting done what I need to for the trip.

See you soon!

Karlee
xoxxo

From: Jack
To: Karlee
Sent: Tuesday, May 24, 2005 3:45 PM
Subject: RE: Hi!

Hi Karlee!

I am ready for you! I know the feeling about those flutters! I have been locked into concentrating on one thing at a time...otherwise, I sit and my mind wanders and...I start to get uncontrollably excited again. I'm also worried that I'll have big time conflicts (or have to go out of town) so I'm trying to "play it cool."

Although, I realized a few days ago that I've practically become a monk...and started thinking about the Wrong Room and a few other things we did and discussed...and I wound up more than thinking about you...multiple times. I haven't done much more than thinking in a while...I practically exhausted myself. So, don't worry...my desire to see you (and more than see you) is stronger than ever...Mmmmm.

What are your accommodation arrangements? Are you going to be spending a lot of time with your friend? This is pure vacation, right? Or will you be doing a seminar?

I've had some interesting fantasies about you lately...one in which someone was watching us! That was something I'd never fantasized about before. Hmmm. Have you had any ideas since we last spoke of such things?

I'll talk to you soon!

--Jack

From: Karlee
To: Jack
Sent: Sunday, June 5, 2005 5:31 PM
Subject: Hi!

Hi Jack,

Well, here I am back in Cleveland and back to email instead of the real thing. How sad!

It was in the mid 90's today. I was at my dad's boat, cleaning the inside. Not the best day for that, but it needed to be done and I didn't want to go through another season without a good cleaning.

I'm glad to hear you didn't get sick like I did. In a way, it worked out that we weren't able to see each other on Tuesday. I had been struggling all day with whether or not I felt good enough to see you. I woke up Tuesday morning and it literally felt like I had two pieces of smoldering charcoal in my throat. Not much fun for my last day in Vegas. I managed to go out on the Strip for a bit with my friend. I was in bed by 11:00PM. On Thursday, I went to a store and bought something my aunt recommended and within a couple of hours I was feeling pretty good. One of the fastest recoveries I've had in a long time!

Speaking of recovering...not yet for me! Monday night, I was walking through a casino and I was thinking about our time in bed earlier that day and one of those "bolts" shot through me. I actually had to stop. You are good! Mmmm—Mmmmm! I realized too that we didn't' have enough time together—I wanted to hear about your fantasy involving someone watching us. Just curious, I guess.

I hope you're doing well.

Karlee

From: Jack
To: Karlee
Sent: Friday, June 10, 2005 11:11 AM
Subject: RE: Hi!

Hi Karlee,

I'm glad you made it back safely, and I trust you're feeling better by now.

It's been a rough week for me. I think I told you about this new job, for which I have had two lengthy phone interviews. I think I also told you that they've blown me off—twice. I'd be given a time for a call, and I'd accept, and they wouldn't call. I'd wait longer than I should, send them a note, and they'd apologize and reschedule. Well, the interviews started the first few days of May. After the last interview, they set up something two weeks later, which would've been this Tuesday.

I sent an email to the secretary who confirmed my appointment and an email to the HR woman who I initially interviewed with. No response on Wednesday.

Nothing. No email, no phone call. They just completely blew me off. My policy is if that happens three times, I don't want to work for a company, because the lack of professionalism is Big Trouble. Nonetheless, I did hear from the HR person late Thursday, and her email said that they didn't feel I was qualified enough for the position.

Anyway, now that hope is gone...I have NO hope of hearing from them again and I've got to move on to something else, but I'm not sure what. I'm in a bit of a scramble. I'm burning out fast.

All that aside, it was great to see you, albeit briefly, and I'm sorry if I wasn't "all there." I want to get settled in somewhere soon and move on with my life. I think I've got to get out of Vegas very soon.

--Jack

From: Karlee
Sent: Monday, June 13, 2005 10:48 AM
To: Jack
Subject: Hi!

Hi Jack,

I was sorry to hear the news about the interview. Have you heard anything more since writing to me on Friday? The whole thing sounds totally unfair not to mention very bizarre. I'm sorry that you invested so much time into something you felt optimistic about, only to have it not turn out.

Any new thoughts about your next step? What's happening with the new book contract?

I heard from the seminar company and they're flying me out to LA to meet with them and sign the contract. I'm excited. I'll probably be on the road starting in August. I'm focusing on all the positive aspects of why this will be good and minimizing the aspects that are less than ideal.

Hmph? When I first read "I want to get settled in somewhere soon and move on with my life," I didn't give it much of a thought. Then I started thinking about it and realized that because the statement was followed by a thought about our time together, that you might be saying to me that you would like to move on (away) from our connection. So I thought I'd check on that with you rather than make my own assumptions.

I hope things brighten up for you soon.

xoxox

From: Jack
To: Karlee
Sent: Tuesday, June 14, 2005 10:46 AM
Subject: RE: Hi!

Congratulations on the seminar work. That must be a relief...it could also lead to new possibilities.

I meant moving on professionally...I'm not enjoying the lack of health insurance or stability. I don't like the fact that I'm paying $15K in rent every year and I can't afford a home in this town ANYWHERE. Like, literally, nowhere.

Oh well. Back to the grindstone!

--Jack

From: Karlee
To: Jack
Sent: Wednesday, June 15, 2005 8:32 PM
Subject: RE: Hi!

Hi Jack,

I hope there's been a bright spot in your week.

I was going through a drawer today and came across a copy of our fantasies. I knew they were in there; I just haven't read them for a while. The reaction was too much and I put them away. I just didn't want to go there at the moment. I wonder if we should think about a One Year Anniversary Repeat Edition! Never in a million years would I have guessed that almost one year later, we'd still be writing. I think I originally posted the ad on Sunday, June 27 and your response arrived on Monday. I don't know why, but I'm feeling like I want to say, "Thank you." I don't know if you have any idea how important and significant our time together last July is to me, and continues to be. For a long time, as I think you know, I had been hoping that there could be more. Now, I have come to accept that it is what it is. I'm not always sure what it is, but I've let go of trying to put what we share into some kind of category. All I know is that I wish I could have sex with you every day!

I don't know what to say about your situation. It doesn't seem possible that one person should have to go through all the rough spots you have had since we've been writing. Is it an option for you to move and still keep those projects that don't require you to physically be in Vegas? Perhaps the right opportunity will show up once you get settled in a place you enjoy. It seems like you have never enjoyed living in Vegas. Maybe once you're someplace you like, the energy will shift.

Last year I went to hear one of my favorite authors speak and he told a story about his daughter wanting to produce a music CD. His repeated message to her every time she would hit an obstacle was, "Contemplate yourself as surrounded by the conditions you wish to produce."

I use it often and it seems to help.

Hang in there!

Love,
Karlee

From: Karlee
To: Jack
Sent: Wednesday, June 22, 2005 5:45 PM

Subject: Hi!

Hi Jack,

My trip to LA was great. Of course, starting it off with time on the phone with you helped! I enjoyed my time with my friend and all went well with the seminar people. Because they schedule so far out, it looks like I won't be going out until the first week of September. I was really hoping to get on the road in August.

xoxxo

From: Karlee
To: Jack
Sent: Sunday, June 26, 2005 2:16 PM
Subject: Remember this?

A year ago on a Sunday morning . . .

Sunday, June 27, 2004 7:55 AM

Hot, Fun Woman Looking for New Experiences—45—w4m

I will be in Las Vegas July 6-10. I am looking to have fun with a young, well-built, clean, attractive male. We can meet for a drink, dinner, or a swim at my hotel pool (I'll be staying at one of the Strip properties) and see where it goes from there. Recently divorced and in need of some exciting sexual experiences! Not looking for anything outrageous; just good, hot sex. Must be willing to wear condoms (I will supply) for both oral and intercourse, provide photos, and have at least one telephone conversation with me before I head out. Non-smokers only. I am attractive, 5' 2", a size 8 with great breasts, blonde hair, and blue eyes, and fun, fun, fun . . .

From: Karlee
To: Jack
Sent: Sunday, June 26, 2005 2:16 PM
Subject: And then this!!!

----- Original Message -----
From: Jack
To: Karlee
Sent: Monday, June 28, 2004 1:25 PM
Subject: Fun in Vegas with a fun guy ... in Vegas

Hi, anonymous craigslist personal ad poster!

I'm guessing that you've probably received hundreds or thousands of responses to your ad by now, but don't delete me yet! Give me the chance to arouse, titillate, annoy, or repulse you first! That's all I ask.

I was supposed to be working, but I'm taking a break. I was distracted and found myself perusing the ads. I have had an ongoing fantasy in my life to have an illicit sexual meeting. I don't know why, but the idea of meeting a stranger and having sex is tremendously exciting for me. You might wonder why, if that's the case, I don't just go off and hire a prostitute—well, I've never done that and it just isn't the same. There's something about a mutual attraction; a raw carnal desire that I'm drawn to.

Throughout my life I've only ever had sex with women that I've gotten to know over time. It's not that I'm shy; I love sex and I've been thinking about sex nearly non-stop since I was...born. Okay, maybe not exactly that long, but pretty close. In any event, other than thinking about it, I've never propositioned anyone for sex, as I always thought it wasn't respectful, or maybe I've had in the back of my head that it wouldn't be meaningful if there wasn't a deep connection to my partner.

So, obviously, I must be trying to change my way of thinking on that matter.

I loved reading your ad. Every six months or so, I'll browse the personals, but I never have written to anyone because I never see an ad that sounds like anything I'd be interested in...until today. I can't imagine a more perfect scenario. I know exactly where you're coming from and I think I would be the perfect choice for you to meet up with. A whole fantasy has popped into my mind from the moment I read your ad, and even while I type this, I'm very excited thinking about the possibility. I don't know what sort of physical specimen you're looking for, or what really "turns you on," but I'm sure that I could go a long way towards your need for some exciting sexual experiences. I'm not into anything "fancy" or "weird," just extremely passionate sex. I would, of course, wear condoms, and I am STD free, too.

I don't know if you've already made other plans. Even if you have, maybe you want to meet up with more than one man. I hope you'd like to know more about me. If so, please let me know. I live here and work here, and I could make time to be available to come to you. I'd be happy to describe some of my fantasies to you, send you a picture, and speak with you on the phone. I would be very happy to take this experience for what it is, and I'm extremely eager to learn more about you. You won't find a guy who's more passionate, and that goes a long way!

I'm 6' 1", 34 years old, and in pretty good shape. I work out regularly.

I hope to hear from you soon!

--Jack

From: Karlee
To: Jack
Sent: Sunday, June 26, 2005 2:20 PM
Subject: You Doctor—Me Patient

Essay #2
YOU: Doctor
ME: Patient

I'm a young female virgin coming in for her first gynecological exam. You're a kind, almost fatherly-like, middle aged doctor. You know I am very frightened about this exam, not knowing what it entails. You begin by having me lie down on the bed and slowly undressing me. You tell me that you're going to help me relax by stroking a feather (I'll get one) all over my body. Soft, gentle, tender caresses. My legs are closed tight because I am so afraid. After some time, you begin examining my breasts. Squeezing, circling, and gently pinching my nipples. You tell me everything looks good there, and that a part of the breast exam involves wearing nipple clamps while you do the rest of the exam. My legs are still closed tight. You tell me that the best way for you to proceed is to let you kiss me "down there" so that I can see that this exam won't hurt. Because you are so kind, I open my legs partly for you to come in with your tongue and mouth. (And if I don't explode by then—hey, when I'm aroused, it doesn't take much, so don't spend too long on any one part!) You tell me it's time to insert the tool for the exam and that I will need to spread my legs wide so that you can do the exam. At that point, you reach for my vibrator which is on the night stand in ice water, (YIKES, I can't believe this is me!), and start to probe.

Your turn...

From: Karlee
To: Jack
Sent: Sunday, June 26, 2005 2:19 PM
Subject: And the fantasies began ...

Anyway, as it plays out in my head, I lean around the corner and you're getting ready for a bath. You don't see me, but I'm so turned on that I unzip my pants quietly and begin to touch myself. You go into the bathroom and I follow, looking at you through the open door. You're so attractive (and soapy!) and I try not to touch myself as I watch you, but the way you move your hands over your body is so sensual. You get out of the tub, and start to dry yourself off, when you catch a glimpse of me in the mirror, my (I'm going to go with the term that seems appropriate here) hard cock in my hand. For a second, it's as if we're both caught in the headlights; we both freeze. I'm vulnerable and embarrassed, as are you, yet we're both intrigued and turned on by what's happening. Neither of us moves for a moment. I open the door all the way and walk towards you slowly. You step up to me so we're face to face. I'm breathing very heavy, unsure of what you want. You touch my chest with your fingers and slowly trace down to my leg, then even more slowly you move your hand up to my cock and caress it. I lean in for a kiss, our bodies push together. I lift you up onto the sink and kiss your breasts, massaging them with my hands as my tongue runs over your nipples. You throw your head back and...

Well, you know. You get the general idea.

From: Karlee
To: Jack
Sent: Sunday, June 26, 2005 2:22 PM
Subject: And the People's Choice Award goes to . . .

For the purposes of this fantasy, each of us are married or with someone, we've never met, and we're all vacationing in Vegas.

You've had a long, relaxing day on your vacation. Your partner went off and did his own thing, playing cards, then said he'd be going out late to check out the night life (probably the strip clubs). You spent the day at the pool, enjoying the solitude. Later on, you went to the spa in the hotel and had a massage, followed by a nice meal, and you decide to go to bed. You change into your comfy satin nightdress and get into bed.

I've had a long day, running around the Strip, attending some convention. I wanted to be having fun, but it's been work. All day, I've been exposed to scantily-clad models and half-naked women trying to sell their products. I've been thinking about sex all day, and I know my partner has been out doing her own thing all day, too. I think she won't be back at the hotel before me; she mentioned going to see a show, and I think that I may use the time alone to pleasure myself because I'm so worked up.

I get back to my massive hotel and look at my card key. I wonder why they don't put the numbers on the keys, and struggle to remember what part of the hotel my room is in. I'm pretty sure it's 872. If you'd been standing there, you could've told me that 872 is YOUR room. But, you were already in bed at that time, and we'd never met.

I find 872 and it looks like the right room from the hallway (they ALL look the same) so I dip my card in. It doesn't open. I try again. Nothing. A housekeeper is rolling her cart past me at that moment and I explain that my card doesn't work, and that I don't want to go all the way down to the front desk, and she very kindly opens the door for me.

I step into the room. It's dark; the curtains are drawn. From the light in the hall, I can see that someone's in the bed, so I know it must be my partner. She must've decided to go to bed earlier than I thought. I close the door and take off my shoes and socks, and very quietly undo my belt so I don't disturb her. You rustle slightly, so tired and relaxed, and fall deeper into your sleep.

I remove my pants and put them on the chair. I'm breathing in short excited breaths. I'm so hard. It's strange; perhaps something about the city has made my libido go through the roof. I step out of my boxers and toss them on the chair, and climb into bed next to you.

You're lying on the right side of the bed, facing away from me. I catch a whiff of your perfume—my partner's perfume. I lay on my back, my cock acting as a tent pole with the sheets. I know I can't sleep like this. I figure you've had a hard day and I don't want to disturb you, so I being to stroke myself slowly. I let out a little sigh, and in your sleep you hear it and also make a little noise. I stop. I whisper, "Are you awake?" as softly as I can. You think you're dreaming; you don't recognize the voice...it's that sleepy, floating sensation. You curl your body a bit more and your rear end rubs against my leg.

I trace my fingers along your back, very lightly. I run my hands up and down, caressing your bottom, brushing up against your inner thighs and the back of your knees. I kiss the back of your neck; you feel my hot breath as it gives you goose bumps. My fingers go down between your legs, ever so gently, touching your pussy. I stroke you softly for several moments as you sleep, until I feel you begin to get wetter and wetter.

You are having an amazing dream...it's not about a person; just about the sensations your body is enjoying. You begin to moan quietly.

As my other hand continues to rub your back and legs, I think how soft your skin is. Maybe you're using a new moisturizer? And you seem to be in better shape. How did I not notice this? Maybe I've

273

been working too hard and neglecting my partner, or maybe I'm just finding myself more drawn to her because I'm feeling the charge of Vegas.

I roll onto my side and my cock brushes up against the outside of your pussy. I can feel your moisture. Still, you're asleep, and I don't want to wake you. I wrap my arm around your waist and hold you, but your pelvis has started to rock back and forth, pushing against me.

You push back and my cock slides slowly inside you. Deeper, deeper, it penetrates you until you feel your whole body is filled up. It's so slow, and wet, and I moan in pleasure. You also moan. I move my arms up and caress your breasts as I begin to thrust in and out of you, slowly and firmly. I notice your breasts seem so much fuller and that makes my cock even harder.

You can't sleep any longer and you have a strange sense of disorientation. You were dreaming, feeling enormous pleasure, and now you realize you're being taken from behind. Your partner came home early, you assume, but this isn't anything like making love to him. It's so...wonderful. You think that maybe Vegas had an impact on him, too.

As we both move together, the pace increases. You grab my hand as I cup your breasts. You become aware that things are different. Those hands are stronger, yet gentler. And something is definitely different about the hard flesh that's inside you. It's different in a good way.

I hear you moan and I wonder why your voice doesn't sound the same. Perhaps the dry air has changed the tone of your voice. That seems unlikely. I reach up and stroke your hair. It's totally different. Maybe you spent the day at the hair stylist?

As we both get closer and closer to orgasm, we call out our partners' names. At that moment, we both realize...what do we do? I freeze, my cock still inside you. My hands still hold your breasts. We're still intertwined, spooning together. Neither of us moves. What do I do? What will you do? I can hear my own heart thumping in my chest. You feel it too, along with your own heart.

We stay completely motionless for what seems like hours. Do we both know that we're in the wrong room? It feels so much better than either of us have ever experienced. We try to convince ourselves that maybe we are in the right place, after all...even though we know it isn't true.

I adjust my hips, ever so slightly and excruciatingly slowly. I want to know what will happen. I don't know what will happen, but I have to find out. You stroke my hand lightly, and then squeeze the muscles inside your pussy, grabbing onto my cock. I again start rotating my hips, thrusting in and out of you, gaining speed, going deeper and deeper. Suddenly, I roll you onto your back and push your legs apart as I climb on top of you. The room is dark, but we can see each other for the first time now...again, we pause...but not for long. I lean in to kiss you as I begin to make love to you more and more passionately. Our hands intertwine, and we look into each others' eyes. We're both screaming now, and I feel your body begin to shake and watch your back arch as you get close to cumming...this sends me over the top, I can no longer control myself, and together we reach the heights of ecstasy. The muscles in our bodies constrict, we throw our heads back, and we pull each other closer together. You feel my cock spasm inside you as my warm cum fills you. We collapse together, breathing hard and caressing each other.

From: Karlee
To: Jack
Sent: Sunday, June 26, 2005 2:23 PM
Subject: Wow!

I think I might come back out!

Hope you are well.

Love,
Karlee

From: Jack
To: Karlee

Sent: Monday, June 27, 2005 1:06 PM
Subject: RE: Wow!

MMMmmmmm!

Thanks for sending these...

You coming back out is an excellent idea!

Mmmmm.

No news from this side. Going over the supposedly final version of the book. I'm going to talk to someone who didn't give me a job today and see if I can gain any insight into what I'm lacking. That'll be fun.

So, do you have any new fantasies?

--Jack

From: Karlee
Sent: Tuesday, June 28, 2005 12:07 PM
To: Jack
Subject: RE: Wow!

Hi Jack,

I'm glad you were happy to receive the emails. Two Mmmmm's in one email from you. I liked that!

How was the conversation with the person who overlooked you for the job? I think you're smart to ask for feedback. I know for me, when I do, sometimes I don't like what I hear, but I always learn from it. Perhaps they'll share one tiny piece that will be the start of everything falling into place.

As far as new fantasies...my legs turned mushy and I had flip flops all evening just thinking about you asking. [For a moment, I was thinking it would be nice if my dentist told me this morning that he decided not to charge me for the permanent crown he put on, but I knew that wasn't the type of fantasy you were looking for!]

I don't know if I have NEW fantasies, but I will share some things I fantasize and think about.

I think it would be really fun for me to come out to Vegas again and reenact our first night together. With some similarities and yet different. I think about me being somewhere, in the casino, at a restaurant, by the pool, and we meet. Either an "on purpose" approach, where one of us approaches the other and we start a conversation, or you "accidentally" bump into me and that starts a conversation. We both feel a charge of energy and we begin to talk. As we chat, the electricity increases, our conversation is laced with suggestive innuendos, and at some point I either find reason to invite you to my room, or excuse myself to go to the rest room and slip you my room key. Depending on the scenario, if the second is what we choose, I rush up to my room thinking I have time to take a quick shower before you arrive. I'm in the shower, you know I want you, and you want me, so you take the liberty of letting yourself in, you take your clothes off and you join me in the shower. (Limbs getting weak here and I'm throbbing while I'm typing!) I'm already soapy and we (having a hard time concentrating on this!) embrace each other and kiss passionately, the water streaming over our bodies. You're hard; I kneel and take your throbbing cock into my mouth. You have a hard time standing and I want you to be inside of me, but there's not enough room. There is a built-in seat/ledge. So I stand, perhaps now you're kneeling, and I lean my body into yours so that you can kiss my throbbing pussy. The intensity is overwhelming. I scream as I cum in delight. We turn off the water and quickly dry each other. We've both been able to gain some composure; the intensity has subsided a bit. You take my hand, lead me to the bed, I lie down, you take me into your arms. We both know we want the X position…you turn, I turn, and you enter me.

So, something like that. I'm thinking a variation of the Stranger/Friendly Las Vegas Host could work so well because I wouldn't have the fears that I had last year. Now that I have been thinking about that, a variation of the Las Vegas Host is coming…

You are a Bellman; you are in my room to deliver my luggage, asking if I need anything before you leave. I tell you I think I'm all set, but as I'm saying that my hand goes to my neck and I complain of a kink in my neck from traveling. You share with me that in addition to working for the hotel, you are a masseuse and offer to see if you can get that kink right out. You're so friendly that I decide it couldn't hurt to let you see if you can relax my neck. You tell me it's probably best if you undress me and I lie on the bed.

I'm too aroused…I'll be back.

20 minutes later…

I'm back. I am enjoying my new (I think it's called) Power Rabbit. As I was in bed, I found myself wishing I would have grabbed my cell phone so that I could have called you.

Anyway…

I think I can continue now. Where was I? Oh yeah, about the Bellman… I am starting to notice a pattern. I evidently have fantasy tendencies toward having sex with some sort of "service" man. Be it a Television Repair Guy, the Bellman, a City Host, heck, perhaps even a landscaping guy.

And…other things I think about doing with you…
—Playing one of those erotic board games
—Camping, and making love in the tent.
—I think about you lightly, and I mean ever so lightly, tying my arms and legs to the bedposts, putting a blind-fold on me and using a soft feather to touch my body all over until I beg you to take me.
—I think about either you shopping and surprising me or us shopping together for an outfit (lingerie or otherwise) for me to wear that would drive you totally wild. Then getting home, putting it on and not letting you touch me until you can't stand it anymore.

—Okay, and even once in awhile, I think it would be fun to take some pictures of each other.

Top of the list—you coming to Cleveland and us being in the Jacuzzi together and just being together for more than three hours, period! Waking up in the middle of the night and making love, perhaps going out to dinner or maybe to a movie or a concert, making dinner together and dining by candlelight, going camping, taking a walk in the park...and more lovemaking. (Not in the park necessarily, but when we come back! Unless you want to make love in the park...I'm sure we could find a spot.)

Sooooo, that's how I've spent some of my time thinking since meeting you last year! And more than thinking!!!

Your turn...

Karlee
xoxoxo

From: Karlee
To: Jack
Sent: Monday, August 1, 2005 11:04 AM
Subject: Thinking of you ...

Hi Jack,

I hope you are well! Are you still in Vegas—maybe you've moved to Alaska!!! I haven't written sooner because I know life has been hectic for you. (And perhaps that's an understatement.) Since several weeks have passed now, I thought I'd at least pop in and say hello.

I am eager to hear good news from you. I hope by now you've gotten or are at least close to a job that you will enjoy.

Not too much is new or exciting here. I'll be going back to LA the week of August 15th for another meeting with the seminar company. I go on the road the first week in September. I've been preparing for this new venture in my life.

I'm still enjoying my new bike. I rode 19 miles on Saturday. My goal is to get to at least 25 or 30 before biking season is over for the year.

Looking forward to hearing from you when you get the chance!

Karlee
xoxox

From: Jack
To: Karlee
Sent: Friday, August 19, 2005 11:27 AM
Subject: RE: Thinking of you...

Hi Karlee!

Yeargh! I'm still alive, I suppose. Still in Vegas...though Alaska sounds better. It's been a tough time as I try to figure out what to do with myself.

I keep trying to plow forward on other projects and interviews, but I'm hitting a wall...I spend so many hours every day networking and emailing and filling out ten page applications, and only rarely do I hear anything back at all (like, even, "we got your resume"). When I do hear something back, I have interviews, prepare more documents, and wait and wait and wait.

I honestly believe that if I didn't follow-up repeatedly, I'd never hear anything back from anyone.

So, I'm in the middle of that process again. I applied for a job I thought would be pretty good, but they're so insulated that I can't even find a person's name to follow-up with. I've had a few "tests" and interviews with another company that isn't my first choice, but desperation has set in.

All this is taking its toll on me. I've had bad insomnia for a couple of weeks now, and I'm trying not to get depressed about the whole ordeal. I find it harder to stay on the healthy eating track when things are ultimately frustrating, but I've hung in there so far.

It's especially frustrating because friends and family want to help, but I've tried everything. It's just a matter of time, I guess, but it feels like it's been an eternity of waiting already.

How goes it with you? Are you ready to "hit the road"? What's your schedule going to be? Are you eager for it or dreading it? Did you make your 25 miles on the bike yet? What else is new, good, or exciting?

Sorry I've been out of touch...time seems to be simultaneously crawling and flying by, and it seems like nothing is happening, so I don't have much to report...other than that I wish you were here right now.

--Jack

From: Karlee
To: Jack
Sent: Sunday, August 21, 2005 12:28 PM
Subject: Hi!

Hi Jack,

It was great hearing from you.

I am sorry that you are still having a challenge with finding a job. The whole process sound excruciatingly frustrating and maddening. I have heard many complaints from my friends and colleagues who depend on responses in order to move forward. I know people are busy and sometimes overwhelmed in their positions; that just doesn't seem to be a viable excuse to not take a moment to respond. Even if the places you send resumes or inquiries to would send a one-second response—"not interested, but thanks anyway."

Anyway, add me to the list of those who send an offer to help. But you're right, it's not like those of us who would like to help can just "give" you a job. It seems that it has to be a matter of time or being at the right place at the right time.

Wow—sounds like the stuff with the book has gotten worse. I thought that would be all behind you now.

My trip to LA was good and I'm pretty much all set to go on the road. As far as dreading it or looking forward to it…I'm somewhere in between! I keep telling myself that this will be a good thing and that it will depend on me keeping my perspective and attitude in check. For now, it looks like a good balance of being on the road and being home.

I haven't hit the 25 miles yet on my bike. And for that matter, I haven't even been on it since the day I wrote that I did [I think] the 19 miles. Not necessarily good ones, but I could offer some excuses! Biggest obstacle is the heat. I just don't get up early enough to get out by 6 or 7 am. And lately, by 8:00, it's already 80 plus degrees. This week is supposed to get unseasonably cool, so perhaps I'll make more of an effort. August has been a busy month for me and riding has lost its priority for the moment. I drove to Wisconsin last weekend for my niece's bridal shower. Then last week I was in LA. Friday, I drove to Youngstown for a funeral of a friend's father, and this week I go to Columbus for two days to stay with my niece and nephew while my brother goes to Germany for his job.

Have you been sleeping any better? That certainly doesn't help on top of everything else. Congratulations on being able to keep on the healthy eating track. That seems to be the hardest for me too when things are out of balance.

And as far as me being there with you…I'm all for that. My birthday is coming up (Sept.) and the thought of flying to Las Vegas had entered my mind. The only reason [this time] would be to see you, so I would only consider it if you thought you'd have more time for us to spend together. Not that a few hours isn't worth it . . . but I think because I was just there, I want to be smart about how I spend my money. Thoughts of you and our time together still turn me to mush. I still get the flutters in my belly (as well as elsewhere). Mmmmmm!

Take good care of yourself. Let me know if I can help. The offer for you to stay here is still open!

Karlee
xoxoxox

From: Jack
To: Karlee
Sent: Sunday, August 21, 2005 1:55 PM
Subject: RE: Hi!

Hi Karlee,

Sounds like everything is coming together with your business travel. Waiting until you get used to it before taking on projects while you're home seems like a smart idea. What sort of places will you be traveling to?

Unfortunately, I'm not sleeping any better...it's been rough lately. I also started to have some lower back problems, but I think that's due to a 100% lack of physical activity. So, I'm starting to exercise a little bit...but I know about the problems of working out when it's hot. Still 100 degrees+ here.

I'm still waiting to hear back on one position...I gave them a bunch of writing samples, and then was given a specific "test." I was given two days to complete it, and I did it in a couple of hours. I guess I thought that I could impress them with the fact that I'm able to turn things around quickly. On the other hand, I imagine that they won't look at anything for a few weeks, so that may have been wasted effort. Oh well.

I'd definitely be up for a visit. I just need to find some time. My hope is that I'll eventually get an offer and have a month or so to get my life adjusted, move, and have some free time. Barring that...there's always winning the lottery!

We should hook up those cameras again someday!

--Jack

From: Karlee
To: Jack
Sent: Sunday, August 21, 2005 7:43 PM
Subject: RE: Hi!

Hi Jack,

Sorry to hear you're not sleeping any better. I can't help but think that if I were there I could have the opportunity to exhaust you enough to a better night's sleep.

As far as places I'll be traveling to, so far it's Indianapolis, Baltimore, Hartford, Miami in November (which will be nice), and Michigan to name a few.

I'm am 100% up for the webcam visit! I am already excited about it—just let me know what works for you.

Tonight I tried to send you a photo via my cell phone, but I got a message that said something like "Invalid address" so I'm guessing you're not set up to receive photos on your phone. It was only one of my breasts and you've seen those, so maybe you're not missing much!

Hope you hear some good news this week!

Karlee
xoxox

From: Jack
To: Karlee
Sent: Wednesday, September 7, 2005 11:12 AM
Subject: I'm alive!

Hi Karlee!

Yikes. Sorry I haven't written in so long. I got your card and your message...I've been non-stop for the last couple of weeks. The good news is, it hasn't been all bad! The bad news is...there hasn't really been any good news.

I've been talking a lot with a company in Portland. Phone interview (which didn't seem to go especially well) followed by a submission of writing samples, followed by another interview on the phone, followed by a request for a writing sample, then a request for a really vague "writing test," followed by a really long phone interview that went well. I followed that up with a thank you letter that included a few ideas for their project and the guy loved the ideas. So, he set up an interview in Portland. Except, he took this entire week off. Then, another big-wig at the company called yesterday because he realized the policy is to have two different people give phone interviews before flying anyone out, so that's today. Anyway, the project sounds pretty interesting.

I've also been looking for places in Portland, just in case. It's ridiculously expensive. Honestly, I don't believe I could ever own a home there...$350,000 seems to be the low end out there. I'm also not sure I want to live in the heart of the city, and I'm definitely sure that I don't want to commute for an hour per day—especially during crunch time when I'd be working 18 hour days.

But, those are the kind of problems to have. And then, I got another call out of the blue from another company I'd applied to months and months ago, and never heard anything from. They're in Madison, WI (closer to Cleveland!) and they spoke to me about a job in the game industry.

That went well too, and I would hope to hear something more from them this week or next, I would guess. Although, they tend to run very hot or very cold...and never call back.

I'm feeling a little bit of optimism for the first time in months, but I'm very worried how I'll feel if neither of these comes through. I'm guessing it won't be good.

So, between doing little jobs to stay alive and repeated interviews and new applications and looking for places to live, it's been hectic. But, there's a chance now that I could wind up in the Midwest, or maybe at least going out there for an interview for a couple of days.

That's the news with me. How are you doing? What's new? What's good?

--Jack

From: Karlee
To: Jack
Sent: Sunday, September 11, 2005 6:52 PM
Subject: RE: I'm alive!

Hi Jack,

Yay! I'm so glad to hear you're still alive! And I was also happy to
hear that you have a couple of promising opportunities in the works.
Portland sounds good, other than you being even farther away from
Cleveland! It appears that the company is excited about what you
would "bring to the table." I certainly hope they realize your
brilliance and how lucky they would be to have you.

I've been to Portland and I've heard a lot of good things about the
city. The only downside I hear is pertaining to the weather and I have
a sense that it wouldn't bother you. As far as owning a $350,000
home—you never know! If you do end up in Portland, I hope you
find something that's reasonable and that you don't have to spend
tons of time commuting. Madison, Wisconsin sounds good, too!

I hope you're still feeling optimistic. Yes, it has been a long time
coming. If you end up coming to the Midwest, even if it's just for an
interview, that would be great!

As far as me…I was in Indianapolis and Columbus, Indiana last week.
All-in-all, the week went very well. I was pleasantly surprised. I'm
home now for a few weeks and go back out the first week of
October. I'll be out eight days in October and for ten days in
November.

I had the opportunity to go to Miami Beach with a friend a couple of
weeks ago. It was fun and I now know another part of the country I
definitely would NOT want to live. Way too hot and muggy for me.
Now I know what people mean when they talk about Las Vegas being
dry heat. (Although I remember a friend of mine once said that an
oven is dry heat and she still wouldn't put her head in one!)

Not too much new. Now that I have my first week behind me, I plan
to spend this few weeks enjoying my time at home. I have a friend

coming to visit me from Minneapolis. She'll be here for three days the weekend of the 24th. My birthday is next weekend, although I don't have anything planned for that.

I lost my beta fish, Vegas. I made a tough decision and practiced euthanasia. According to my amateur diagnosis with the help of one of the clerks at the pet store, it appears that he (she?) developed a bacterial infection. Started with losing the top fin. Little by little, he started to lose his color and vibrancy. Then every day he just looked worse and worse and it was starting to give me an upset stomach. I decided since he was probably going to die anyway that I would (hopefully) put him out of his misery.

As far as what's good...YOU! I was thinking today that now since the evenings are getting cooler, it's almost time to think Jacuzzi again! Although I'm becoming doubtful about an official christening with you, I'm still mildly optimistic!

I look forward to hearing from you again soon!

I miss you.

Love,
Karlee

From: Jack
To: Karlee
Sent: Friday, September 16, 2005 10:54 AM
Subject: RE: I'm alive!

Hi Karlee!

Here's the latest news...

Nothin'.

I'm hoping that by the end of the day, I'll have heard something from someone. I was supposed to have flown out for an interview this week to Portland, but they pushed things back. They've given me, to date, five writing tests. Last I heard they want me to do something to one of the samples, but they didn't follow up.

I had a long conference call interview the other day with another company. I don't like interviewing on a conference call. In my experience, it's always very awkward—three or more people in a room don't really listen to what you're saying. They've scheduled a block of time, and they all sit together, and you know they're going down the list, giving 30-45 minutes to each candidate. They read prepared questions, and no one seems into it...so I don't think I nailed that one. Supposedly I should hear something today, but...doesn't seem likely.

I think that by October 1, I'm going to make some serious plans. Everyone I've dealt with professionally for...oh...at least three years has just dragged things on. I'll give it a couple of more weeks, but I'm not going to wait around for six months to hear about any of these jobs. I guess as of October 1, I'm going to make some kind of plan. Don't know what it will be, but I can't take this anymore. I know I've been in that boat for a long time...but it's really time to jump overboard.

Less than three weeks. Then, a plan. That's my plan. See, I've been so stressed and scrambling so hard just to keep my head above water that I don't have the time or energy to think about good stuff, like you! That's no good. Gotta change.

--Jack

From: Karlee
To: Jack
Sent: Sunday, September 18, 2005 9:29 AM
Subject: Hi!
("My Birthday is Friday" photo attached)

Hi Jack,

I was happy to hear from you. Sorry that you weren't [yet] able to share some exciting news regarding a job. Did you ever hear anything by end of day on Friday? Seems like the company in Portland is definitely interested. Five writing tests—that's a lot1 And perhaps another interview. Might just need to wait a bit longer.

Wow—sounds like you're serious regarding a plan by/on October 1. It will be interesting to see what you come up with. Do you have any ideas as of yet? What have you been considering? Back to Chicago, or perhaps Cleveland? (!) I should probably be more optimistic and supportive that the job in Portland or another one will come through before that. But, I do agree with your realization that it might be time to get out of "that boat" and into another one (like on Lake Erie!)

My birthday is not actually Friday, per the attached photo. It was yesterday, but I remembered how much fun it was to send that photo to you last year (and the one I received in return!). I thought I'd send it again—just in case you haven't seen me for awhile! Wouldn't want you to forget what I look like!

I had a nice celebration. Friday night I went out with family and friends and last night went to see a movie with two friends and then to the Cheesecake Factory for dinner. If we could have been together, we could have made love 47 times—one for each year. Okay, so maybe not 47 times; maybe just the 4 or 7. Okay, one would have been wonderful! Mmmmmm!

Not too much is new. I've been working on projects around here. Getting ready to be gone a couple of weeks in October and November. In addition to going to Michigan and Connecticut for the seminar company, I'll also be going to Wisconsin for a few days for my niece's wedding.

Have you had a chance to do anything fun for yourself? I hope you have.

I'm looking forward to a telephone or webcam visit soon!

Love,
Karlee
xoxoxox

From: Jack
To: Karlee
Sent: Sunday, September 18, 2005 12:28 PM
Subject: RE: Hi!

HAPPY BIRTHDAY!

I'm the world's worst person with birthdays. Someday, I'm going to use a computer calendar, and that will all change. But, what can you do? I often forget my own birthday...it's a family tradition.

I have a bad feeling that none of the jobs will be offered to me. Had a talk with the first guy I spoke with in Portland...he is fighting for me, but the other guy didn't like my writing samples. The first guy, by the way, doesn't like the taste/writing of the second guy, which brings up the frequent problem I've hit in getting writing gigs...it's entirely subjective. Though I'm willing to "sell out" and shoot for the lowest common denominator, I think only really good stuff comes from being true to yourself. But, we'll see. I'm doing another pass this weekend...although, I'm aware that trying to overcome someone's negative first impression of your work is often futile.

Well, I was very happy indeed to get that photo again! I've been so wrapped up and stressed out about where I'm going/what I'm doing that I haven't spent nearly enough time thinking about the great things in life...like you!

That photo instantly reminded me, so I took a little break to do some...remembering.

I would like to chat/webcam soon. Unfortunately my week is fairly miserable. How's your Tuesday? Will you be around in the afternoon, or will you be off in some exotic far-off land?

In any event, I'll check back...it would be very nice to see you! It would, of course, be infinitely better to do that in person...I'm working on it.

--Jack

From: Karlee
To: Jack
Sent: Monday, September 19, 2005 11:37 AM
Subject: RE: Hi!

Hi Jack,

I hope some good news came through this weekend regarding a job.
I agree with you when it comes to writing styles. Subjective for sure,
and I think even more so today with there being so many new rules
and so few people really knowing the "old" rules. I am confident that
someday soon someone will see the brilliant side of you! And then
there will be someone (besides me), saying, "We want this man!"

Thanks for the birthday wishes. Glad you enjoyed seeing the photo
again and that it prompted you to take a well deserved break.
Tuesday afternoon works for me for a visit. No exotic destinations
for this week.

See you soon! I hope I can figure out my webcam again. I haven't
used it since the last time we visited.

xoxxo

From: Karlee
To: Jack
Sent: Friday, September 30, 2005 12:57 PM
Subject: Hi!

Hi Jack,

How goes it? Any news yet? Good news only, I hope.

I'm getting ready to go on the road again. I leave on Sunday for Ann
Arbor and Troy, Michigan for the week. I've enjoyed my time at
home and I'm actually looking forward to being on the road again.

I was trying to get a few more bike rides in this week, but I did
something to goof up the left side brake and I need to take it to a

shop to have it adjusted. So at this point I'm not sure if I'll have an opportunity to go out again this year. At least next year I'll have an earlier start since I already have the bike. I'm also planning to buy a rack for my car so that I don't have to take it apart to put into my car. I live really close to the parkway, so sometimes I just ride it down there. There's another path I like better, and to get to that, I prefer to drive the car.

Since it's been a couple of weeks since we last visited, I feel like I should have more to write about. (Maybe by the time I return, you'll be telling me that you've decided to take me up on my offer to live here…then THAT will be some excitement!) Now that I think about it, I just remembered…I was in my closet today looking for a Michigan map and came across my Canyon Ranch Spa brochure. I immediately had one of those flip flops in my stomach… remembering you standing behind me, showing me the brochure… Even as I type, I can feel your body up against mine and your breath on my neck. Mmmm—Mmmmm!

Karlee

From: Jack
To: Karlee
Sent: Saturday, October 1, 2005 11:25 AM
Subject: RE: Hi!

Hello Sexy Karlee...

Argh! Why me? There is some news. Some bad; some not so good. I think I may be cursed.

One company called me back and told me I was not going to be getting the job. That was bad, but I think they're the first company I've dealt within the last...say two years (?) to have the courtesy to let me know that. Of course, the way they did it wasn't exactly well-executed. I had an email saying that they'd tried to reach me via phone but couldn't, and would I please call them right away. But, at least I know.

As for the other company...I had another phone interview with another person. This fellow is taking over for the second guy I interviewed with, who apparently has left the company. We had a long chat and I pushed for information. Apparently, they really like me, but they didn't think I had the best writing sample. I pointed out that I sent another writing test to their specifications, but I don't know if anyone looked at it. So we talked, and now the first guy is going to call me again on Monday. They need to hire someone right away...they've told me that their production schedule is stalled by not having a person...and I get the impression that they don't think I have the best samples...so I'm not sure why they keep talking to me. Or, why they don't fly me out to meet me. But it keeps dragging on and on and on...

I'm trying to get moving on what my next (desperate) step will be. I think I'm pulling the plug on Monday on this job...it's felt like it's not going to happen for a while now. I have applied for a number of other jobs, and I have to make my exit plan in case none of those come through. That's been continually pushed back, thanks to the single threads of hope, and I've got to get realistic. Let's see. In this particular industry, I've had many interviews with several companies, and the trend is phone interview, writing sample, phone interview, writing sample, wait a month, repeat, then hear nothing. So, time for plan B, whatever that will be.

Your trip sounds like a fun trip. Let me know what you think of Ann Arbor. I thought about moving there at some point.

Mmmmmmm...the Spa brochure and me standing behind you. I remember that like it was yesterday! Much more fun thinking about that than work!

--Jack

From: Karlee
To: Jack
Sent: Friday, October 7, 2005 12:31 PM
Subject: Good news yet?

Hello Hot Jack...

Well, I'm back at home after my week on the road. All-in-all it was a good trip, and I'm really glad to be home. As far as Ann Arbor, I really didn't see much of it. I was not at all close to the U of M campus or what would be the heart of the city. Troy was very nice; the city is only 50 years old. Quite a different feel than Cleveland. They have a beautiful mall that has two anchor stores on one side of the street and two on the other. It was connected by a moving skywalk that crossed over six lanes of traffic. Very upscale, even for my taste! Definitely nice though.

I don't think you're cursed, yet I can see how you could be feeling that way. Now that almost a week has gone by…any news? It sounded like the one company is interested in you, even if they had some disagreement on your writing sample. Was it the company in Portland that called you back?

I hope you hear some good news soon. You've got to be close! No one should have to go through the process that you've been dealing with for so long.

I am sad that you have not been able to enjoy the things you enjoy. This will change soon. However, knowing you haven't played poker for months could be good news for me. You see, I have a fantasy about us playing strip poker. But, my knowledge (and skills) in playing are extremely limited. I always figured you would win immediately and—poor me, I'd be there all naked and you'd have all your clothes on. You not playing for a while might give me a chance! (Of course, if I ever have the opportunity to play strip poker with you—I know either way—it will be a very pleasurable experience! And, I'll be a winner whether I win or not!)

xoKarlee

From: Jack
To: Karlee
Sent: Saturday, October 8, 2005 12:06 PM
Subject: RE: Good news yet?

Hi Karlee,

That shopping center sounds pretty fancy. There was some talk about making the "new" biggest mall in the country about an hour from where I grew up. I think I'm easily impressed by big sprawling malls, but that fades within a few minutes. That's why I never went to the Mall of America, but some people plan an entire vacation around it.

I'm still going back at forth with the company in Portland. I think they're trying to line me up for a position that is supposed to open up in the beginning of next year.

But...I know they're already four months behind schedule, so it seems unlikely they'll be ready then. We'll see. I have another phone interview with a different company on Monday for a job that I don't think I'm even remotely qualified for...but it will be my second phone interview, and I won't argue if they give me the job.

Hmmm...Poker...this is an interesting fantasy! But, you know, any advantage I have is in the long haul. One-on-one poker has a lot of fluctuation due to luck.

Of course, we could just deal out two hands and see who has the better hand; winner gets a piece of clothing! Mmmm. Much better than casino poker.

I'll have to give more thought to fantasies...been focused only on survival for too long. Actually, you and me on a deserted island...mmmm...

--Jack

From: Karlee
To: Jack
Sent: Saturday, October 15, 2005 4:19 PM
Subject: Hi!

Hi Jack,

I hope you are doing well.

How goes it? What's the latest? Have you moved to Portland? How was the phone interview with the other company on Monday?

I had a good week in Connecticut. Two really good groups; one in Waterbury and one in Hartford. When I left yesterday, the people in Connecticut were on their eighth consecutive day of rain. The sun was out when I left Cleveland on Monday and I never saw it again until this morning.

I'm home now for two weeks, with the exception of a trip to Wisconsin for my niece's wedding next Saturday. She's the oldest and it's the first wedding in the next generation so we're all very excited.

You and I on a deserted island sounds good! Heck, being anywhere with you sounds good!

I've been horny today. Perhaps you can feel the energy from me spending a lot of time looking at and touching your pictures. I was thinking about us being in my hotel the first night and you saying something like, "Maybe it would help if I kissed you." Then you stood up and leaned across and lifted my hair and kissed me ever so gently on the neck. Why do thoughts of those little things still send quivers through my body? It's not fair!

Karlee

From: Jack
To: Karlee
Sent: Monday, October 17, 2005 7:27 PM
Subject: RE: Hi!

Hi Karlee!

Argh! I just don't get it. I'm at a total loss. The latest is this: I had the phone interview, which was a three-on-one conference call. I thought it went poorly. It probably didn't help that my patience for these things is quickly dwindling, so I took an early opportunity to point out that if the set of skills they were looking for was (B), I wasn't their guy.

But, if they wanted someone with skills (A), who could certainly learn (B) in about a month, they'd do no better than me. But, if I were them, I'd hire someone with the (B) skills. They said they wanted (A) and (B). I thought it didn't go particularly well...I had no read on them whatsoever, so I assumed I didn't get it. However, I've heard that they've contacted a couple of my references, so I'm not sure what to think. No word from them last week at all.

I did get a call to fly to Portland for another company, but...I'm not sure if that's happening either. They asked me for dates; I got back to them immediately...no reply. I followed up, they changed the dates...no reply. I followed up again...they passed me to someone else...no reply. I picked dates, times, flights...was asked to confirm. I did...no reply. Now I'm supposed to be out there next Sunday through Tuesday. I've asked repeatedly to know what my interview schedule will be. They said it would only be part of one day. Which one? I don't know. No reply. WHAT IS GOING ON?!

On top of that, today came another rent increase from my horrible apartment complex. They raise the rent every month. I have to give them notice by November 1 to get out of here. I would like nothing more...but I have nowhere to go. I had some lead on a horrible little job in my home town...maybe it's time to pull those strings. At least I'd be closer to Cleveland!

Ah well. I have no idea what to try next. Maybe I'll get lucky and something will come through before November 1, but it's getting to be time to try desperate measures. Argh.

>>*Why do thoughts of those little things still send quivers through my body? It's not fair!*

Thoughts of our first night together send quivers though my body. Well, more like some other reaction.

We should webcam again soon...

--Jack

From: Karlee
To: Jack
Sent: Tuesday, October 18, 2005 7:13 PM
Subject: Hi!

Hi Jack,

I almost called you back tonight. I was even more aroused after we hung up. I kept thinking about our webcam visit and how I wanted more! Can I possibly be the same woman who was terrified to even go out and buy the camera? And now look; you've got me hooked! Of course the fact that I played that deserted island fantasy in my head with quite a bit more detail didn't help!

I hope you hear some good news yet this week.

By the way, how was your shower? Mmmmmm? It's been way too long since I've had the opportunity to wash your hair! I love your hair and running my fingers through it.

Good night,
xoxox

From: Karlee
To: Jack
Sent: Wednesday, October 26, 2005 7:10 AM
Subject: How was Portland?

Hi Jack,

I hope you're doing well. How was the trip to Portland? Was there a trip to Portland!? After the rigmarole you went through the week before, maybe you didn't even go.

My niece's wedding was fun, fun, fun. She looked absolutely beautiful. I got home Sunday night. The trip went well. I flew from Cleveland to Midway and picked up a rental car and drove the rest of the way to my sister's, which is about 40 miles north of Milwaukee.

I'm home this week and head back on the road Monday. First week of the month is Baltimore and Annapolis. The second week is Ft. Pierce and Miami, Florida. Then a big trip the third week to Lima, Ohio. I hope by the time I go to Florida that things will have settled down from the hurricane. The news said it will probably be a couple of weeks before things are back to normal.

Looking forward to hearing your update. Hope you've had some good news.

Love,
Karlee

From: Jack
To: Karlee
Sent: Thursday, October 27, 2005 11:19 AM
Subject: RE: How was Portland?

Hi Karlee!

I'm back!

I did go to Portland, in fact. I didn't have my appointment confirmed until the day before, but I did go. It was an interesting trip. It turned out that I didn't have a reserved seat on the plane....and it was totally full. I got there two hours early, but apparently the company didn't pick a seat or something. Anyway, they booted about 8 people off the plane (free tickets for them) and I made it. When I got to the hotel, I found that in addition to giving me an extra day on the plane, they had made an extra night's reservation at the hotel... something I had quite specifically NOT asked them to do. I'd planned on spending one day in Portland and the second night in Redmond (about 1/2 hour away) so that I could spend the full day there. But, they made a reservation for two nights. When I told the hotel I'd only need one, they said that it was less than 24 hours of cancellation notice (which wouldn't have been a problem if my plane hadn't been delayed), so that I would be charged for both nights.

The folks I met with were very casual. It was a chance to have lunch and see their facilities...no pressure, no interview, just hanging out and getting to know folks. That was nice. I also got to see Redmond which I enjoyed a lot, but was crazy with traffic. I got stuck for 20 minutes on a highway at 2pm on a Tuesday. No accident...just normal traffic.

Anyway, it was something. I told both people that if they wanted to do something with me, I wanted/needed to know ASAP. If I don't hear something before 10/31, I'll be locked in for another month here (through December 31). If neither of these pan out, I assume I will be stuck in Vegas through the end of the year, since most people stop hiring soon. So, I'm looking at other options (Cleveland, too!) and with any luck something will pan out.

I'll keep you posted if there's any news from these meetings...they say two weeks...I asked for one week...I imagine it will be four weeks or more, given how things have gone so far.

--Jack

From: Karlee
To: Jack
Sent: Friday, November 4, 2005 8:16 PM
Subject: I'm hot for you!

Hi Jack,

I hope all is well with you. I just returned from my week on the road. I am glad to be home. On my return flight, there was an annoying [to me] guy sitting across the aisle that couldn't seem to sit still. I just kept closing my eyes, playing a montage in my head of our (you and me—not the guy across the aisle) times together. A lot of our first night together, thinking about how you helped towel me off when I came out of the shower and then when you lifted me up onto the bathroom countertop and put your mouth on me and I came in about two minutes. Those thoughts were much more fun than dealing with the fidgety guy. But the bad news is that I arrived home all hot and bothered and you're not here! So I'm writing to you instead to at least feel like I'm talking to you!

Thanks for the update on the Portland trip. Sounded like it was part productive and part frustrating. Have you heard anything yet? I know you said you thought it might be several weeks. I was thinking that since almost a week has gone by, you might have some good news.

I don't have much else to write about since I was on the road all week. Baltimore was nice. One evening, I took a walk from the hotel down to the Inner Harbor area and had dinner. The weather was great—70 degrees and sunny! I didn't see much of Annapolis. How about this—in January the client has me going to Fargo, North Dakota!!! Maybe that would be a good trip for you to take with me, since I haven't been booked for the Caribbean yet! Ha!

I'm home tomorrow and the get on a plane again on Sunday for the week in Florida.

Hope you have a great weekend!

xoxxo

From: Jack
To: Karlee
Sent: Sunday, November 6, 2005 11:51 AM
Subject: RE: I'm hot for you!

Welcome back, although you've probably already left again. I can sympathize with your struggling with annoying people on the plane.

I was thinking about that whole scenario of us and our first night together (and the wrong room) just the other day myself! Mmmmm....we need to revisit those SOON.

I have news, but it's all bad. I pushed both companies to get back to me, and on Friday (within two minutes of one another) I got two rejection emails. I guess the "good" news is that one of the companies said that a producer wanted to know if I'd be interested in a different project...which he'd be hiring for in EIGHT OR NINE MONTHS. Yeah. Swell. I'm sure they'll call. I'll be waiting by the phone.

So, there are a few other things I've got out there, but nothing I feel confident about. I was looking through old positions I'd applied for and found one that had offered to send me an on-line "test" before a formal interview, but they never sent it, so I asked them again.

Nothing else in the frying pan. I guess I may do a trip back to see my parents and see if there are any jobs there...maybe I can find a way to incorporate a trip to Cleveland somehow? What's your schedule like in December?

I hope you enjoy Florida...everything should be back to normal by now, with any luck. I'll write more soon...going to go panic for a while, and come up with plan B. Oh wait, I'm on to plan F by now...it's time for plan G.

--Jack

From: Karlee
To: Jack
Sent: Wednesday, November 9, 2005 6:26 PM
Subject: Greetings from Miami!

Hi Jack,

How are you? I was sorry to read the news about the job—both jobs. Both gone within two minutes of each other. Must have been a fun day. Have you received the on-line test from the company you spoke about?

A visit from you in December sounds wonderful! I hope we can make it work. I don't have my exact schedule with me. I know I go out the last week of November which carries into the first week of December. The second week I'm out for two days and the same for the third week. I think my last day of training for the month of December is the 16th. Then I'm home until sometime in January. Plenty of time for us to re-visit the Wrong Room fantasy! (As well as any others we may want to add!) That's of course assuming I let you leave the Jacuzzi! I've got the flutters just thinking about it!

Mmmmmm!

Good night,
xoKarlee

From: Jack
To: Karlee
Sent: Thursday, November 10, 2005 3:09 PM
Subject: RE: Greetings from Miami!

Hi Karlee...

Well, this has been a rough week. I didn't hear back about the on-line test...it's yet another company that varies between rush-rush-rush and "we'll talk to you again in two months."

Then I sent an application for a tech writing job. I didn't have my relevant samples (because I did them 10 years ago). It's another local job.

I'm not sure what I'm going to do, but things seem bleak. I suppose I've missed out on enough jobs that it's affected my confidence. I've never had this much trouble, especially getting jobs I don't even really want!

Ah well. I'm glad you have email. I had a very strange fantasy about you.

I was thinking I'd call you while you're down in Florida, maybe on a break from work. I'd tell you to go to the restroom in the hotel, and enter a stall. Then I'd have you pull down your panties and step out of them. Then slip out of your skirt. Next I'd have you unbutton your blouse, and remove your bra, so that you'd be completely naked inside the stall of the restroom. Then I'd have you touch yourself, while I did the same, and listened to you on the phone. Afterwards, you'd get dressed and resume your work...I liked the thought of you being totally exposed for me.

Then I thought I'd do this a few more times. And then one day, I'd secretly show up to the town you were in, and be waiting outside the ladies' room. Once you said you were completely nude, I'd come in and knock on your stall door. You'd hear my voice, and let me in. I'd scoop you in my arms and kiss you, then remove my pants and slide my cock into your wet pussy. After making you cum, I'd go up to your room and wait for you to finish work, and we'd make love all night. The Right Room fantasy!

Hmmm...Anyway, despite all the frustrations of other stuff, I've been thinking about you, and it would be great to see you again...SOON!

--Jack

From: Karlee
To: Jack
Sent: Friday, November 11, 2005 8:18 PM
Subject: I'm back in Ohio!

Hi Jack,

Sorry to hear you had a rough week.

Don't give up! I can certainly understand how having all of these disappointments could affect your confidence. I hope you're still able to recognize and remember all of your positive attributes and how any organization would be lucky to have you. You are smart, intelligent, and bright, you work hard, and I'm guessing you are extremely knowledgeable in the fields in which you have experience. These traits will be valuable to an organization eventually. As to why it's taking so long, who knows.

Thank you for sharing the fantasy with me; I love the idea of a Right Room fantasy! (Not that there was anything wrong with the Wrong Room fantasy!) Of course as I read it, I immediately turned to mush. You still have that very strong affect on me. I love the idea of you secretly showing up when I'm out of town. (It's not too late for the Lima, Ohio trip!) I thought about you being with me when I was in Miami; the room I had was very nice and it had a wonderful king bed. Of course I think about you being with me no matter where I am. And after reading your fantasy, I started to let my mind wander in the direction of other things that could have happened in Miami…

After training all day, I decide I'm going to take advantage of the warm temperature and go to the pool. I'm changing from my work clothes into my bathing suit, and once my clothes are off, I think about how fun it would be to go skinning dipping with you. But you're not in Miami—you're in Las Vegas. So I decide I probably will skip that. Perhaps I'll just swim laps instead and that will help me to burn off some of my sexual tension that has come up thinking about skinning dipping with you.

I take the elevator down to the 7th floor and go through the doors to the pool area. No one is there. I wonder if the pool might be closed. I check the sign. It's open until 6:00 p.m.; it's just after 5:00. I figure that swimming in November is most likely to be done only by tourists from the north. How often do I get to be by a pool in November? I decide to stay, even though I'm a little bit leery of the fact that I'm the only one out by the pool. I lie down on the lounge chair and sigh with a feeling of relaxation as the sun warms my skin. Mmmmmm. I immediately am reminded of how aroused I was as I left my room. "If only Jack were here…" I feel myself throbbing as I imagine you rubbing sunscreen all over my body. You're so gentle and erotic with your hands. You intentionally slide a finger or two inside my suit as you're covering my inner thighs with the lotion. You go far inside the top of my suit as you're covering my chest and ever so gently come in contact with my breasts. You gently pinch my nipples. Now I'm hot. I can't tell if it's from the sun or my mind wandering. Doesn't matter. I decide I need to cool off. The thought of swimming naked comes to my mind again. "What the heck," I say to myself. No one is around. It's starting to get dark by now. I stand and stretch, feeling totally relaxed. As I start to ever so slowly slide my bathing suit off, I notice the silhouette of a person near the window on an upper level floor of the office building across the street. "Could they be watching me?" I ask myself. I tell myself that even if they were looking in this direction, they wouldn't be able to see that much from the distance. Then I decide to imagine that it's you up in that office building. I adjust my body so that, just in case you can see me, you see all of me. My suit is off now, and I stretch again. The sun feels so good on my naked body; I want to just enjoy the feel of the heat on my breasts. I touch my breasts, imagining that my hands are your hands. You squeeze gently at first; then you take one in your mouth. I lift one of my breasts to my mouth and suck. I want to feel it in your mouth; I need to have your mouth on my breast. Then I remember I'm outside and in public. Embarrassed, I jump into to the pool and try to hide, just in case anyone did see me. The warm water feels heavenly on my naked body. I'm shaking with desire. I swim to a part of the pool where there seems to be very little light. I need to self-pleasure to release the tension and the throbbing in my pussy, but I have to be careful. Someone could be watching. I prop one of my arms up on the side of the pool. I'm in the shallow end. I take my other hand and put it between my legs. I'm wet with moisture. A different kind of wet than the water. I lean my head back and imagine that you are there with me. I move my finger in and out of my throbbing pussy. It feels so good because I'm imagining that it is really you in between my legs. I'm moaning now, so between the sounds that I'm making and the humming of the filter in the pool, I don't hear you step into the water. It WAS you in the building across the street and now you are in the pool with me, naked. Just as I'm about to cum, you grab me by my waist, take me into your arms and move my hand from between my legs and gently thrust your rock-hard cock into me. I scream in delight, as I am brought to ecstasy over and over again.

Yes, it seems like a good time to talk about seeing you again SOON!

Karlee

From: Jack
To: Karlee
Sent: Saturday, November 12, 2005 10:23 AM
Subject: RE: I'm back in Ohio!

Hello again!

Well, all I can say is WOW. Mmmmmmmmmmm.

That email certainly got me worked up. My heart is beating...I'm breathing heavily...and my cock was so hard that I had to pull down my shorts and let it out...I thought it could burst through, like the Incredible Hulk.

Hmmmm. You'll have to keep me up to date with your travel schedule!

I was going to write about other things, but now I can't think about anything other than watching you by the pool, then joining you. You know how to push all the right buttons with me.

Okay. Let' see...I did take the programming test. I was supposed to get there at 3:30. It's a half-hour drive. At 12:30, I got a call from someone else that wanted to give me a test for another job. I'd spoken to them two months ago, and they never sent the test. I followed up and they asked when I would want to take it. I listed several days and asked them to let me know. I guess they missed the "let me know" part because at 12:30 they said, "An email is on the way. You have three hours to do the test." Except I had less than two hours because I needed to shower and get to another job test, but...I didn't want to lose out on an opportunity.

The three-hour test seemed to go well. I got it done in about an hour and a half, which was good, because a maintenance guy showed up to fix my toilet (I don't have fantasies about the maintenance guy seeing ME in the shower...) I rushed down for my written test and...

Well, I rang the buzzer and a woman opened the door. I told her I had an appointment at 3:30. She asked, "Who are you with?" and I said "Myself. It's a job interview/programming test." She asked who I was going to see. I said "John." She seemed to have no idea who or what I was talking about.

I said that maybe I had the wrong place, but eventually she found him. This office was COMPLETELY EMPTY—imagine a giant central workspace with NOTHING IN IT, except for one of their slot machines, all the way against the back wall, and a vacuum cleaner in the corner. New office, apparently.

I took the test. Eight questions. Question one: I had no idea. None.

Didn't know what they were referring to. Question two: I knew what they were referring to, but I haven't done programming of any serious nature for...four years? I had to transcribe motion from a straight line to a circle, and there's a formula to do that, but I couldn't remember it. It'd take me thirty seconds to find the formula on Google, but that wasn't an option. So, I wrote what I'd do, then came up with a working solution. The other questions were all over the place...some were ridiculously easy, others just random trivia. More importantly, I was listening to people talk as I was working, and it doesn't sound like it would be a great place for me. Weird conflicts already exist.

I gave him the test and said I didn't know the first question. He tried to explain to me what he was looking for without giving it away, and I couldn't get it. So he told me what he was looking for, and I didn't know the answer. I think he wanted me to spend the time I had remaining to do the best I could, but...I dunno...perhaps this isn't helping my situation, but my tolerance for these kinds of tests are pretty low. I'm a grown-up. I'm happy to tell him what I can do or can't do. The fact is that I had a cell phone and could have gotten all the info I needed to get a perfect score with one call, or five minutes on the net. What does that test? I suppose the most interesting thing about the job is that it would involve travel to the UK for a month...but the rest of it...well, I won't be sad if I don't get it. "What was Napoleon's favorite color?" I dunno. Can I look it up?

No. You must know it. Ah well.

This week was like being back in college...except without sex or fun. So, the timing of your email was very good....it turned things around!

--Jack

From: Karlee
To: Jack
Sent: Sunday, November 13, 2005 1:43 PM
Subject: Mmmmmm!

Hi Jack,

You sent the Right Room fantasy and that got me all worked up. Then I sent you the pool fantasy and got you worked up. Now I'm worked up again thinking about you being worked up. I keep thinking about you being hard and having to pull your shorts down. I immediately had an image of me being on my knees between your legs, helping to get your shorts off and then taking you in my mouth. Mmmmmm! I've self-pleasured twice since receiving your email, and even as I'm writing this, I still have an uncomfortable throbbing—I can't seem to make it go away on my own! Can you help me? Perhaps I need to see a doctor. No, can't think about that or that will bring on another fantasy!

Wow—a lot of tests for these job interviews. I can see why you felt like you were in college again last week. It will be interesting to find out what you hear from the slot machine people. What's happening this week? Any new leads or follow up?

It's been nice to be home for a few days to get caught up on mail, etc. Last night I went out with some friends to listen to a band. I was skeptical since I have such a low tolerance for loud music, but the band was actually very good.

I was going through my mail and had an advertisement from the Mirage. The outside of the self-mailer read, "Special offer enclosed." I opened it and on the inside it read, "Live it again." I thought, "how did they know?" I would like to…and I do…live it again, over and over and over!

Tomorrow I head to Lima. I'm just out two days this week and I will be driving (about 175 miles) which means not having to deal with air travel. Yay!

Off to make some homemade chili. My mom's recipe. I haven't cooked for a long time. It will be nice to eat a real meal.

Love,
Karlee

From: Jack

To: Karlee
Sent: Monday, November 14, 2005 1:03 PM
Subject: RE: Mmmmmm!

Hi Karlee,

Too late! Now you'll have to tell me about that fantasy, too. I'm having the same effect...you get worked up reading about me getting worked up, and it works me up again. Fortunately I have a phone meeting shortly...that works like a bucket of ice water. But only for a little while.

I'm sure my mind will wander back to you moments after hanging up with them. Especially if I go through a hotel and near a pool!

A few more interviews and more applying. I'm looking at jobs in my home town...not sure if those will lead anywhere or not. I don't think I have any optimism left...I'm just going through the motions, trying to sound interested and positive to employers, but not expecting anything to come through. I've been amazed by how long it takes most people to get back to me, so I kind of forget about jobs once I've applied/had an interview. I keep notes to follow-up, but...let's just say I'm not packing for any of those jobs. I'd be shocked to hear back from the slot machine people...but that's just as well.

Maybe you should be the spokes model for the Mirage! They can publish that story...I'm sure a lot of people would go to Vegas if they thought they could have the experience we had! You'll be rich!

Well, 175 mile drive is better than flying. I don't like flying these days. It's slow, depressing, and aggravating. But, I'd fly to see you. We'd just have to find some way to UN-aggravate and de-depress me. I have a few ideas.

I hope the chili came out good. I always associate chili with winter, even though it's from the southwest. Or maybe it's from Chile. I never thought about it.

By the way, I'm starting to get a conditioned response from my webcam. We've only used it a couple of times, but it's sitting next to my computer monitor. Many times I've looked at it while I was working and I'll suddenly be unable to stop myself from thinking about our webcam meetings...which has a very immediate effect on me. Like now. Mmmmm.

--Jack

From: Karlee
To: Jack
Sent: Thursday, November 17, 2005 8:15 AM
Subject: Back from exciting Lima, Ohio!

Hi Jack,

I'm back from Lima! Very quiet there. About the most excitement was the tornado warning for the area on Tuesday evening. I take that back...the fact that the seminar room was directly across from the pool added excitement. One morning as I was sitting at the registration table looking at the pool, I imagined you in the hallway, peering around the corner, naked, your cock in your hand, just like when I was in the shower at the Mirage! I couldn't go there for too long; I was afraid my knees would feel too much like Jell-O and make it difficult for me to stand and present.

Now the Golden Nugget... Do you think someone out there is watching us? Yesterday, I received something in the mail from the Golden Nugget and it reads in big, one-inch letters, "WHAT'S YOUR FANTASY?" The tag line was about some sort of Football Parlay Card, but when I first saw it, I thought, "Another one?!!" Can't seem to get away from it!

>>But, I'd fly to see you. We'd just have to find some way to UN-aggravate and de-depress me. I have a few ideas.

Just a few ideas? I have 3,217! Not really, but maybe you should share your ideas so that I can make sure I'll be able to accommodate you before you go through the process. I'd hate for you to get all the way here and find out that I wasn't able to UN-aggravate or de-depress you.

Maybe that's why I take my web cam down after our cam visits. Yet I'm happy to re-hook it up any time for you!

Karlee
xoxox

P.S. I think you're sexy.

From: Jack
To: Karlee
Sent: Thursday, November 17, 2005 11:55 AM
Subject: RE: Back from exciting Lima, Ohio!

Hi Karlee,

Well, nothing much new here. I'm going to go to visit my parents for Christmas, but it took long enough for my father to get back to me that I can't use frequent flier miles, and the choices were extremely limited.

I'm going to meet a couple of people when I'm home. There was a job there, but apparently it's "on hold." I'll meet them anyway and see what the deal is.

I had an interview on the phone for a job in Baltimore. Turns out, it isn't a real job...they call it an internship. But, you don't have to be in school. See, rather than hire people and pay a salary, they'll hire people as interns, pay them next-to-nothing, and then promote the ones they want to keep after a few months. But, if I'm offered that, I'd just have to go there: no in-person interview. Just show up and hope it's good. It's all taking a toll on me. I usually go on a ski trip with my friends...can't justify the expense. Couldn't justify it last year, either. I don't feel like I'm living...I feel like I'm always waiting for everything. I suppose the thing that's getting to me is that I'm doing everything I can...nothing's working. So what do you do? Baltimore is a lot closer to Cleveland...but...I tell you, I have absolutely no confidence that any interview will go anywhere. I keep doing it and plugging away, but prior to this stretch, if I had an interview, I always got the job. I keep trying, but...I no longer feel like I've got any marketable skills. I suppose the worst thing is that I keep lowering the bar. I left high-paying jobs to pursue things that gave me professional satisfaction but were unstable. Now I want stability. My high-paying skills are out of date and not in demand, which means I'm looking at very low level jobs. And, I'm overqualified for those. Plus, it's almost the holidays, and things get slower through January. Argh.

Ah well. Got to keep pushing along. Maybe I can find out how much it would cost to reroute over to Cleveland for a couple of days on the way back. That'd be something to look forward to!

--Jack

From: Karlee
To: Jack
Sent: Friday, November 18, 2005 6:45 AM
Subject: Hello ...

Hi Jack,

Sorry to hear you didn't have more optimistic news to report.

What you've been going through would take a toll on most. Especially because you feel that you are doing everything that you can. Something will work eventually.

Perhaps taking a ski trip with your friends would be a good idea. Despite the cost, you still deserve to have some fun in your life. And a change of scenery and activity would probably do some good. It might shift the energy around a bit.

I remember you mentioning quite awhile ago that someone thought you should play poker professionally. Is that something you would ever consider? Of course, now that I'm writing that, it sounds like a silly question. I guess if you would consider it, you'd probably already be doing it!

It would be great if you could jump over to Cleveland on your way back after visiting your parents. It would be the best news I've had for a long time. I've got the flutters just thinking about it. What better a place for you to UN-aggravate and de-depress after being in the airport. I'll start filling the Jacuzzi!

xoKarlee

From: Jack
To: Karlee
Sent: Friday, November 18, 2005 1:57 PM
Subject: RE: Hello . . .

Hi again...

Don't fill the Jacuzzi just yet. I called the airline, and believe it or not, to re-route my return through Cleveland for a few extra days costs more than my entire round-trip ticket! So, I'd be better off just going out to see you directly. I asked why the fee was so high (even with the credit from my original ticket—it's $500). Evidently during the Christmas through New Year's week, a lot of people travel, and the prices are higher.

What about January some time? What's your schedule like then? If I don't have a job (which it seems like I won't) I'll be free and needing some R&R.

The ski trip would be fun, and I'd stay with friends and eat canned tuna, but the ski passes are pricey. Maybe I'll play in a few tournaments in the coming weeks and see how I do.

Hmmm...I didn't think about checking to see if it would work for me to fly to Cleveland first before I go home. I'm going home early (19th), which is just about a month away, but maybe there's something around the 16th or 17th? I'll check as soon as I get the chance. Got to finish up some documents and have a few more phone meetings. I'm awfully busy to be not-quite getting by. Seeing you would definitely be something to look forward to!

--Jack

From: Karlee
Sent: Friday, November 18, 2005 3:03 PM
To: Jack
Subject: RE: Hello...

Hi Jack,

As far as my schedule in December, I'm away the 15th and 16th.
One good night of rest and I can be ready for you on the 17th! As far
as January, I'm scheduled for the 17th and 18th, and I'll be in
Orlando for a few days the first week of the month. Other than that,
I plan to be around.

Any good news out of your phone meetings today?

Karlee

From: Karlee
To: Jack
Sent: Thursday, November 24, 2005 11:22 AM
Subject: Hi!

Hi Jack,

Happy Thanksgiving! How was dinner with your friends?

It was great "seeing" you yesterday. All of you. I'm still feeling the
effects of our webcam visit. Mmmmmmm! Last night, even after a
shower, I was still wet.

Winter has definitely arrived here. Cold, snowy, and blustery today.
Glad I'm not going far. It would be a good day to make love in front
of the fireplace—with you!

I head out on the road again on Sunday. I'm going to Washington,
DC and Reston, VA. It should be an interesting trip.

Thanks for making yesterday so great!

Karlee
xoxxo

From: Jack
To: Karlee
Sent: Sunday, November 27, 2005 6:56 PM
Subject: RE: Hi!

Hi Karlee,

Dinner was fine...ate lots of turkey and all the usual side dishes. I'm
now trying to find a way to get an interview in Lake Tahoe so I can
justify a ski trip which I can't afford.

Mmmmm—making love in front of the fireplace? Agreed! It turned
cold here last night. Low 40's. I think I read that there's an
overnight low of 34 tonight. That's crazy for Vegas. I was out late
and didn't bring a jacket. Glad my heater works, though making
love by the fire is a much better idea.

I hope your trip goes well.

The job hunt resumes Monday...we'll see what happens.

Hopefully, something. Anything.

--Jack

From: Karlee
To: Jack
Sent: Monday, November 28, 2005 8:42 PM
Subject: Pool on Roof!

Hi Sexy,

I'm in Washington, DC...not that I will have had a chance to see
much of our nation's capital. I did see the Washington Monument
and the Capital building when I flew in last night. The hotel I'm at is

316

actually pretty close to the White House, although I probably won't see it while I'm here.

I've thought of you a few times since I've been here. First, when I noticed that the pool is on the roof—ninth floor! That could be fun! And...there's a new building being constructed right across the street from the hotel. I have a view from my room. I was visualizing you as a construction worker and seeing you across the street wearing nothing but a hard on—I mean a hard hat. And I was imagining that you would notice me from across the street and walk over to the hotel and...Mmmmmmmmm! I bet we could write yet another book titled something like *Travel Erotica*. It seems so easy to think of a variety of scenarios for us while I'm on the road. When I was in my room this evening, I was thinking about your fantasy of me going into the ladies' room for you! Mmmmmm again!

I hope you find a way to make it to Lake Tahoe. You deserve a break! Maybe I'll come out there so that I can interview you. You'd have to take your clothes off.

I miss you!
oxoxoxo

From: Jack
To: Karlee
Sent: Sunday, December 4, 2005 1:46 PM
Subject: RE: Pool on Roof!

Are you back from DC? Ah, if only I could've been down there to join you at the rooftop pool.

Not too much exciting here. I was slated to take a pre-employment test, but I got the notice last Wednesday that it would happen in Portland at 8am this Monday. I would've had to stay over a night in Portland, and airfare was prohibitively expensive (especially for a PRE employment screening) but fortunately they found a place I could take it right here in Las Vegas. That's good.

Nothing else terribly interesting to report. I've been trying to line up interviews in Lake Tahoe. I was just about to commit to it, when my friends all decided to possibly abandon Tahoe because it's too warm and wet to ski. That would mean no cheap lodging. Now they're talking about renting a condo for a week. I was hoping maybe you'd fly out and join me, but I doubt I'm going now, and six people in a two-bedroom condo probably wouldn't be a lot of fun anyway.

I hope your trip was/is good. I'll keep you posted as to what's going on.

--Jack

From: Karlee
To: Jack
Sent: Monday, December 5, 2005 3:03 PM
Subject: Hi!

Hi Jack!

Yes, I'm back from DC. Had a great week, enjoyed being home for a few days and I go back out tomorrow. I'm headed to Traverse City, MI. Should be nice and cold up there! Brrrrrrrrr!

Did you take the pre-employment test? It's good that you were able to stay in Las Vegas and take it locally. Is this for one of the companies you met with on one of your visits?

I hope the ski trip works out. I know you enjoy skiing. And…I definitely would have been excited about joining you! Of course rather than being in a condo with other people, I would have suggested our own place so that I could ravish you with kisses, etc. That's assuming you'd have energy left after skiing! Either way, it would be fun!

Are your plans all set for your trip to Chicago? How long will you be gone?

Looks like it's going to be a quiet holiday season again here. My sister in Wisconsin is not coming down at all and my other sister just announced that she and her boyfriend are going to Las Vegas for Christmas. I'll be heading down to Columbus to my brother's.

I guess I'll just have to use my imagination and think about waking up Christmas day and finding you under the tree with nothing on but a bow! Mmmm—that would be fun to untie!

xoxxoxo

From: Jack
To: Karlee
Sent: Tuesday, December 6, 2005 2:36 PM
Subject: RE: Hi!

Hi Karlee,

Yes, it will be cold in Michigan. Hmmm...nice and cold. I miss cold. I bet your nipples get hard in the cold. See why I like the cold?

I still don't know if I'm going on the trip. And yes, it would be fun! Waiting to hear on some other things I applied for. I applied for something in California, because the job sounded great, but...I HATE California. Even moving to California for my dream job would be a difficult decision. If things work out, I may wind up driving (8-12 hours!) up to join my friends and ski, but it's been too warm there (40's) and I don't know how much sense it makes to go up there to sit in a room.

If YOU were there, it'd be different, of course. Totally worth it! Watching the snow, sitting by the fire...mmmmm.

My plans for Chicago are still up in the air, too. I've got an appointment on the 21st (for a job that's currently 'on hold')...I think I'll be gone the 19th–27th or so.

A quiet holiday sounds nice too, to me! I'm not in much of a Christmas mood. Maybe that'll change with my trip. It's hardly a winter wonderland here.

I'll mail myself to you if I can find a box big enough. Mmmm...I can imagine you coming down the stairs and taking off my bow...I think it's better to give than receive!

--Jack

From: Karlee
To: Jack
Sent: Wednesday, December 7, 2005 6:04 PM
Subject: Let it snow, let it snow . . .

Hi Jack,

I'm here in Traverse City. It's beautiful, cold, and snowy! After the seminar, I changed clothes, put on my new boots and took a walk around the downtown area. It was snowing and the sidewalks were covered but I didn't mind because I love my new boots! My feet never felt cold. While I was walking I was thinking about how you would probably have loved being here because of the snow and the cold. It is a winter wonderland. And yes, you're right...my nipples do get hard in the cold. And they also get hard when I'm not cold but thinking about you. I had a wet dream [with you] this morning. A wonderful orgasm just before I woke up. I was dreaming that we were in my bed and you put your hand between my legs and I came. Talk about a wake-up call. Do men have wet dreams or is it just something that happens in adolescent boys? I never really hear anyone talk about them. And I wonder if men know that women have them, too!

So what is your dream job?

I love California—for visiting! After being in Santa Barbara a few times I thought I might want to live out there at some point. I have since changed my mind. I'd still like to go back to visit some of my favorite parts of the state.

I guess we'll both give and receive! Just a matter of who goes first—and it doesn't matter to me!

Off to take a hot shower. Then I'll be crawling under the covers; this room is a bit chilly. Last night I felt more like I was camping because it was so cold. I'm in one of those "historic" hotels, so you know how that goes. At least I'll have thoughts of you (and my wet dream) to keep me warm!

Back home tomorrow. Good night.
xoxoxo
Karlee

From: Jack
To: Karlee
Sent: Saturday, December 8, 2007 7:15 PM
Subject: RE: Mmmm . . .

Hi Karlee!

I'm sorry I missed your call....hmmmm....I don't have the webcam set up but re-borrowed it in exchange for a shovel (we got snow here finally, and it came all at once).

I've been kind of busy, but will get back to you soon...Strangely, I have seen a spike in people wanting to talk to me. I don't think anyone will actually do anything before January 1, but at least I've got a couple of prospects. Spent most of the day working on a sample piece for one group, so we'll see....

I wish I'd gotten your call! I was probably shoveling...I'd much rather have talked to you!

--Jack

From: Jack
To: Karlee
Sent: Thursday, December 8, 2005 12:10 PM
Subject: RE: Let it snow, let it snow...

Argh!

I just discovered that holding the shift key and moving my mouse wheel will make the browser go back or forward. This was an accident. I was trying to scroll through a message I just wrote to you. But, instead, it erased everything I wrote! Blast.

Let's see...I said something about liking the idea of Traverse City, but not liking the bitter cold as much as the snow. 29 and snow seems good; 10 below and snow seems...less good.

I also wrote something about wet dreams. I only remember having one wet dream, and that was as a freshman in college. I'd given up masturbation because I had a roommate, and the idea of being walked in on wasn't very appealing (being caught by him, at least). After several weeks, I had this amazingly intense dream and I woke up at the end and I'd cum, explosively. It was a powerful experience, though also embarrassing. It hasn't happened since, though it was a more memorable event than touching myself. It's kind of too bad. I think that'd be a great way to wake up! I've had fantasies that involved being woken up by you, touching me, or taking me in your mouth, or climbing on top of me...too bad I'm such a light sleeper. I'm getting all worked up thinking about it. Maybe you could inspire a wet dream....

Mmmmm! Between thinking about you in a hot shower, and your wet dream, and my fantasy about you making me cum while I sleep...I'm all worked up! I guess I'll have to touch myself now...I wouldn't want to fall asleep during the test and have a wet dream.

That might hurt my candidacy.

On the other hand...I do sort of feel like touching myself so you can see.

Hmmm.

I hope you had (have) a good flight!

--Jack

From: Karlee
To: Jack
Sent: Thursday, December 8, 2005 6:04 PM
Subject: Still here!

Hi Jack,

Thank you for the good flight wishes. Actually, I've had no flight yet. I'm stuck in Traverse City. I got to the airport only to find out that the plane was delayed coming in from Detroit. Therefore, my outbound flight was of course delayed. I would have most likely missed my connecting flight in Detroit, so the airline put me up at a hotel and gave me vouchers for ground transportation. Frustrating, but manageable. I was originally supposed to leave at 6:56 PM. Then it changed to 7:42—then to 8:12, arriving in Detroit at 9:30. My connecting flight was scheduled to leave at 9:22. It was either sleep here in a bed, or take a chance of having to sleep at the Detroit airport, since the airlines in Traverse City were told there were no hotel rooms left in Detroit. "Don't send any more people," is what they were told." Ahh, the pleasures of business travel! Now I get to leave this hotel at 6:00 AM to catch a 7:00 AM flight. I'm due to arrive back in Cleveland at 9:38 in the morning.

You would have liked Traverse City. It was in the 20's and not bad at all. I was expecting it would be a lot colder up here. They have had a lot of snow already.

Waking up next to you and making love first thing in the morning...I'm throbbing just thinking about it. Now, I'm not claiming to be a sleep expert, however, I'd like to suggest that if you would spend a considerable amount of time sleeping with me, you would most likely be having a considerable amount of sex, which could in turn result in a more sound sleep for you. Just my theory! Perhaps you'd like to test it!?

Yes, touching yourself during the test would most likely hurt your candidacy. But, at least you'd go down with a smile on your face!

Believe me, I like seeing! (Not to mention touching and tasting, and hearing!) Mmmmmmm! Maybe I should start traveling with my web camera!

Karlee

From: Jack
To: Karlee
Sent: Friday, December 9, 2005 10:45 AM
Subject: RE: Still here!

Did you make it back? I always used to like getting snowed in at airports...I suppose I'm strange that way. Free hotel! Weee!

So, naturally...I'm planning to take a trip for a couple of interviews...just about to make it happen today, and I wake up to find a message on my machine. Another person wanted to do a phone interview for a job I applied to quite a while ago. He didn't leave a name or number, so I can't get back in touch with him. I'm hoping he calls today some time; otherwise I'll be worried that I'll miss a potential interview if I'm not around. Ack.

I hope you've made it back home by now. I'll let you know what happens.

--Jack

From: Karlee
To: Jack
Sent: Sunday, December 18, 2005 10:14 PM
Subject: Hi!

Hi Jack,

How are you? How was Lake Tahoe? Did you have fun? Get to ski much? How'd the interviews go?

Okay, so enough questions!

I was in St. Louis last week; got home Friday night. No more seminar work until the middle of January and they only have me scheduled for two days. Good news and not so good news, since of course I don't get paid if I'm not working.

We had a "partial" early Christmas celebration today. My dad's birthday is Tuesday and since my one sister is going to be in Las Vegas on Christmas, we were together today. My brother came up with his two kids, along with my dad and his girlfriend, me, and my sister and her boyfriend…well, now I should say fiancé—they got engaged this morning!

Not too much new here. I'm looking forward to a quiet week. And Christmas day will be really quiet. My dad just told me tonight that he's going to be at my brother's just in the morning, as he plans to drive back to Cleveland to have dinner with his girlfriend's family. That means it will be just me and my brother for dinner. Maybe I'll suggest to my brother that we just cook a couple of steaks on the grill, make a nice salad, maybe baked potatoes and that will probably be it. How about you? Does your mom cook a traditional Christmas meal? Do you have aunts/uncles/grandparents that are a part of your family tradition for the holidays?

Looking forward to hearing from you. I hope you have some exciting updates on the job search.

Karlee

From: Jack
To: Karlee
Sent: Friday, December 23, 2005 2:30 PM
Subject: RE: Hi!

Hi there…

I don't know if it's the cold or time difference or what, but I've not been sleeping much and am completely exhausted while I'm here. I guess I've also been doing a lot of running around, cooking, errands, and having meetings in an attempt to get a job.

Regardless, I've done some looking for airline tickets. I'm trying to arrange for an interview in Orlando (against my better judgment) and due to the holiday, this has become quite tricky. But, if I can do it, maybe I can piggyback a trip to Cleveland! Or, maybe I can just go out there directly for a few days. The more I think about that idea, the more I like it. So...keep some time open. Maybe I can find a job at KFC out there. I always liked their Cole slaw.

Have a happy holiday! No big excitement here, which is a good thing!

Talk to you soon...

--Jack

From: Karlee
To: Jack
Sent: Friday, December 23, 2005 7:30 PM
Subject: RE: Hi!

Hi Jack,

Sorry to hear you're feeling exhausted. Perhaps it's a combination of all three—the time change, the weather change, and all the running around you've been doing. I hope you get a chance to relax a bit before you head back to Las Vegas.

There's a KFC right down the road! See, you should come and live with me.

Believe me—I've got time open for you! My car is already programmed for the airport! Keep me posted on what you'd like to do.

I was going to send the attached on Christmas day, but since you mentioned you were exhausted, I thought maybe this would pep you up a bit!

Happy Holidays to you, too!

xoxoxoxox

From: Jack
To: Karlee
Sent: Saturday, December 24, 2005 2:52 PM
Subject: RE: Hi!

Pep me up indeed!

WOW! You definitely know what I like...secondary only to being
with you and having you in my arms, this picture is the perfect gift!
And it keeps on giving!

You're so sexy. Did you see this photo? Mmmmmm! You look
amazing...so sexy.

I'm very sad that I don't get a moment's privacy here! I'm going to
have to find a way to sneak off and pleasure myself in the back yard
in the cold and snow!

Things here aren't going well...some serious problems with my
father's health. We called an ambulance for him and took him to
the emergency room...some internal bleeding, and that's never
good. It may, in fact, be "relatively" minor due to irritation from too
much ibuprofen, but they're doing an endoscopy tomorrow morning
(Christmas day!) so I'll know more soon, I hope. He lost quite a bit of
blood and was dizzy and his pulse was racing a bit...he's staying
overnight in the hospital. Great.

So, I suppose the good news (if there is any) is that if I have to stay
longer here, maybe I can get the ticket changed with a jump over to
Cleveland. Or, we'll just plan a separate trip out there. The more I
think about that idea, the more I like it. Maybe a long weekend or
something coming up. Then I can give you your Christmas
present...I'm eager to give it to you. Repeatedly!

Thanks again for the photo...you really do know how to make me
smile! And I needed it today!

--Jack

From: Jack
To: Karlee
Sent: Sunday, December 25, 2005 11:54 PM
Subject: RE: Any news?

Hi Karlee...

Merry Christmas! My father's still in the hospital, though we're
hoping he can come home tomorrow some time, depending on test
results. Looks like everything will be okay...probably no surgery,
which is always a good thing (except for the surgeons).

>*As far as your visit...Mmmm....I'm sure we can make it work however it works
out. Perhaps you'll end up in Cleveland for New Year's Eve. I've had many
fantasies about that since...well, probably last New Year's Eve! A quiet evening
in, perhaps champagne, a nice bubble bath, and making love with nothing on but
the Christmas tree lights.*

MMmmm! I read this earlier and it makes me very happy to image.
In fact, I looked at your picture again after reading that...

It was terrible. I went out to walk the dog, and I was alone (except
for the dog) and my mind started to wander. I was wearing these
polar-fleece pants, and looked down to see that the material was all
stretched to a point thanks to a raging, throbbing erection. I'm glad
the streets were empty on Christmas. I was thinking that I'd have to
sneak off into the bushes by the road and touch myself...but I
couldn't figure out what to do with the dog. So I tried to think of
other things, and needless to say it was a long walk for the poor little
dog. I even tried calling you but I think your phone was shut off.

Of course, now that I'm back home and in bed, thinking about you
again, the problem has reappeared! Sometimes being a man is a
hassle...it sure would be nice to satisfy my urges without making
such a noticeable mess. That, and I do make quite a bit of noise.

Anyway, I keep thinking about the fantasy I wrote you about...where
we share this intense sexual tension, "accidentally" seeing each
other...catching each other...walking in at the "wrong moment"...
over and over. MMmmm...it drives me wild. Partly because I guess I
feel like that's what's been going on for the last several months. I

guess maybe it's because I get so impossibly turned on from our little video-chat sessions...or maybe it reminds me of our first two fantasies in different ways. I get so aroused watching you...and I get so aroused showing myself to you.

Send me the dates that you're free in January. I think I need to get out there SOON. I may have to go to Florida for a few days in late January, so maybe I can do it before, or maybe I'll just go to Cleveland before. Drill those keyholes in all your doors!

Mmmm....nothing on but the Christmas lights. Wow. I can't even imagine what that would be like. I'm guessing that "amazing" wouldn't even begin to describe it.

Oh, I need to go to Cleveland now.

--Jack

From: Karlee
To: Jack
Sent: Monday, December 26, 2005 11:57 AM
Subject: The Cleveland Hostess—kind of like a Las Vegas Host Reversal!!!

Hi Jack,

How's your dad? Is he home yet? Good news about surgery most likely not being necessary. I hope everything is looking up and that he's feeling well.

WOW! I have been breathing heavy and worked up all morning…

It all started before I was even out of bed. For some reason, I found myself thinking about your penis. Just your penis. I spent what seemed like several minutes thinking about what it looks like, how perfect its shape and size, how it feels in my hands and in my mouth, and especially seeing it go into me as we move into the X position. I guess it was like going into a candy store and just delighting in all the sites without even really eating any; enjoying the experience just because I know how yummy my favorite candies taste to me. Then I turned on my computer and read your email about your erections yesterday. Hmmm? I must have been picking up the wavelengths while I was sleeping! Just the thought of feeling your hard cock through the softness of those polar-fleece pants…Mmmm!

Then I found myself sitting on my couch thinking about your fantasy (reality!) regarding us sharing an intense sexual tension. I created my own version, beginning with picking you up at the airport.

I was imagining that you are a friend of one of my friends. We've never met. My friend mentions that his friend (you) is coming to Cleveland for some sort of business-related something. He also mentions that he waited too long to make a hotel reservation and was having a difficult time finding a place to stay. So being the nice person that I am, I offer to have him (you) stay here.

I meet you in the baggage claim area. I see you and think, "Wow, he's cute. This could be fun." I immediately tell myself that any kind of sexual activity would be totally inappropriate, because you are here for business, plus the fact that you're a friend of ___'s." We shake hands. On the drive home, we engage in small talk about our work, what brought you to Cleveland, and how we each know our mutual friend.

Shortly after we get here, you mention that you'd like to take a nap. You were up late the night before, now you're in a different time zone, and you have a function you need to attend that evening for work.

As your hostess, I insist that you will be sleeping in my room and I will be sleeping in my office on a very comfortable blow-up bed. So off you go to take your nap.

I decide to curl up on my favorite chair and read while you're sleeping. I want to be as quiet as possible so that you can rest. After about a half an hour, I remember that I need to make a phone call and the information regarding that call is on my bedroom dresser. Thank goodness—although you've closed my bedroom door, you left it open just a bit. I don't want to disturb you, but I must go in. I know I can be quiet. I very gently open the door, and tiptoe in. I'm figuring you'll be under the covers, sound asleep. Much to my surprise (and delight), you're totally naked and sleeping on top of the covers! I'm in now and I don't have time to think about staying or leaving; I grab the piece of paper off my dresser and get out. Before I close the door, I take another quick look. "Wow, I'd love to just pounce on him."

A bit shaken, partly because I wouldn't want you to think I was being rude and infringing on your privacy, and partly because it's been so long since I've seen a man completely naked. And in my bed! I go back to my reading, but I can't concentrate. I'm fantasizing about what it would have been like if you had awaken and invited me to the bed to nap with you and how you would have slowly undressed me and made love to me. "That's crazy; I've only known this man for less than two hours," I tell myself.

I'm still shaking a bit, mostly from my thoughts, when you awake from your nap. You tell me you'd like to take a shower before you leave for your business function. Thank goodness I hear you close the bathroom door…totally closed. I hear the water running, and only a few moments go by when I hear you call out my name. In just that split second, I panic between fear of why you might be calling my name, and the excitement in the fact that you're calling for me while you're in the shower. I go to the door, but don't dare open it. "Yes, Jack, what do you need?" "There doesn't appear to be any soap in here." Agh, I forgot to put a fresh bar in when I cleaned. "Just a minute, I'll get one." "Okay, now how do you want me to get this to you?" "Come on in, I'm sure you've seen a naked man before." He's right, I have, and I can be mature about this! This would be all fine and good, since most people would just wrap the shower curtain around them, and most likely you wouldn't even see anything. But there is no curtain. It's a clear glass door. I step in toward the shower, you open the shower door and extend your hand, and I place the bar of soap in it. You appear embarrassed as my eyes can't help but wander down to your huge erection. We both quickly look away. I leave the bathroom.

You head off to your business function and I'm home alone for the evening. And although it's still somewhat early, I decide to take a hot shower and head for bed. "Jack probably won't be back for at least another hour or so. No need to be concerned with that," I think. Although I'll be sleeping in another room, I head to my room to undress and shower. I'm still worked up from seeing you naked. I decide to enjoy the eroticism of my thoughts and start to think about how it would be if you were there, watching me. I pretend that you're on the other side of the door. I undress, very slowly, rubbing my hands over my body, touching myself, massaging my breasts. I'm starting to breath heavy. I realize I'm getting overly worked up. I stop myself and head to the shower. I think I'll take my vibrator. I'll never be able to fall asleep with this man in my house, all worked up like this. I'm in the shower, enjoying the vibration between my legs, thinking about seeing you in the shower earlier that day and how beautiful your cock looked fully erect, so different from when you were sleeping, and how wonderful it would be if you were actually in the shower with me. "Stop it, Karlee," I tell myself. "You can't be with this man. He's a friend of ___'s." I go back to concentrating on my own self-pleasuring and scream in delight, yet with a sense of frustration that I'm alone and not with you.

I turn the water off, step out of the shower, and am just beginning to dry myself off, when you walk in. I'm startled and I scream. As soon as I realize it's you, I relax a bit, yet I'm still pretty shaken. I wasn't expecting you so early. (You came home, saw the office door closed, and assumed I was already asleep in bed.) You feel bad that you have scared me and your natural instinct is to approach me, take me in your arms and hold me, as a way a letting me know that I'm not in any harm. You don't even take a moment to think about the fact that I'm naked. It's just your natural response. Feeling your strong arms around me relaxes me, and my natural response is to let go of my towel and reciprocate your gentle embrace. It feels so good and I don't want to let go. You evidently are feeling very comfortable as well. We just stand there, relishing in the moment. I'm just about to pull away, when I feel your now rock-hard cock through your trousers. You lean into me; I'm still warm and moist from the shower. My arms and legs go weak. "This would be wrong. This is ___'s friend," I think to myself. I quickly pull away and pick up my towel and turn around. You're not certain about what to do. You apologize for scaring me and leave the bathroom.

I finish getting ready for bed and head to the office, where I will be sleeping. My mind wanders back to the scene in the bathroom. I'm relaxed now, and enjoying the headiness of the feeling and moan as I stretch out to sleep. In the meantime, you're still feeling bad about frightening me earlier and decide to check on me before you head to bed. You've already taken off all your clothes, since you sleep in the nude, but you figure I'll be asleep so it's no big deal. You approach my office, just as I let out another moan of delight, thinking about how good it felt to be held by you in the bathroom, you fully clothed, and the feel of your erection against my naked body...

That's about as far as I got. I realized if I wanted to, I could have had this scenario go on for days and I knew I had to eventually get something done around here.

But now in the last hour, I find myself thinking about your tongue. I'll tell you about that in my next email. I had to change my panties once already today. Not the same hassle you talked about, but something to deal with nonetheless!

Now, on to those dates in January, so we can get you out here...(which now really can't be soon enough!)

I'll be in Orlando Jan. 4-7. That leaves Jan. 8-14 open. I need to block out January 15-18 for my work in Fargo. Anytime between Thursday the 19th and Monday the 23rd works great as well. I head back on the road January 29th.

As far as number of days (and nights!), I'm open. The more the better!

By the way...if you go for a walk today, perhaps it would be best to leave that poor little dog at home!

Mmmmmm!

xoxxo

From: Karlee

To: Jack
Sent: Monday, December 26, 2005 12:13 PM
Subject: Any news?

Hi Jack,

I'm sorry to hear the news about your dad. Any test results yet? What a way to spend Christmas Eve and morning. And not to take away from the concerns of your father, but this is not something you need on top the stress of looking for a job.

I'm glad you liked the picture and I'm glad I sent it when I did. Looks like it was good timing with the situation with your dad. It puts a smile on my face to think that I put a smile on your face. And I am looking forward to the present that you have for me... I think it was the word "repeatedly" that put another big smile on my face!

I'm at my brother's as I'm writing this. The kids had fun opening their presents. Now they're playing with them. I'm not sure yet if I'm driving back tonight or in the morning. I'm leaning toward heading home tonight.

As far as your visit...Mmmm...I'm sure we can make it work however it works out. Perhaps you'll end up in Cleveland for New Year's Eve. I've had many fantasies about that since...well, probably last New Year's Eve! A quiet evening in, perhaps champagne, a nice bubble bath, and making love with nothing on but the Christmas tree lights.

I'd better stop now. I don't have any privacy here either!

Hope your day has at least a bit of a bright spot in it. If you're at the hospital all day, that could be doubtful. But you never know.

Take good care of yourself!

Love,
Karlee
xoxxoxo

From: Jack
To: Karlee
Sent: Monday, December 26, 2005 2:19 PM
Subject: RE: The Cleveland Hostess—kind of like a Las Vegas Host Reversal!!!

Hi Karlee,

Hmmmm....it's been a while since we've exchanged these detailed fantasies, hasn't it? It still amazes me how you and I are *exactly* on the same wavelength...everything you described was so exciting to me; I literally couldn't take it (in a good way). Parts of what you described are exactly what I've been thinking about, and the other parts were better than what I'd been imagining! I can't even tell you how worked up I am. Flushed, breathing heavy, heart racing. I hope I'm not having a heart attack! I also know that these comfortable pants make hiding an erection completely impossible.

Mmmm...everything you said...I can't even tell you. I think you know what I mean...it's a sort of fantasy that you can play in your head over and over again, and everything just builds and builds. I suppose I have a lot of thoughts about lounging around in loose clothing and "accidentally" catching glimpses...having breakfast in our robes, and, I guess I didn't tie it as tightly as I thought, and who wears anything under a robe anyway? Like on our video chat, I got so excited watching you look at me as I leaned back and crossed my legs. Seeing my cock throb below the thin layer of terrycloth. Mmmm. I also love the idea of having breakfast with you, you leaning over to pour me some water, and catching a glimpse down your shirt, seeing your perfect breasts. Oh...I can't even tell you how worked up I am!

I also like the thought of your wearing a robe...and I "innocently" drop my napkin on the floor...you notice that I seem to be taking a very long time to pick it up, and you spread your legs a bit under the table in case I am looking. I love imagining watching you in the shower, or through a window, or getting dressed. I love the idea of pressing up against you as I help you do something; reach a box on a high shelf, or to fix something that's broken. Mmmm.

Whew. And I can't even begin to tell you what happens when I imagine finally being able to touch you, to feel you, to taste you, and to slide inside you. Maybe this fantasy is so potent because we've been apart for so long.

I've thought about the other thing you said too, where we're having a sexy video chat, but we're next door to each other. I've imagined that because we're both so worked up, we each decide to go on-line and look for someone to have cyber sex with. We go to an anonymous site and see each other, but only from the neck down because we're both afraid of being recognized. We chat a bit, take off our clothes, and begin to pleasure ourselves, and then I move in such a way that you recognize me as your house guest...you hadn't recognized that the man you're watching is in your own bedroom! You come by the room and knock on the door and I scramble to pull on a towel...I see you, wearing only a robe...and we both realize what's going on. Mmmm.

So...anyway. As for dates, I'll have a better idea once I'm back and can look at my calendar. Sometime in the 8-14th might work. As it turns out, there's a chance that I may go to Orlando for an interview...I'd thought that maybe we'd both be there at the same time, but my trip will almost certainly be later. And...well...while I could come earlier than my appointment, I think I'd rather have your full attention, so a time when you're not busy with work is probably best.

If I can get Orlando set up for the 13-17th, I could come to Cleveland first for the 10th-13th or so. Or, maybe I can do Orlando before the 19th and come to Cleveland on the way back...personally, sooner is better than later...because I don't know how much longer I can take it! Of course, Orlando may not happen, and I may have a conflict during one of those weekends...but tentatively, let's plan on those dates.

Hmmm...mutual friend...generous host...yes, perfect. You're too sexy. Tell me more! I'll spend my entire visit here doing job interviews, waiting at the hospital, and repeatedly touching myself in the bathroom, trying not to moan. Believe it or not, in the time that I wrote this, I've been driven to a frenzy yet again. At least I'm getting a lot of exercise!

--Jack

From: Karlee
To: Jack
Sent: Monday, December 26, 2005 7:36 PM
Subject: Whew!

Hi Jack,

I'm spent. I hardly have the energy to write! I guess I got a little worked up between writing to you and reading your response. I spent a good part of the evening in a daze. I'm not sure this is healthy. Or perhaps it's that I just haven't been on **this** kind of health kick for some time! You're right as far as it being some time since we shared such detailed fantasies. Ya know, now that I'm thinking about it, the way I felt today was very similar to some of the feelings I was having almost two years ago when you responded to my ad.

Looks like we'd be in good shape for either of the two time frames we seem to be looking at—somewhere between Jan. 8-14 or after the 19th. Of course we both know that can change based on availability as the days go by. I wouldn't think a whole bunch of flights will be sold out between now and the 28th, when you'll be back in Las Vegas and can check your calendar.

I'll write more when I regain my composure! Of course, at this point I doubt I will regain it. Just thinking about the reality of you coming for a visit has put my mind into full gear!

I've already started to move everything in the kitchen to the highest shelf I CAN'T reach! Mmmmmmmm!

Karlee

From: Jack
To: Karlee
Sent: Tuesday, December 27, 2005 9:21 AM
Subject: RE: Whew!

Hi Karlee,

Feelings like you had two years ago? Oh no! Does that mean you're going to get cold feet and cancel a few times? I hope not! But if it makes you feel better, you can take your wine with you into the bathroom in Cleveland.

I'd say that arriving January 9th in the evening (or 10th earlier in the day) and returning on the 12th in the evening would probably be the best for me. Let me know if that's good for you.

My mind is in full gear, too. I think I'm even more excited than I was before our first meeting...which is something I didn't think would be possible.

Mmmm. I've started trying to sleep naked on top of the sheets without an erection, but I don't think that's possible. Don't forget to remove the soap from the bathroom!

The really difficult thing is to imagine how long we can control ourselves. As it runs through my mind, I can't control myself...but I do like the idea. I imagine that when we do give into our desires, it'll be amazing. I imagine the most explosive, most passionate, and best lovemaking either of us has ever experienced. Not to set the bar too high, of course! But...I don't know. The already built-up sexual tension may put me over the top!

Maybe after you tiptoed into my room and saw me sleeping there naked...later that night...you'd go to sleep. Maybe you'd partially awake, and see me standing by your bed, in the darkness, completely nude and completely hard, watching you...I might silently move around, watching you, drawing a little bit closer, but then suddenly realize "what am I doing? This woman doesn't know me, she's my host! She's my friend's friend! She'll think I'm trying to rape her!" and I slip away. But you're tired, and not sure if it's a dream or I was really there.

Though you are probably unlikely to have saved these on your computer, I love the idea of asking you to borrow your laptop...you turn it on for me, and leave me in your office...and you hear me making some noise. You tiptoe in and see me from behind, and on the monitor you see the photo you sent me on the screen... something you'd forgotten was on there...you also see me doing something. I quickly cover up and close the image...I apologize; I accidentally opened it and "didn't really see anything." I'm not sure whether I'm more embarrassed for having been looking at your picture or nearly getting caught touching myself while fantasizing about you.

Hmmmm....of course I just thought of another potentially interesting piece of the puzzle...maybe my job is working in the medical field. So, you could rationalize that my seeing you is no big deal because in the medical field, naked bodies are no big deal (this is why I could never be a doctor). And maybe at some point, you decide to ask me for an exam. Since you've been so nice, I'm sure I'd be happy to oblige.

Let's see...here's another thing...you don't have to read these all at once, of course...I just have been lying around fantasizing about one situation after another...just gets better and better.

Maybe our mutual friend is having an anniversary and we think we should go out and get him a gift. His wife is about your size, so we decide to go look at lingerie. We decide that together, we'd probably be able to find something they'd both like, so we go looking at things, and eventually decide that it'd be easier to tell if you tried something on, and maybe I should look at it, too. No need to be shy around me. You bring me to the changing room and we pick out something. You'd probably get a little worried that I wasn't feeling well, because you'd see me flushed and breathing heavily. And, of course, some of those sexy lingerie pieces are hard to get into, so I might have to stand very close to you, nose to nose, so I could reach around back and unhook a tricky bra.

Mmmmm.

Okay, I have to go again. Mmmmmm.

--Jack

From: Karlee

To: Jack
Sent: Tuesday, December 27, 2005 2:59 PM
Subject: RE: Whew!

Hey Sexy,

I'm feeling much better today! I actually wasn't getting cold feet AT
ALL! (Quite the opposite—everything is HOT!) When I said I was
having similar feelings, I was talking about physically. I guess I'd
describe it as such an intense sexual charge that it's almost to the
point of uncomfortable. Heart racing, cheeks flushed, and weak
limbs, not to mention the throbbing and heavy secretions between my
legs. There will be no canceling on this end and none of that "should
I—or shouldn't I" dance I did a million times last July. But, that being
said, I appreciate you giving me permission to take my wine into the
bathroom! The thought of remembering that and that you
remembered made me smile.

I'm more excited too than our first time. Mostly because I'm not
dealing with the fear issues I had when we first met. That, plus the
fact that I already know what you look like, that I like you, and that
you're an amazing lover! I didn't know any of that when we first
met. I had suspected that the sex would be good based on the emails
we shared, but thinking back, there was always the possibility that
neither of us would have found the other exciting, stimulating, and
satisfying. Now we know!

Actually, now that I think about it, the idea of seeing you asleep with
an erection really turns me on! As far as the soap, I'm throwing it all
away!

I'd like to put you over the top! As far as how long we can control
ourselves…Hmmm? I've got mixed emotions on that one. On one
hand, I love the idea of waiting as long as we can. The built-up
tension is definitely a turn on for me, too. On the other hand, since
you're not going to be here for a month, I don't want to wait too
long, because that doesn't leave as much time for the other good stuff
and more fantasies! Plus, prior to us starting this new string of
fantasies, I had always imagined if you ever did come to Cleveland, I
would ravish you even before we left the airport. I don't know if I

like the idea of giving you a handshake rather than the passionate kiss I always imagined. I have a feeling we'll figure it out and it will be amazing, regardless! Being with you has already been the best lovemaking I've ever experienced, and I'm all for raising the bar! Hmmm? I like your idea, other than the part about me sleeping in another room! Perhaps from there, I then get out of bed to check on you, to find out if I was dreaming or if you were really there. When I go to your room, I find you in my bed looking at pictures of me that you 'accidentally' picked up off of my desk while you were doing some paper work in my office. [I could print copies (I think I may still have a couple of them) and have them under some papers, getting ready to mail them to someone I know in Las Vegas!]

Here we are…on the same wavelength again! Yesterday I was thinking about the possibility of you going to a lingerie store with me while you're here. When I go there, which is occasionally, I am always intrigued by the couples that come in together. So the thought of actually going with you has been appealing to me. I actually went there before Christmas. I was hoping to find some sort of really sexy Santa thing to wear for the photo of me under the tree. I didn't find anything I liked, but I did have thoughts of you while I was in there. I also like the idea of us shopping and picking out something new that might be exciting for both of us. Not necessarily lingerie, but perhaps a toy, lotion, etc. I'm not sure about the dressing room scene. I love the idea; I just don't know if I could control myself! Perhaps we could improvise—take a piece of my own lingerie with us in the car, still go into the store, look for what we think our friend's wife would like, and then when we get back here, I could try it on to make certain we like the selection.

Here's something else I think about that really turns me on. I wouldn't really call it a fantasy. It's just something I have always hoped I would have a chance to do someday. I'm lying naked on a blanket on the floor in front of my fireplace. You're naked too, but not lying down. I'm stretched out, but in somewhat of a closed way. My legs and feet are together and my arms are tight next to my body. I'm blindfolded. You're kneeling next to me. There's a song playing on a CD…a piece by my favorite composer. (The music plays a big part in this fantasy.) Using a feather, you start touching me, feet first, very slowly and softly. Feet, legs, stomach, between my legs, my arms, my breasts, my neck, my face. You might do this a time or two; I'm not sure how it will need to be timed with the music. Next, you do the same thing, but instead of using a feather, you use the tip of your tongue. Slowly and softly. This time my legs and arms are spread out, not all the way, but definitely not close to my torso. And this time, when you get to my pussy, you spend just a bit more time there, teasing. (Believe me, not too much or I'll cum too early). Same with my breasts. Now one more time, but this time, you use your cock. You're straddled above me, just touching my body with your cock. My face, between my breasts, and then just before the climax of the musical piece, you thrust your cock into me and I cum along with the height of the music. I don't know if this is humanly possible, but I've loved this piece for a long time and always thought it would be neat to cum as the cymbals clash. When you get here, I'll place the piece and see what you think. Even if the timing doesn't work for an orgasm at just the right place, all the rest of it would be amazing as well!

Mmmmmm! Now I've got to go.

xoxoxxo

From: Karlee
To: Jack
Sent: Tuesday, December 27, 2005 3:01 PM
Subject: Your dad?

Hi Jack,

How's your dad?

I just couldn't bring myself to ask that at the end of the last email I sent. It just didn't fit in, but I have been wondering!

Karlee

From: Jack
To: Karlee

Sent: Tuesday, December 27, 2005 4:04 PM
Subject: RE: Your dad?

Hi Karlee,

Hmm...I read this email first, so I wonder what's in the other email...
My dad's doing okay. They probably won't have the results of the
biopsy for another week-ish, so I'm going to proceed as though
everything is fine. He's in no pain (never was) which is good. His
symptoms have abated, and other than being a bit frail, he's good.

The lack of a good explanation for all of this is what's most
disturbing to me, but we'll see.

--Jack

From: Jack
To: Karlee
Sent: Tuesday, December 27, 2005 4:27 PM
Subject: RE: Whew!

It's me again!

Well, fortunately I'll be playing the part of a medical professional, so
not to worry about all the physical reactions! I have a special
medical instrument I can use to revive you.

Yes, knowing what we know makes a huge difference. I hadn't
thought about it. Makes perfect sense. It's one thing to be excited
about a possibility with a lot of unknowns...could be good, could be
bad. But now...you're right. I know what I'm getting! Mmmm!

On the other hand, at this point just seeing you in the airport could
lead to a big scene. I don't know if I could stop at just a passionate
kiss, and we wouldn't want to get arrested for indecent exposure. I
have a feeling I'll be saying (in the context of the fantasy) "Oh, I'm
sorry...I don't know what came over me..." a lot!

The store sounds like a great idea. I didn't know they sold other
things. That could be extremely fun, too.

That musical piece seems like it could be an interesting challenge! I'm definitely interested in trying. What's the piece? I'll start learning my cues.

--Jack

From: Karlee
To: Jack
Sent: Tuesday, December 27, 2005 8:39 PM
Subject: Keeps getting better and better...

Hi Jack,

Our talking about your visit has given a whole different meaning to the rooms in my condo. Now instead of seeing my dining room table as "just a table," I see it as the table we'll be sitting at in our robes, naked underneath, having breakfast. Today I found myself wondering if you'll like the idea that my table is made out of glass! I can always put a tablecloth on it so that we can't see through. Or maybe you will like the idea of being able to see through it! When I was in the shower, I was thinking about all that might take place there! I even checked out the "view" of the shower from the door. It's actually a great view, via the mirror. Just as you love the idea of watching me in the shower, I love the idea of watching you! And then joining you! And the kitchen...what I see there is mostly that "accidental" bumping into each other (it's not that big) while we're cooking or getting something to drink. Mmmmm! And then there's the great room, where the couch and fireplace are. And as far as the bedroom, too soon to tell all that might go on in there! And let us not forget the Jacuzzi! Mmmm—Mmmm—Mmmmm!

I cannot even tell you how worked up this has me. I don't know why. When I wrote that doctor fantasy a year and a half ago before we met in Las Vegas, I found it exciting. But this whole thing...my excitement level has been heightened tenfold! I think you originally suggested that I ask you for an exam. How about the idea of you having to give a "practice" exam as a part of your coursework, and you asking me if I would be willing to volunteer? (Isn't it interesting how sometimes just tweaking an idea a bit can make it all the more exciting?!)

Actually, it would probably add to my excitement, having a sense up front that my friend's friend is attracted to me, knowing that it would be "inappropriate" for either of us to act on it. After all, he's a guest. He came to town for business, and nothing else.

I was on the couch with my eyes closed, imagining the timing of the song. Not sure it will work. All along, I always felt like it was a longer piece. It's only four minutes and some seconds to the cymbal clash. That could be tricky. Of course I suppose we could start the whole thing on an earlier track. I just listened to it again. It might work better as more of a ravenous lovemaking song. Some parts are fast paced and more intense. When I listened to it a second time, I was imaging us being able to look at each other while it's playing and we're making love, almost like using the music as a guide as to when to go fast and hard and when to go soft and slow. The whole thing is totally erotic to me. Plus, there's a really nice soft piece right after that which would be perfect!

Thanks for the update on your dad.

I'd better get to bed. I can see I'm going to need a lot of rest over the next couple of weeks to prepare for all the energy I'll be expending soon! And I can't wait!

Good night!
xoxoxo

P.S. Just think, in a couple of weeks, instead of saying good night via email, I'll actually be crawling into bed and saying it to you!

From: Karlee
To: Jack
Sent: Tuesday, December 27, 2005 8:41 PM
Subject: P.S.

I hope you have a good trip back to Las Vegas today. Safe travels.

Karlee

From: Jack
To: Karlee
Sent: Tuesday, December 27, 2005 11:10 PM
Subject: RE: Keeps getting better and better . . .

Seeing through the glass table sounds good! I can imagine going over to pour you orange juice, and noticing through the table that your robe is open and I could see your pussy....Mmmmm...I wouldn't be able to pour the juice with my hands shaking!

All these options in your condo—why would you want to sell that place? It sounds perfect to me.

MMMmmm...yeah. I like the suggestion on the doctor exam. Since you're such a good host, I'm sure you'd oblige. It'd have to be a full body exam, of course. I'm sure I could come up with some good tests.

Oh, the more I play it over in my mind, I can easily see throwing you down and making love to you, then embarrassedly apologizing and making an excuse ('must've been the wine, I don't remember much, it was an accident, sorry') and then building the tension again. Round and round. I'd wonder if you were upset that we'd gone "too far" and think maybe it was the wine...and we'd both pretend it didn't happen. Mmm. But it might happen again. And again.

I'd better get to bed, too. I'm completely exhausted. I think the last time I was anywhere near this worked up was when we were talking before our first visit. It's kind of strange...the stress and frustration of job/life has kind of prevented me from thinking too much about happier things...and now, it's like I've just discovered my penis. Unfortunately, I'm at my parents' home, which makes it all the more awkward and tricky...but maybe being away has helped get me out of my mental rut. Either way, I'm amazed just how much more excited I am. I'd wake up feeling like I was about to have a wet dream! I touch myself, read an email from you, and start over again. It's kind of embarrassing...but also kind of nice. I feel like I've just discovered sexual arousal!

Mmmm. Nice thought—you crawling into bed with me. Gee, it'd almost be like the Wrong Room fantasy...never having been to your place before, I might get confused and get into your bed by mistake! And if I should accidentally have something happen while we were both in the same bed...well...neither of us would be to blame, right?

Mmmm...

So, I guess I should ask a bit about how we want to handle protection. I know I told you my desire to be inside you with nothing on...but having never done that, I don't know what we would do to be safe and responsible. How would this work? I can certainly bring condoms, but guess we should talk about how this might work. I'm a virgin in this department. I guess thinking about it is both scary and new and exciting for me...I guess it also fits in with this impulsive part of the fantasy...not being able to control ourselves and being swept up in the moment. But, I don't know what we need to know. Do you?

It's a little bit silly, but I'm a bit nervous thinking about being inside you without a condom...nervous in a good way...wondering if it feels as good as it does with a condom, what will happen without one? I'm worried I might come instantly...I don't know. I'm not sure what to expect, and I like it!

--Jack

From: Karlee
To: Jack
Sent: Wednesday, December 28, 2005 9:06 AM
Subject: Hi!

Good Morning, Jack! Or shall I call you Dr. Jack?

I just got done using my vibrator—again! I was going to see if from today on I could hold off until you get here. Really let that tension build. No way! Who was I kidding? I would never have made it.

As I was lying in bed, I was wondering if you would like to watch me while you're here. I remember you mentioning that in one of your emails when we first started writing to each other. If I recall, it was more about both of us self-pleasuring at the same time. I was thinking perhaps this might be something else as a part of your "medical professional" coursework—you need to observe a person having an orgasm so that you'll be able to identify all the signs as you move forward in your profession. Just a thought!

One of the [many] reasons I was so worked up was because I spent a good part of the morning playing the scenarios we've created in my head. I also found myself adding some little surprises for you along the way.

I don't think I'll be able to eat at my table anymore until you get here. My mind goes wild! I can't even talk about the doctor fantasy. It's way too much for me—I'm so flippin' excited just thinking about it.

Something else that's on my mind…a few times you mentioned the idea of "getting caught" touching yourself. I'm totally fine with that. What I don't have figured out yet, is how you might expect me to respond or react. Would you expect I would be afraid, disgusted, intrigued, or "Oh, let me help you with that; you shouldn't have to do that by yourself," or just walk away and pretend like I never saw it? I guess I'm looking for what you would expect to see happening next.

Perhaps this is just what the doctor would have ordered! I never thought in a million years that my sending that photo would have led to what we've just shared since a day or two before Christmas! Good move, Karlee, if I must say so myself!

What would a trip be without some variation of our Wrong Room fantasy? It should be a tradition!

Hmmm? The fun subject of protection. I had already been thinking of that as well, primarily because of you sharing your desire earlier with me. I don't know if I have all the answers, but this is how I look at it. There are basically two categories of risks involved:
1. Pregnancy 2. STD's. Do you have a sense of which of these make you the most nervous, or are they equally frightening? For me, I am generally more concerned about STD's than getting pregnant. It's

still physically possible of course, but because of my age (Ugh!), it's more than unlikely, especially as long as I'm not ovulating. (And if I thought I was, I would probably suggest we not take the chance.) BUT, as far as I can tell, I won't be ovulating while you're here. As far as STD's, I think I mentioned I just had an HIV test as well as some others that my gynecologist does as routine for his patients who are sexually active. Everything came back negative, which I imagined it would. But what I don't know for me is your history. I have nothing to go on except what you tell me—and trust. My instinct would be that if you have never been inside a woman without a condom, I shouldn't have much to worry about. However, we both know there are other ways to contact disease. For a year and a half, I have been placing a great degree of trust in you to be truthful with me; however, although we know each other more intimately than I've ever known anyone, I still don't know much about your day-to-day activities and the possibility of relationships along the way. I remember you told me some time ago that you don't look at me as a girlfriend, so I've always taken that to mean that you could/are possibly sexual with other women. So, without laboring this for hours, hmmm, what do I say? Frankly, I love the thought of going without, too. I love the idea of the spontaneity. Condoms are an option, of course. One other thought is the spermicidal products. I've never used one. Have you ever been with someone who has? I could stop at a drug store and see what those are all about as far as use, possible side effects, effectiveness, etc. I do know they're for preventing pregnancy and don't offer any protection for preventing STD's. And I wonder about taste. I don't want to do anything that would get in the way of oral sex. Gee, this can be complicated! I have no doubt that we've taken way more time on this than the average person, and I'm glad. A big part of the enjoyment for me is not having to worry.

Don't worry about cumming instantly. If you do, I'll take it as a compliment. It would be my honor!

Hope you have a safe, uneventful flight home.

Karlee
xoxxo

From: Jack
To: Karlee
Sent: Wednesday, December 28, 2005 11:02 AM
Subject: RE: Hi!

Hi Karlee,

You don't have to call me Dr. Jack...unless we're in the middle of an exam!

I'm with you on the vibrator thing. I'll be surprised if I make it all the way home. I may have to join the 2,640 foot club... (1/2 of the mile-high club). Long flight with lots of time to think...

Um, YES, I would be very interested in watching you pleasure yourself. Yes, yes I would. And observing you for my profession sounds like an excellent idea...I appreciate your willingness to help me with my studies. It's making me want to go to med school for real!

I'm not sure, exactly, about your reaction to catching me touch myself. It varies. Never REALLY disgusted. Maybe embarrassed or startled. Maybe curious/excited/intrigued. Maybe afraid of noticing that I noticed you and pretending it never happened. I guess I don't imagine you saying "let me help you with that" so much...I'm not sure why. I guess I like the idea that we're both so turned on in this scenario that we can't control ourselves, but yet we're both controlled. We rationalize to ourselves how everything that happens is just accidental, and neither of us wants to take the initiative because it would be "wrong," and so we tell ourselves that it's just something else. In my fantasy, we're both so attracted to each other that we can't believe that the other would actually be interested, too. So, even though you might see me, stroking my cock while looking at photos of you, you tell yourself it must be something else I'm thinking about. And when you catch me peeping on you in the shower and begin to rub your breasts, I think that maybe you didn't see me. I also imagine that when we "cross the line," there will also be some excuses that we both make and agree to, so that it never happened. Maybe after catching me touching myself, we talk for a while and decide for some reason (it's cold in one room) that we should sleep in the same bed...we're both adults, after all. And, in the middle of the night, you hear me ask a few times if you're asleep. You feel me slowly move around, as I pull your nightgown up, above your thighs, above your ass. I pull the front out slowly so that I can see your breasts moving up and down as you're "sleeping"...then...maybe I slowly rub my rock hard cock up against you, until I position you in such a way (like, an X) that I can slide inside you and we make love...we both know what's happening. But in the morning, we realize we're both out of our clothes and are embarrassed...must've both been hot and peeled them off without realizing it. We each try to cover up and don't talk about what actually happened.

I think pregnancy is what I'm most worried about. I don't have and have never had an STD. I've never been with a woman without a condom...even for a moment. Not even by accident. I get the impression from my friends that I'm the only man on the planet for whom this is true. I have had oral sex without a condom in the past, but (partly from my time working with physicians) I was very compulsive about getting checked.

I have not had any new partners, and unless one can get an STD from masturbation, I'm safe! But I don't know enough about the risks of pregnancy (always used condoms with spermicidal lubricant) to know what happens. I know that a spermicidal can react badly with some people, and I do know it has a taste (a bad taste) and that's all unpleasant.

Thanks for the good flight wishes. I'd write more but it's time to pack, and there are people everywhere...I'll write more when I get home. I trust that we're both clear since our last partners (since we met), and as for pregnancy...I guess I'd like to know what we'll do and what happens if my high-powered sperm manage to get past your feminine defenses! Actually, for all I know, I may be sterile...but I'd rather not find out the hard way!

--Jack

From: Karlee
To: Jack
Sent: Wednesday, December 28, 2005 8:51 PM

351

Subject: Back safe, I hope?

Hi Jack,

I hope your trip back went smoothly and that the airport treated you well.

Mmmm! Actually, becoming a member of the mile-high club is on my list of things I'd like to do in this lifetime. (Another good reason for you to take a trip with me!)

Your fantasy sounds wonderful! I'll be very eager to fall asleep!

I went shopping tonight for some "sexy" clothes. That was very exciting for me and it also gave me an opportunity to think up a few other scenarios that could be fun. Surprise, surprise! I guess my thought is that since we'll be having more time when you're here than during my visits to Las Vegas, I'd like to keep a few things under my hat. It's not like we have to fit ten hours worth of fantasies into three hours. Yay!!!

What will we do if your high-powered sperm manage to get past my feminine defenses? Wow, this is what they call a "loaded" question, I guess—literally! I once attended a seminar that had a section titled, *How to Answer a Question When You Don't Know the Answer or When You Don't Want to Answer*. The training material actually suggests posing a question back. So I could ask, as it would be in this case, "What would you want us to do?" But, that just doesn't feel like the right thing to do. I've been pondering my response most of the day. It's not something to take lightly. Do you know what your answer is; are you waiting to see what I would say? Or do you not know? While I've been sitting here, I've started to write what I'd like to say a couple of times, and I just can't find the right words to put onto paper. I think I prefer to have this conversation on the telephone. I'm concerned about the possibility of a misinterpretation of my response.

Sleep well.

xoKarlee

From: Jack
To: Karlee
Sent: Thursday, December 29, 2005 1:53 PM
Subject: RE: Back safe, I hope?

Hi Karlee,

The Mile High Club for us? Well, I don't think we need any more good reasons, but I'll add it to the list anyway! On the flight I was imagining that we were together...it seems like it is a tricky club to gain membership in...especially on a full flight! There didn't seem to be a subtle way to get two people in or out of the restroom. Of course, they do give you little blankets. When everyone was asleep, I could cover myself with a blanket, and then pull down my jeans around my hips. You could wear a skirt with no underwear, and start to slide by me, and just sit on top of me for a moment...but people would certainly notice! I wonder what the air marshals are trained to do then.

Hmmm...I don't think I'd misinterpret your response. As for what my answer is...I don't really know. I suppose being realistic I know...I've occasionally had thoughts about having a family and all that, but given how things have been going for me professionally and my financial situation, I'd say that it would be a big mistake for me to have a child. I find the prospect very sad, but I think it won't happen for me. If it did...I think I wouldn't be able to give a child the necessities. I guess that's my feeling, and I've never really thought all that much about it (I suppose I should have). What are your thoughts? Why would I misinterpret? You do a good job of explaining things...

I'd have called you, except...I used up my minutes from all the calls with my parents. I'm sure we'll talk soon, probably this weekend, but I'm curious what you were pondering.

--Jack

From: Jack
To: Karlee
Sent: Thursday, December 29, 2005 1:58 PM

Subject: Dates

Hi Karlee,

So, I'm waiting to hear on a possible interview...two dates were given to me. I picked the one that would have worked perfectly, and they wrote back and seemed to have withdrawn the good one in favor of the bad one. It also turns out that the bad time (when I have something else scheduled) is also around Martin Luther King's birthday, apparently. I thought that was a holiday?

The dates are close to overlapping when I thought I'd come to Cleveland...as soon as I hear back, I think we should make plans! I'm still thinking about January 8-11 or 9-12. I'm pushing to know as soon as possible.

--Jack

From: Karlee
To: Jack
Sent: Thursday, December 29, 2005 8:47 PM
Subject: Hi!

Hi Jack,

Glad you made it back!

Now that's what I call flying the "friendly skies"! Now if you came to Fargo with me, my guess is that it wouldn't be a very full flight.

Perhaps misinterpretation was not the best word to use. I guess I was just feeling like my answering the question would have been too much like a one-sided conversation. I believe it's really something for both parties to discuss together. Unless, of course, one person is very set on absolutely only one option—which is actually not the case for me. For example, yesterday, I could have answered, "We'd get married and raise the baby together." And you could have said, "No way." Then really we wouldn't be any closer to the answer to the question. That being said, I don't have one pat answer. Too many variables, etc. What I can say is that I would see the options as (and in no particular order of preference) 1. We get married and raise the baby together. 2. We don't get married, but raise the baby together 3. I have the baby and you raise it (if you didn't want to marry me or live with me but really wanted to raise a child) 4. I could have the baby and I raise it by myself (probably my least desirable option) 5. I could have an abortion 6. We/I could have the baby and put it up for adoption. See, when you look at all that, doesn't it almost become overwhelming? (No wonder people don't take time to think it through!)

Since my divorce, I have been asked more than once if I would ever consider having a baby if I got married again. My response was, "I really don't think so," and…I've learned to never say never. I would then go on to say, that if I really felt like I was with the right person, and it felt like the right thing to do, I would consider it. But I think the last time I was asked, I was a couple of years younger than I am now! Since I'm not exactly in my "prime" child-bearing years, there would be higher risk factors for me and a baby. Lots to consider.

January 8-11 or 9-12 both sound great!!! Either, or, or both! In the spirit of maintaining my excellent standards in being a hostess, I have a few questions…regarding food! Since I'm leaving for Orlando on Wednesday and coming back on the 7th, I'd like to have as much done before I leave, especially if you arrive on the 8th. We've been talking so much about all the sexy stuff, (Mmmmm!) that we haven't really talked about what we're going to do when we're not having sex. Probably just recover! And our recovery periods should probably include some meals! So I'll try to not make this too complicated, but I'd like to know a bit about your food preferences. Any favorites? Anything that you usually have on a daily basis and would miss if it wasn't here? Anything that is definitely a NO WAY? What about coffee? Do you drink milk, and if so, what kind? How about other types of beverages? Pop? (I think you mentioned Diet Coke once.) Alcohol? Wine, (white, red?), beer, margaritas, mixed drinks? What do you eat for breakfast? Should we cook together or should I prepare a few things ahead of time and put them in the freezer? Should we plan to go out for some meals? I know that's a lot of questions. And, you can skip answering them and we can shop when you get here. But I will tell you, I have very little food in the house at any given time. So I was thinking it might be nice to have at least a few things when you arrive. (Especially in case we end up never leaving the place!)

Now, one more thing and then I'll stop with the questions! Aside from hours and hours of incredible, wonderful, amazing, etc. lovemaking and fantasy fulfillment, do you want to do anything else while you're here? Have you been to Cleveland before? Do you have any interest in seeing any parts of the city, etc? Not that any or all of it has to be planned, and I'm not trying to become Miss AAA, I'm just curious more than anything.

Karlee
xoxox

From: Jack
To: Karlee
Sent: Friday, December 30, 2005 11:36 AM
Subject: RE: Hi!

Hi Karlee,

Well, I think you covered all the pregnancy options. I think. Hmmmm. I tend to think that right now, pregnancy is something that would be better avoided. As for how to best go about doing that...I'm not sure. What about something like a diaphragm or sponge? Do they even make those anymore? I suppose I need more research! I'll have to ask some teenagers.

I think the best plan is for me to fly out on the afternoon of January 8 and fly back on the 10th in the early evening. If I can find something that meets the above, I'll get the ticket! Yay! Then...the Long Wait begins! Longest week ever...

As for food, I'm usually pretty easy. I'm not a big fan of asparagus, but that's about it, and I'll even enjoy that on occasion. Oh, I guess shrimp, too...had a bad shrimp experience many years ago. I still eat it on occasion, but it seems wasted on me. I usually eat a lot of sliced turkey. I'll drink V8 and orange juice (not mixed together), and I do have one particular orange juice quirk—I like Tropicana

Light and Healthy, Some Pulp. It's about the only orange juice I can drink, but I'm not sure why. If you can't find it, no problem. I drink water, soda (usually caffeine free anything), and other juices. I even like broccoli. I'm not much of a booze drinker, but I'll have whatever is around. I don't drink coffee. If I'm cooking for myself, I make Egg Beater omelets, usually, and chicken breasts with broccoli. But, I'll eat just about anything.

As for things to do in Cleveland...I'd be perfectly happy never leaving your condo, or maybe going out to a restaurant. I've been there before a few times...about the only thing I have on my "list" is to see the Cavs play some day, but I assume you're not a basketball fan (never seen you wearing a jersey) and the tickets are usually crazy expensive. So, I'd say we should hope that we get snowed in.

Keep me posted! I'm VERY excited to see you.

I guess the only other question is...what will be the story on our mutual "friend" that introduced us?!

--Jack

From: Jack
To: Karlee
Sent: Friday, December 30, 2005 11:38 AM
Subject: RE: Hi!

Mmmmm...I just got the gift you sent me. Mmmmm. How'd you know EXACTLY what I want?

I can't imagine a better present. Because, you know...having a photo on the computer is great, but not terribly convenient! Mmmmm.

I'm going to make good use of that photo RIGHT NOW! Too bad you're not online!

--Jack

From: Karlee

To: Jack
Sent: Friday, December 30, 2005 2:16 PM
Subject: Hello....

Hi Jack,

Glad you like the gift! I had a feeling you might.

I have a really bad headache at the moment, so I'm not going to write much.

I found some information regarding other methods of birth control. There are of course others, but they're either something I would not be interested in using or require a doctor's visit, for which I don't think there is enough time. The Pill probably would have been the most desirable for me. Considering I was just to the doctor, I could probably get him to order a prescription over the phone. But...I should really be on it for at least a month and have one period before considering it "safe." So, what do you think about others, such as the female condom, the contraceptive sponge, and there's also emergency contraception.

The concern with the sponge is I don't know if I'm sensitive to Nonoxynol-9. Plus, I'm not thrilled about leaving it in for at least six hours after intercourse.

The reason I have a headache is because I'm just starting my period. This is great news—meaning I won't have it when you're here. It's also good news as far as your visit being a "safe" time according to the Rhythm Method. If we wanted to bank on this, I could purchase what's called an Ovulation Predictor Kit. They're available at the drugstore. It's used to test my urine to identify hormones that indicate ovulation is about to occur. If it is, then we'd probably have to jump to you wearing a condom.

My vote would probably be the Emergency Contraception, IF my doctor would be willing to write the prescription without a visit, or the Rhythm Method with the kit, since I am 99.9% certain that we'd be safe based on my cycle. But, hey, you can't mess with Mother Nature!

I was thinking about our mutual friend, too. More so, just wondering what name we should give him. I'll think about the story a bit when I'm feeling better. I've had bits and pieces of one come to mind as I've been thinking about other parts of your visit.

Thanks for the input on the food. And I would totally be into a Cavs game. I actually am very fond of basketball even though I don't follow it very closely. I'll at least take a look at the schedule and see if they're even in town.

Love,
Karlee

From: Karlee
To: Jack
Sent: Friday, December 30, 2005 2:18 PM
Subject:

Forget the idea of the Emergency Pill. I just found this!

The "Morning After" Pill. Are there side effects?
Nausea and vomiting are the most common side effects. These side effects can persist from a few hours to a few days. Serious side effects such as blood clots, heart attack and stroke are extremely rare.

From: Jack
To: Karlee
Sent: Friday, December 30, 2005 3:19 PM
Subject: RE: Ticket on hold!

Hi Karlee!

I'm sorry to hear about your headache...hopefully you'll feel better soon knowing that I'll be there in...a week?! Wow.

I booked the ticket!

I read your two notes. I've heard about the "morning after" pill from a friend. It's essentially a big dose of hormones which prevent the egg from attaching to the uterine wall. The side effects I've heard about are generally mild, though some people do react badly to the hormones (meaning they feel ill) but it's very short-lived. The risks (heart problems, stroke) are, as I understand it, comparable to the pill or other hormonal birth controls—I think your doctor would know more about this.

Hmmm... We'll talk more about this when you feel better. I'll do more reading, too....

I'm coming to Cleveland! Yay!

--Jack

From: Karlee
To: Jack
Sent: Saturday, December 31, 2005 2:04 PM
Subject: Let the countdown begin!

Hi Jack,

Headache is gone. I'm feeling great today! My mind has been racing a million miles a minute with thoughts of you. It's just been one of those busy days and this is the first I've been able to sit at my computer. I hope I can remember all the thoughts I had that I wanted to share with you.

Oh, one, before I forget—what do you think about us playing some type of "strip" game? Strip poker, strip rummy, strip Monopoly, strip Chutes-n-Ladders (did you play that as a kid?). I've never played strip poker or any kind of strip game and I think it would be fun. Not that we don't already have enough fun things to do!

I was also thinking that we might need to adjust our fantasies a bit based on your arrival time. Since it wouldn't make sense for you to be "taking a nap" at 10:30 at night... I've thought of some other scenarios, but I'm not sure if they lend to as much "tension build up"! What about something like this...

I pick you up as our mutual friend's friend, bring you back here. I have just landed an exciting something professionally, a new book, a great client, something big, and I tell you I am going to celebrate by drinking champagne and relaxing in my Jacuzzi. I'm a bit shy, so although I've thought about it, I don't saying anything to you about including you. You pick up on that and offer to just read or watch TV while I'm in the tub. Sounds good to me. Then I say that I of course would like to at least have you join me for the champagne part. So we open the bottle and have a glass. We are really enjoying each other's company, sitting on the couch, getting to know one another and talking a little bit about our mutual friend, and the fascinations of your "medical professional" coursework! At some point, I excuse myself to start my bath. While I'm undressing, I decide I could really use some help with a piece of clothing and why should I struggle by myself when I have another person in the house that could help? So I go back out to where you are reading or whatever, only partially clothed now and ask you to help me with all of "these darn snaps." You are happy to help. Your hands happen to slip just a bit. (Here would be a great place to do an, "Oh pardon me, I don't know what came over me!") I finally get into the Jacuzzi. A few minutes later, you innocently decide you're going to change clothes, or do something that requires you to go into my bedroom, which is where you're sleeping. You come into the bedroom and can't help but notice that I've left the bathroom door open, just a bit. "Just enough for me to take a peek," you say to yourself. "If she catches me, I'll just say that I just came in a second ago to change clothes," or some sort of alibi. A bit more time goes by, and I notice you again. This time, I tell you to come in so that we don't have to talk through the door. After all, it's easy for me to "cover up" with my arms while I'm sitting in the tub. At this point, you might already have your clothes off or partially off since you originally came in to change clothes. If you have clothes on, I can't help but notice the huge erection through your clothing. (If your clothes are off, well, then it would be obvious!) I'm uncomfortable with the fact that you have an erection, and also partially intrigued and turned on. I decide to invite you to join me. After all, celebrating would be more fun with two. I'll leave the Jacuzzi scene to your imagination! Not sure what will come after the Jacuzzi, but eventually it will come time that we decide we're going to go to sleep. The tension is mounting! I'm really comfortable with you by now and I'm also feeling drawn to you, almost like a protector. I've been living on my own for so long and my boyfriend is overseas and I haven't been with a man for a very long time… I'm okay during the day, but I tell you that I really don't like sleeping alone and ask if you would mind if I slept with you. "Of course," you reply. You're totally comfortable with that. And then you tell me that you have a live-in girlfriend and you're used to having someone in bed with you each night, so me being with you would actually be more natural. (And then I fall asleep as fast as I can so that you can wake me up like we talked about before!) Mmmmm!

Then, on Monday, we could bring in all or a combination of all we talked about for the last week…the breakfast table, you taking a nap, me seeing you naked, you coming home and finding me in the shower, shopping at the adult store, me "volunteering" for your projects…

I think it could all fit together quite nicely!

As far as our mutual friend…how about the name John? Would it work for you to know John from college and I know him from high school? As far as other details, as I see it in my mind, the story would just kind of unfold as it needs to and we would both pick up on those cues and play along. Like I might say, "Did John tell you I…?" and it won't matter how you answer because it will work either way. Or I might say, "I'm sure John told you…" and you would say, "Yes, he did." Make sense? I'm open to other ideas if something would work better for you.

Any more thoughts/research on the birth control? I've been curious about what made you change your mind from "okay without" to "better not." Or maybe I am assuming that at one point you were okay; maybe you were never there.

Happy New Year! Doing anything fun to celebrate? There must be a million choices in Las Vegas. I'm staying home, and that's fine. After all, I'll be celebrating next week! Mmmmm!

Any more news about your dad?

Karlee

XOXOXXO

From: Jack
To: Karlee
Sent: Saturday, December 31, 2005 3:05 PM
Subject: RE: Let the countdown begin!

Hi Karlee,

Happy New Year! And what better way to ring in the New Year than to know that in one week, I'll be there with you!

I'm glad you're feeling better. I thought I was feeling a bit off yesterday, but it may have been the return to dryness. Then again, today it's cloudy and looks like it may rain! I wonder if one can make oneself sick from too much self-pleasuring? If so...I may be in trouble over the next week.

As far as playing strip games, I'd be up for that! It's always tricky figuring out a fair way to do that...unless both people have the same number of clothes on. Then again, I suppose it's not as much about fair play as it is about having fun.

Mmmm... All you wrote about my arrival evening sounds good to me. You know, another piece of clothing I always thought was very sexy was the one-piece short dress...comes up to above the knees...shows a little cleavage. A long zipper down the back. I love the idea of unzipping you and having you step out of something like that. Not sure if you have any clothing like that. But, who am I kidding? I love the idea of you getting out of ANY type of clothing. The other thing I've been picturing you in is...again, I'm not sure what it's called, but I think it's a "baby doll nightie"...thin straps, sort of very light material that just barely hangs to the very top of your upper thigh...mmmm.

I love the idea of us talking while you're in the tub. Can you see into your bedroom from the tub, too?

I saw a movie the other night which had a scene that seemed to be ripped directly from a fantasy I was telling you about...a college student is spending the summer with a writer, and he has a crush on the writer's wife.

He has her bra and panties laid out on the bed, and he's touching himself. She walks in on him and sees him from behind, his pants and underwear pulled down. She jumps and says, "Oh!" and spins around and leaves the room, but stops in the doorway. He pulls up his pants and sheepishly returns her clothes to the drawer, embarrassed. She starts talking to him, saying that she's not mad; she understands that he's curious, etc., etc. He doesn't say anything. She says she's flattered that someone would think about her...not that she's assuming he was thinking about her, maybe he was thinking about someone else. He says that he does think about her, remembering the first time he saw her, and the sweater she was wearing. She invites him to sit next to her on the couch and they talk for a bit. They agree to move on.

Later on, he comes to the room and finds that she's laid out her bra and panties on the bed, surrounded by the sweater she wore when he first saw her. Hmmmm. I guess I'm not the only one with these fantasies!

At some point, I do want you to "catch me." I'm not sure if it should be the first night or not. If you could see into the bedroom from the bath...maybe you'd realize what was happening and then invite me in? Or maybe the next night you'd walk in on me when I'm looking at your pictures on the desk. Mmmm...either way. Both ways! It's all making my heart race again.

As far as our mutual friend...everything is good except for the name. I know a few John's, and had a roommate in college named John. How about Neil...do you know any Neils? I'll know him from college...I just don't want to be thinking about someone I know! It'll just confuse me. "John said that? Really? Weird."

Now about the birth control—I don't know...still like the idea of not using anything, but having no experience in that realm, I'm not sure what to think. I suppose if we had a spermicidal handy, that might be okay...is that inserted immediately beforehand or can you have it in for a while? I don't think you're allergic to it, because the condoms we used had Nonoxynol-9 on them, I thought.

I guess to get back to the discussion we started in an earlier message... I'd think that getting married because you were pregnant would be something I'd be very wary of. I think that's the worst reason in the world to get married...but, I come from parents that aren't exactly the most loving towards each other, so that may have jaded me. I think the only reason two people should get married is because they love each other and know they want to spend the rest of their lives together. I think having that process accelerated or skipped "for the good of the child" isn't a good idea...I think it's much tougher on the child. So, while it's unlikely that we'd wind up having to worry about this at all, it's my nature to worry about such things. That's why I think it's worth talking about beforehand...

No big plans for new years. Continuing to fill out resumes and applications. I filled out an application at one place and it didn't recognize my login and wouldn't email me my password (even though it said repeatedly it would). I'm also getting things lined up for a meeting in about two weeks.

Are you home? Maybe I'll give you a quick call!

I can't wait to see you. Mmmm. I'll have to remember to bring my robe.

--Jack

From: Karlee
To: Jack
Sent: Saturday, December 31, 2005 9:33 PM
Subject: Happy New Year!

Hi Jack,

Happy New Year to you! And yes, I agree, no better way to bring in the new year than knowing that in one, did I say one (!!?) week, you'll be here with me!

Did you end up doing anything tonight? (Or last night depending on when you read this). It's 11:25 PM right now. I might actually still be up at midnight. WhooHoo! I had a nice and quiet enjoyable evening, spent mostly daydreaming about your visit and reading.

I wouldn't think self-pleasuring would make you sick, other than you might spend a lot of time with your clothes off and get cold. Stay healthy!

I think I might actually have a dress similar to what you described. I've been giving thought to what I'll be wearing while you're here. I hope you like what I select! And I'm still thinking about a couple of other fun/sexy pieces.

Is that movie you watched one I might find at a video store? Sounds very erotic and I like that! Plus, I like the idea of watching something that is similar to your fantasy.

As far as catching you—I'd say either way would be good. I'm still a little nervous on this one. I guess I haven't yet gotten clear on how I will react and what I would say, etc. Will any of that have an effect on how much enjoyment there is in it for you? I don't want to do it wrong! Maybe that's why I like the idea of watching the movie and seeing how the woman responded, even though I know you already told me.

Yes, bring your robe. That should be about all you need! I'll have to turn the thermostat up. I have a feeling we won't be wearing much warm clothing. I know I don't plan to!

Okay, so now it's an official Happy New Year! I just took a break to watch the ball drop. Looks like fun at Times Square, if you like being around a bazillion people! So today is now Sunday and I see you NEXT Sunday! I'm glad I'm going to Florida; that will make the time go by much more quickly for me, since I'll be busy having to pay attention to other things...other than when I'm on the plane!

Do you like lasagna?

Do you have any fantasies including edibles? Whipped cream, chocolate sauce? It could fun other than the calories!

I've been thinking about the doctor's exam. I can barely stand it, but

I do manage! I was imaging that I could prepare a "tray" with all the "tools" you would/could/might need. Is there anything you can think of that I should be sure to not leave off the list? (Ohhh, I hope so!)

On that note, I think I'll go to bed with my Happy Birthday, Karlee picture of you and work towards my first orgasm of the New Year! Well, might need to do that in the shower. I'll have to leave your picture out. But that doesn't matter since I've looked at it so many times, I know what it looks like. And in one week, I'll see you and the same thing I see in that picture! Mmmmmmmmmmmm!

xoxoxo

From: Karlee
To: Jack
Sent: Sunday, January 1, 2006 8:32 AM
Subject: What an image!

Hi Jack,

I think I got it! I was just going through some of my lingerie and I got a vision of how the whole "catching you" scenario could work! See, once I can get a picture, then I'm fine. Up until now, I wasn't getting a picture.

Oh my, am I turned on!

Back to my lingerie…

Karlee

From: Jack
To: Karlee
Sent: Sunday, January 1, 2006 12:56 PM
Subject: RE: Happy New Year!

Hi Karlee,

I went out to see the fireworks...it was really windy and raining here earlier in the day, so they thought they might have to cancel them, but I decided to take a walk and check out the view. It was pretty good. Then I fell asleep...been tired lately...I think you're wearing me out already!

I do like lasagna!

As far as fantasies including edibles... You know, I had some experience with edibles and it's never really been that intriguing for me. If you want to try something, I'd be up for it, but in general I think that even though I enjoy sex and food separately, together is less enjoyable. Messy, sticky, distracting...but maybe I did something wrong.

And the doctor's exam tray—Hmmm...something tickly (like a feather), something warm, something cold (ice cube?), something that vibrates, something soft...I'll keep thinking.

See you soon!

--Jack

From: Karlee
To: Jack
Sent: Sunday, January 1, 2006 8:40 PM
Subject: One week from tonight . . .

Hi Jack,

It's 11:28 PM. Next week by this time, assuming your flight arrives on time, you'll be HERE! Wonder what we'll be doing at 11:28 PM next Sunday? Mmmmm! The couch, the tub, the bed, the kitchen floor?

As far as already wearing you out...I hope not! Should we implement a "no self-pleasuring until next week" rule?!!! (One thought about the doctor fantasy and I'd break it anyway.) I hope you are able to get some good rest this week. I'm hoping I'll be able to sleep for a short bit on Sunday afternoon. I'm really not a nap taker and I hardly get tired during the day. But with the three hour difference our bodies will be on, I hope I can stay awake long enough to do all I want to do Sunday night! Of course I know the sooner I fall asleep, the sooner it will be the middle of the night, and I might hear you ask a few times if I'm asleep. And then I'll feel you slowly move around, as you pull my nightgown up, above my thighs, above my ass. Then maybe you'll pull the front out slowly so that you can see my breasts moving up and down as I'm "sleeping"...maybe you'll slowly rub your rock hard cock up against me, until you position me in such a way (like, an X) that you can slide inside me and we'll make love...

I did some birth control shopping today. I didn't buy anything, but I did learn a lot! There were three products that looked promising. The ovulation kit looks good. It appeared to be easy to use, easy to figure out if you're basically safe or not. There were two spermicidal products I looked at. One was a solid something that you inserted and it dissolves. The other was actually a film. I'm guessing that basically they all do the same thing. The difference to consider is that each one seems to have different "directions" as far as how many minutes prior to intercourse you can or cannot insert, for what duration they are effective, etc. I think the one was good for three hours. The other said to put in every time you had intercourse. But—one it was okay to insert up to an hour before. The other you weren't supposed to put in until 15 minutes prior. So a few things to consider, but all-in-all, they didn't look like a bad way to go, with the exception of the oral sex component.

I had no attachment to bringing food into our time together. I was mostly asking in case you did. Although if this did interest you, I probably would have known by now!

Have you been able to get any of your other interviews lined up yet? I'm guessing probably not too much with it still being holiday season. I know here, a lot of people are still off tomorrow.

Anything else you've always wanted to do that you'd like to put into the mix? Not that we don't already have enough! And if we end up going to the lingerie/toy store, maybe we'll see something we haven't even thought of yet!

Anything else we need to talk about?

Good night.
Karlee

From: Jack
To: Karlee
Sent: Monday, January 2, 2006 11:43 AM
Subject: RE: One week from tonight . . .

Hi Karlee,

Hmm? Next week at this time? I'm sure wherever it is, we'll both be glad we're there!

A no self-pleasuring until next week rule? It'll never work! It sounds like a nice idea, but I'd never make it. Not even close. I'll try as long as I can...but I don't think I'll make it past lunch.

Sounds like the birth control shopping went well. That's a good sign! I can also bring condoms, just in case...I mean, I may also discover that being inside you without a condom is too intense for me to take! I don't know! While I remember you said that if I only lasted a minute without a condom, you'd take it as a complement...I don't think that would be good repeatedly! Not that I'm changing my mind...but it doesn't hurt to have them handy.

Of course, there is another method that in and of itself isn't very effective...withdrawal. I suppose you remember from the Wrong Room fantasy...when I pulled out and came all over you...I rather like that...I'm not sure why. Mmmm. Definitely won't make it a week without self-pleasuring. I'll be lucky to make it through this email!

No interviews lined up yet. My other interview has been delayed. I did find some new jobs to apply for. I don't know...I still do the work and make a very concerted effort to appear positive and upbeat, but...I'm greatly concerned, as you may have guessed!

Other things to put in the mix? Oh, many things. I was thinking about lying on top of the sheets, sleeping...maybe you come into the

370

room to get something, and you tiptoe closer for a better look. Maybe you sit on the edge of the bed, and then decide to slowly put my cock in your mouth while I'm sleeping. Just a little...but maybe you enjoy it and keep going...until I wake up. Mmmm.

I guess I've also had the fantasy about videotaping ourselves...and ...oh, there are other things, too. Not sure if I'd be able to go through with that. But, I like thinking about it.

Definitely won't make it to Sunday.

Oh, I forgot something...garlic! I have trouble digesting garlic, so I've been trying to stay away from it (even though I love it).

Mmmmm. Long week ahead, for sure.

--Jack

From: Karlee
To: Jack
Sent: Monday, January 2, 2006 7:59 PM
Subject: Six days!

Hi Jack,

See, the week is shorter already!

I know what you mean about the no self-pleasuring not working. I was in my car today, just driving, and I started thinking about you being in the car with me driving home from the airport and the throbbing started again! Then I found myself reminiscing about our time in Las Vegas in May and had an image of us in the X position on my bed at the hotel and I had what I call a full-body flutter! Why I was thinking about us together at that hotel, I have no idea!

No need to bring condoms. I'll buy some here. As far as lasting only a minute repeatedly, I appreciate your consideration! Now here's something I was thinking about along those same lines. I've never been in a situation like I'm imagining our time here will be. I guess I would say it could be looked at as somewhat of a sex marathon! Being with you, our first two times together, is probably the longest I've ever been in a lovemaking session with someone. Maybe there have been some that were that long or longer, but I'm not recalling any. So I have no idea how long I can last! I can only think of a couple of times where I've been with someone long enough to move into a second orgasm for me, you being one of them. I can't imagine that I'll ever get tired, but I just don't know what to expect. And I can't wait to find out!

Yes, the withdrawal method is one of the riskiest, from what I've heard. But, if you'd like, you can certainly repeat that part of the Wrong Room fantasy, not for birth control methods—just for your own enjoyment! Pure pleasure, perhaps!

Good that you found some new jobs to apply for. Have you heard anything back on the government job?

And you lying on top of the sheet…I like this a lot. Will you really be sleeping or will we "pretend?" This came up before, as far as me taking you in my mouth while you're asleep, or crawling on top of you. I love the idea as long as you're not someone who gets startled when they are awakened from sleep and swing in defense. When we were kids, my mom would say, "Wake your father up for dinner," if he happened to be napping. None of us ever wanted to because he'd get mad. So we'd just say very loudly from a distance, "Dad, wake up!"

I, myself, am not very fond of garlic; I never buy it to add to my cooking. But sometimes there are traces of it in some foods, like spaghetti sauce. Usually an ingredient might be listed as garlic power or garlic salt. Would that bother you? I was thinking about making lasagna for Monday night. I usually use a combination of ground meat and sausage. The sausage could have garlic in it, but I wouldn't buy anything where it was specifically labeled as such. I do know how to make other dishes if you'd rather not have that. Reality is, almost anything with any amount of flavoring seems to have some touch of garlic.

Do you like waffles? What do you generally put in your Egg Beater omelets?

Mmmmm! I'm so looking forward to feeling you in my arms again...

xoxox

From: Jack
To: Karlee
Sent: Friday, January 6, 2006 3:07 PM
Subject: For Karlee

Hi Karlee...

I'm Neil's friend, Jack. I'll be coming to town on Continental flight 760, arriving in Cleveland at 9:58pm this Sunday, January 8th.

Neil's told me all about you...he's had many great things to say. The fact that you're being so kind as to not only put me up at your place for a few days but to also give me a ride to the airport tells me you're even more generous than his description!

I certainly look forward to meeting you in person, and I can't thank you enough for your hospitality. If there's ever anything I can do for you, please don't hesitate to ask! As a struggling student, your help is tremendously appreciated!

So you'll recognize me, I'm 6'1" and I wear glasses. I'll have a red rolling carry-on with me. I'll look for you in baggage claim, if that works for you.

Thanks again and I can't wait to meet you!

--Jack

From: Karlee
To: Jack
Sent: Friday, January 6, 2006 8:45 PM
Subject: RE: For Karlee

Hi Jack,

Nice to hear from you. Thanks for the note. I spoke with Neil today and he said I'd be hearing from you.

I too am looking forward to meeting you! Hmmm? You said Neil told you all about me—he told me all about you! We'll have to compare notes when you get here. He has said nothing but great things about you, too, including that he suspected the two of us would "get along quite nicely." He told me you're a really nice guy and that I need to behave myself. He knows me too well! Ha-ha!

Let me know if there's anything I can do before you arrive to make your stay more comfortable while you're here. All hard-working medical students deserve great hospitality! I've got your guest room ready. I'm actually looking forward to having another person in the house for a few days. Sometimes it gets a bit too quiet around here. I'm happy to pick you up at the airport. When you get off the plane, just follow the signs to the baggage claim area. I'll meet you at the bottom of the escalator. I'm 5'2" with blonde hair and blue eyes. I'll be wearing a green raincoat.

Safe travels.

Karlee

Continued in Book Two...

TRAPPED IN A FANTASY
Soul Mates or Scammed?

ABOUT THE AUTHOR

Karlee Christopher is the founder of a life advice program dedicated to personal transformation and the psychology of success. She has worked with and inspired people from all walks of life, including CEOs, business owners, entrepreneurs, speakers, authors, and people in transition. An internationally published author and avid reader who loves bicycling and travel, Karlee currently resides in Columbus, Ohio.